AIRPOWER
OVER THE
RHINE

TITLES IN THE SERIES

Airpower Reborn: The Strategic Concepts of John Warden and John Boyd

The Bridge to Airpower: Logistics Support for Royal Flying Corps Operations on the Western Front, 1914–18

Airpower Applied: U.S., NATO, and Israeli Combat Experience

The Origins of American Strategic Bombing Theory

Beyond the Beach: The Allied Air War against France

"The Man Who Took the Rap": Sir Robert Brooke-Popham and the Fall of Singapore

Flight Risk: The Coalition's Air Advisory Mission in Afghanistan, 2005–2015

Winning Armageddon: Curtis LeMay and Strategic Air Command, 1948–1957

Rear Admiral Herbert V. Wiley: A Career in Airships and Battleships

From Kites to Cold War: The Evolution of Manned Airborne Reconnaissance

Airpower over Gallipoli, 1915–1916

Selling Schweinfurt: Targeting, Assessment, and Marketing in the Air Campaign against German Industry

Airpower in the War against ISIS

To Rule the Skies: General Thomas S. Power and the Rise of Strategic Air Command in the Cold War

Rise of the War Machines: The Birth of Precision Bombing in World War II

At the Dawn of Airpower: The U.S. Army, Navy, and Marine Corps' Approach to the Military Airplane, 1907–1917

The Birth of British Airpower: Hugh Trenchard, World War I, and the Royal Air Force

THE HISTORY OF MILITARY AVIATION
Paul J. Springer, editor

This series is designed to explore previously ignored facets of the history of airpower. It includes a wide variety of disciplinary approaches, scholarly perspectives, and argumentative styles. Its fundamental goal is to analyze the past, present, and potential future utility of airpower and to enhance our understanding of the changing roles played by aerial assets in the formulation and execution of national military strategies. It encompasses the incredibly diverse roles played by airpower, which include but are not limited to efforts to achieve air superiority; strategic attack; intelligence, surveillance, and reconnaissance missions; airlift operations; close-air support; and more. Of course, airpower does not exist in a vacuum. There are myriad terrestrial support operations required to make airpower functional, and examinations of these missions is also a goal of this series.

In less than a century, airpower developed from flights measured in minutes to the ability to circumnavigate the globe without landing. Airpower has become the military tool of choice for rapid responses to enemy activity, the primary deterrent to aggression by peer competitors, and a key enabler to military missions on the land and sea. This series provides an opportunity to examine many of the key issues associated with its usage in the past and present, and to influence its development for the future.

AIRPOWER OVER THE RHINE

THE LUFTWAFFE, THE FRENCH AIR FORCE, AND THE BATTLE OF FRANCE

JAMES F. SLAUGHTER III

Naval Institute Press
Annapolis, Maryland

Naval Institute Press
291 Wood Road
Annapolis, MD 21402

© 2025 by the U.S. Naval Institute
All rights reserved. No part of this book may be reproduced or utilized in any form or by any means, electronic or mechanical, including photocopying and recording, or by any information storage and retrieval system, without permission in writing from the publisher.

Library of Congress Cataloging-in-Publication Data

Names: Slaughter, James F., III, author.
Title: Airpower over the Rhine : the Luftwaffe, the French Air Force, and the Battle of France / James F. Slaughter III.
Other titles: Air power over the Rhine
Description: Annapolis, Maryland : Naval Institute Press, [2025] | Series: History of military aviation | Includes bibliographical references and index.
Identifiers: LCCN 2024059372 (print) | LCCN 2024059373 (ebook) | ISBN 9781682477946 (hardback) | ISBN 9781682470954 (ebook)
Subjects: LCSH: World War, 1939–1945—Aerial operations, French. | France. Armée de l'air. | Germany. Luftwaffe. | Air power—France—History—20th century. | Air power—Germany—History—20th century. | World War, 1939–1945—Aerial operations, German. | World War, 1939–1945—Campaigns—France.
Classification: LCC D788 .S64 2025 (print) | LCC D788 (ebook) | DDC 940.54/4944—dc23 /eng/20250203
LC record available at https://lccn.loc.gov/2024059372
LC ebook record available at https://lccn.loc.gov/2024059373

♾ Print editions meet the requirements of ANSI/NISO z39.48-1992 (Permanence of Paper).
Printed in the United States of America.

10 9 8 7 6 5 4 3 2 1

To My Family

Contents

Acknowledgments	xi
The Airspace and Geography of the Battle of France	xiii
Introduction	1
CHAPTER 1. Combat Aircraft: A Technical Analysis	8
CHAPTER 2. The French and German Aircraft Industries	31
CHAPTER 3. French and German Intelligence, 1934 to 1940	56
CHAPTER 4. The French Air Force, the Luftwaffe, and the Spanish Civil War	78
CHAPTER 5. French Doctrine and Training, 1934 to 1940	106
CHAPTER 6. Luftwaffe Doctrine and Training, 1934 to 1940	138
CHAPTER 7. Politics and Airpower in France: A Nation and Its Services Divided	158
CHAPTER 8. Reassessing the Air Battle over France in 1940	181
Conclusion	204
Notes	213
Bibliography	235
Index	243

Acknowledgments

IT IS IMPOSSIBLE to research historical events without the assistance of others. Anyone who conducts primary-source research for events beyond twenty to thirty years ago is reliant on a great many people and organizations who assist in one way or another along the way. During the course of researching and writing this book, many organizations were vital. In the United States, the National Archives, the archives of the National Air and Space Museum, the Air Force Historical Research Agency, and the library of the U.S. Army Command and General Staff College all played a role in discovery or refinement.

In Britain, the Liddell Hart Archive at King's College, the Imperial War Museum, and the archives at the Royal Air Force Museum were extremely helpful. In France the Service Historique de l'Armée de l'Air at Vincennes and the archives at Sciences Po were both gracious and extremely helpful over the course of multiple visits; they expanded my view as greatly as the cuisine in Paris expanded my waistline.

While there are multitudes of people to whom I owe a thank you for help along the way, whether for finding a document, pointing out an error, or simply offering a smile after a tough day, a few deserve special consideration.

First and foremost, I could not have finished this work without the support of my family. My mother and father instilled the love of learning in me that led to this point, and my wife Stacy and son Logan continue to support this manifestation. The number of weekends and evenings I told my son, "I have to write" seem innumerable. I owe them all a debt I cannot repay and time I cannot give back.

My first mentor, Dr. John Maxwell of West Virginia University, who tragically departed far too soon, always had more faith in me than I did and pushed me to go outside my comfort zone; nothing I did academically after losing him was comfortable, but it was worth it. My excellent friends Johannes Allert and Carole Butcher not only provided encouragement for this project, but also were there along with the rest of the Norwich Mafia. John Buckley at the University of Wolverhampton, my PhD advisor, was vital during the process that generated a significant portion of this book. In addition, Martin Alexander provided crucial research tips, having navigated the world of French military archives beforehand, and Chris Robinson provided an excellent map to help define the battlespace I needed to describe for this book.

Everything positive in this work I owe to those above, while I personally own the negatives.

The Airspace and Geography of the Battle of France

THE AREA of northwest France has been an invasion route since time out of mind. The Romans fought over it as did the Celts and Germans beforehand. While not without challenges, the region presents armies with good routes of travel and in less modern times, some natural resources from which to draw. The area is key to breaking into the easy terrain of central France and in the northern sector, the North German Plain. The area was contested throughout the modern period, and many of the key points and nodes from at least Frederick's time forward were of such salient importance they were contested in every major conflict. The area around Sedan, Stonne, and Verdun, and the Meuse River were key points in two centuries of conflict between France and Prussia and later Germany under Prussian dominance.

The bulk of World War I in the West was fought in this area. The addition of airpower complicated rather than resolved the battle space, which now became three dimensional. The deadlocks of late 1914 to early 1918 witnessed these key areas and points maintain their importance. Following World War I, both potential adversaries looked to the same areas to provide victory.

France bet its national security on the Maginot Line and a fundamentally altered army in 1928 that reduced the time of conscription to one year until well into the 1930s. After Germany's recovery and rearmament, it followed suit with the Westwall. Both countries bet that fortifications could potentially play an important part in the next war. France's plans were complicated by a vacillating Belgium, while Germany's plans evolved an increasingly offensive path and as such sought ways to overcome obstacles such as the Maginot Line. The *Bewegungskrieg*, which was developed to incorporate cooperative land forces and airpower, after much gnashing of teeth helped along by unfortunate happenstance, went around the Maginot Line and through the "impassible" Ardennes in the Fall Gelb plan.

France had little doubt about what to cover, the debate was how to cover it. The army perceived that its various permutations would meet the German attack successfully. None of the plans called for dealing with a massive mechanized German blow through the Ardennes. The French air force's (FAF) mission, regardless of army plans, remained largely the same and its initial deployment prior to 1938 into zones under air force control, that although lacking radar, was deployed to deal with a major German effort in the area. Production problems aside, the FAF seemed reasonably well deployed in early 1938 before reversion to army control as part of the massive internal crisis that witnessed the arrest of many French communists and politicians on the far left.

The massive differences in outlook and operational communication and cohesiveness between the FAF and the army made covering the area in May and June 1940 a virtual impossibility. The FAF was forced to react in dribs and drabs as it labored under the control of an army that had no idea how to use it and was technophobic in general especially regarding radio communication. Thus, in May 1940, the FAF was ill prepared to assault stalled German columns, even if it had been given permission to do so. Coordination over such a vast area with poor or restricted communications was virtually impossible. The FAF's squadrons, groups, and wings were too dispersed to properly coordinate in a meaningful way.

There was no lack of ingenuity, know-how, or competence. France matched Germany blow-for-blow as the air war developed during World War I. Further, the French demonstrated exceptional forethought and innovation in the cooperation and coordination of land and air units during the Rif War. While French airmen, especially under Pierre Cot, put too much emphasis on strategic airpower that was likely to never be used because of national sensitivities, its pre–1938 structure would arguably have been extremely well suited to contest the airspace in question had it been left alone. As it was, individual squadron commanders had to wait for orders from often ill-trained army officers who had no idea how to use, integrate, or control airpower, or simply take off and hope they encountered an enemy to fight.

When Sedan was threatened and the Meuse crossed, the FAF and the Royal Air Force (RAF) assaulted the German bridges and crossings piecemeal, in predictable low-level and often slow attacks, and in the face of murderous flak and airborne German defenses. One can only speculate at how much differently the Battle of France might have evolved in the same battlespace had the FAF and the army coordinated and trained along the same lines as the Luftwaffe and the Heer. Although the French made a costly and noble stand in Stonne, it was simply outflanked and overwhelmed, and with the unhinging of French defenses, the FAF had to retreat pell-mell to scattered airfields around France, often losing aircraft, parts, and valuable technicians to the sweeping German advances.

The irony again was that this piece of land was too utterly predictable as a battlefield, that even the most amateurish military enthusiast could have guessed it as the most likely conflict zone based upon rapid and cursory surveys of the history. The Maginot Line was designed to cover the area and stopped close to the Belgian border originally because Belgium was allied to France in the interwar period. Belgium's switch to neutrality to placate Germany resulted in a rapid and improvised extension of the Maginot Line that was mostly composed of blockhouses and pillboxes, not the intricate defenses found farther south. The fact that the Germans exploited the Ardennes (again, as a secondary plan) proved that innovation is still to be had in the most predictable of environments.

INTRODUCTION

ANALYSIS OF THE CONFLICT that evolved into World War II began as early as the fall of 1939. Mass media generated untold quantities of print journalism, radio broadcasts, and both still and motion pictures covering the war in near real time until the German surrender on 8 May 1945. Interpretations of events began almost as soon as the last shot was fired—victories and defeats from Poland to Pearl Harbor, from El Alamein to Berlin—resulting in a dense mass of material in multiple languages that no one person can ever hope to completely examine, even concerning just a single battle or campaign.

With hindsight and access to fresh material (bolstered by the interest and support of the general public), historians began to reshape the accepted narrative in the 1990s. The collapse of the Soviet Union provided access to untapped archives yielding fresh perspectives. The most notable changes began with the destruction of the "clean Wehrmacht" myth. Introspective German examination and works such as Geoffrey P. Megargee's *War of Annihilation*[1] began to dismantle the sanitized view of German war efforts and aims willingly provided and carefully edited by German soldiers and officers, aided by the crusade against Communism and the formation of NATO, the Bundesrepublik, and the Bundeswehr.

Access to Soviet archives and seminal works such as *The Stalingrad Trilogy*, by David M. Glantz, not only refuted the monolithic paradigm established in the West, it set scholars and the public on a new course, reexamining World War II in its totality.[2] The most notable shift in scholarship to date concerns actions on the eastern front in the European theater of operations. Perhaps it is the contempt bred by familiarity or the excitement over previously "forbidden" information that rendered certain events less well examined and subject to accepted mythology, and of these the French Campaign in 1940 is most notable.

The general outline of the French defeat is well known: the Germans pushed armored divisions through the Ardennes Forest (circumventing the Maginot Line), cracked the feeble French defenses in the Sedan sector, and raced to the sea, isolating the best French divisions and forcing the British Expeditionary Force (BEF) to huddle on the beaches at Dunkirk. The evacuation of the BEF by a plucky fleet of military and civilian craft turned a potential disaster into a moral victory cemented into British cultural dogma, much as the Alamo in the United States. All the while, the French army melted away under ceaseless bombardment by the Luftwaffe (German air force, GAF) because the Armée de l'Air (French air force, FAF) was a nonentity; it was nowhere to be seen.

Part of this work began as a dissertation addressing the fundamental question: "Why did the French air force fail in 1940?" Like most research questions, it evolved and took on a life of its own, ultimately becoming a comparison of the Luftwaffe and the Armée de l'Air. Unlike the air war from 1939 to 1945, which witnessed evolution and development on both sides, the six-week French Campaign was a relatively brief and isolated event; there were only six weeks of committed combat between 10 May 1940 and 25 June 1940. There was virtually no time for the belligerents to reconsider. The campaign was primarily a product of the previous work in France, Britain, and Germany; the fighters trained for six years for one winner-take-all fight that ended with no possibility of a rematch. What did both sides do right and wrong? This is the fundamental question.

The answers lie in the development of both forces from 1934 to 1940. Under the Versailles treaty restrictions, Germany had no legitimate air force before 1934 and France had an anemic and antiquated air force attached to the army as an auxiliary. The independence of the FAF and the GAF genesis under Hitler properly initiate the analysis. The seemingly simple right versus wrong question belies a series of complex questions examining the development of both forces in detail. The answers are often more complex, and some of them serve as a challenge and a warning for modern organizations facing complex military problems that frequently have sociopolitical inputs steering the outcomes.

This work examines six fundamental areas that affected the development of the FAF and the GAF: aircraft and equipment, the aircraft industries, intelligence, the Spanish Civil War, doctrine and training, and last but not least, politics and airpower. Each area had dramatic effects on the efficacy of each force during the campaign.

Aircraft and Equipment

Technology is often given too much credit for victory or defeat, but it is a measurable factor in warfare. French planes were noticeably outclassed in 1940. While promising designs such as the Dewoitine 520 entered production in time for the campaign, they were too few in number to have a dramatic effect on the outcome of the air battle. French fighter pilots rose to defend France in dated and marginal American Curtiss Hawks, and the Morane-Saulnier 406, which was often as dangerous to the pilot as the enemy. French bombers were simply abysmal. Although promising designs sat on the drawing board, the FAF fought the air battle at a distinct disadvantage to continually refined and upgraded German Messerschmitt Bf 109, Heinkel He 111, and Junkers Ju 87 Stuka (a dive bomber and a concept that the French considered but abandoned).

Why were French aircraft noticeably inferior, why did France procure older American designs, why were the German aircraft noticeably superior, and why did the Messerschmitt Bf 110 and the French *bombardement, combat, reconnaissance* (BCR, of which the Bloch MB.131 was a salient example) "wallow in the same mud"? What overall effects did aircraft designs have on the outcome of the battle? These are all questions worthy of our attention.

Aircraft Industries

France ended World War I with arguably the most successful combat aircraft industry in the world. French designs equipped all Allied nations to some extent, and considering the disadvantages under which the French industry operated, it was remarkably prolific with designs, technology, and numbers produced. French aircraft were so highly regarded that Germany actively scavenged the battlefield to recover French aircraft parts. With the German military aircraft industry effectively eliminated following the Versailles treaty, the French aircraft industry should have remained dominant. Yet with war clouds on the horizon, French production lagged far behind that of Germany from 1938 to 1940. Why was the French aircraft industry so inefficient? What internal sociopolitical problems affected the French aircraft industry? How was the German aircraft industry able to not only catch, but dramatically surpass the French aircraft industry in less than a decade?

Intelligence

Understanding potential adversaries is vital. France increasingly anticipated conflict with Germany throughout the 1930s. Following the Munich agreement, war was considered unavoidable by many. What did French intelligence know about German intentions? What did the French know about German armament, doctrine, training, organization, and infrastructure—and vice versa? When the French Campaign began in May 1940, how well did each side's intelligence services prepare for conflict and what effects did this have on the campaign and the outcome of the air battle?

The Spanish Civil War

The Spanish Civil War is still largely overlooked and misinterpreted. While the Spanish Civil War captured the world's attention in the late 1930s as a proxy war between fascism and communism, World War II eclipsed the Spanish conflict almost entirely. Following a decade of post–World War II analysis in the West, the Spanish Civil War was mislabeled as a sort of laboratory for blitzkrieg, something it most certainly was not. However, the Spanish Civil War was a formative and informative experience for both France and Germany. Some in the French military sought to understand and interpret the war while actively avoiding participation; French sociopolitical divisions were such that it was feared any active involvement might spread the war to France. The German Condor Legion played an active role alongside Italy in supporting Franco's Nationalists in their struggle against the leftist Republicans. While subordinate to Spanish control, the Condor Legion made use of the active experience to refine ideas and equipment. How did both France and Germany read the lessons of the Spanish Civil War, and did these interpretations affect the outcome of the French Campaign?

Doctrine and Training

The interwar period was awash with military theory and doctrinal developments. Ideas that predated the technology upon which their implementation—not to mention success— hinged, continually developed from the late nineteenth century onward. Technical developments during World War I—such as aircraft, tanks, the radio, and poison gas, among others—made science fiction a reality. Total war moved one step closer to reality and machines now existed that could bring the war to the enemy at every level; the army and navy became a shield that could simply be flown over. The next war would involve entire populaces engaging against each other at every level. In light of these developments, how did France and Germany approach airpower doctrine and training in the interwar period? How did French colonial operations dismiss or reinforce airpower concepts left immature in 1918? Why did French and German airpower doctrines develop as they did in the 1930s—what were the influences, and how did Germany come from seemingly far behind to dominate France in 1940? Were the French backward in their thinking, or did other influences affect the outcome of the French Campaign?

Leadership, Politics, and Airpower

Militaries do not exist in isolation; they are the products of the countries that create them. France and Germany went to war in 1940 with militaries directly influenced by politics. In Germany, Hitler and the Nazi regime thrust rearmament to the forefront. A deeply divided France changed governments so frequently that one needs a chart ready at hand to keep track of the heads of state through the 1930s. In both cases the politics, and through politics, culture and society made themselves felt during rearmament and preparation for war. Although Hitler was reviled following World War II, and often blamed for every military mishap, the Wehrmacht did very well in 1940 under his (but always his) hand through the 1930s, whereas France was the epitome of the "weak liberal democracy," continually divided by deep social rifts and squabbling politicians. Further, France's deep mistrust between military and politics dating to at least the time of the Dreyfus affair, created factions the likes of which were unseen in Nazi Germany. While the money trail is easy to follow in military aircraft production, sociopolitical influences can be difficult to discern when it comes to topics such as doctrine, yet they still exist. How did French and German politics influence airpower from planes to doctrine?

French Air Minister Pierre Cot is a virtually unknown name in the United States. While at one point he was vocal and to a degree prominent in his exile following the fall of France, he has faded into obscurity. Cot was an intellectual from a generally conservative family and he saw service during World War I. He rose to political prominence in the interwar years, and he advocated an "air minded" France. He was influential in establishing Air France, and he was the prime mover in government responsible for the establishment of an independent French air force in 1933 and 1934. Cot's politics changed over time; he moved further to the left the longer his political career endured, and once suspected, he is now known to have actively spied for the Soviet Union. In a paranoid France with deep political divides, Cot's mark on the Armée de l'Air was notable, and the conservatives in France were all too cognizant of this fact. How did Cot's proximity to the FAF contribute to its successes and ultimate failure?

A Reconsideration

This book argues that the Armée de l'Air was outmatched by the Luftwaffe due more to internal than external problems. That is to say that the aerial defeat over France, based upon the above factors was more due to what the French did wrong than the Germans did right; the air war post–1940, a topic well considered, thoroughly demonstrated that the Luftwaffe specifically, but Germany in general, was not prepared to engage in the type of air war required to win on a strategic or grand strategic level. However, in six weeks, German airpower dominated the air (and the press' and subsequent historians' imaginations) as a key component of the Wehrmacht's victory, but at a higher cost than previously considered, especially in the anglophone world. Although Britain contributed significantly and sacrificed greatly to defend France and Belgium, the primary burden of the battle fell upon the French military, and that is the primary concern of this work.

The FAF trailed the Luftwaffe technically and numerically, and possessed modern written doctrine, but it was ill-suited at critical points for French defense. Despite these disadvantages and disruptions due to internal political turmoil, the FAF fought a disorganized but brutal battle against a Luftwaffe that had its own problems (though critically fewer than the FAF). Further, the French army deserves perhaps as much blame for overall defeat in the air battle as the FAF. The army's shameful theater at the Riom Trials, one of the worst examples of collaboration during World War II, was the beginning of the defamation unfairly levied against the FAF. A united Germany (admittedly under a vicious and repressive regime) with significant interest in airpower and well-placed advocates, produced a Luftwaffe best designed for an operation such as Fall Gelb (the German designation for the Battle of France). Conversely, France was deeply divided (with an unfortunate air force as a focus) and it represented the "weak democracy" that dictatorial and repressive regimes tend to mock as incapable. The squabbling affected everything from doctrine to aircraft production in France, and it proved fatal in May and June of 1940.

— 1 —
COMBAT AIRCRAFT
A Technical Analysis

WORLD WAR I was an "industrial war." More specifically, by 1918, World War I had arguably become an "industrial/technical war." Embryonic technologies such as the airplane and the radio matured rapidly between 1914 and 1918. Similarly, new weapons platforms—the tank being a prime example—were conceived, designed, built, and improved during the war. Although concepts such as J. F. C. Fuller's "Plan 1919" never made it past the drawing board, the battles from August to November 1918 portended an increased role for technology on the battlefield, which could hardly have been dreamed of in 1914.

After World War I ended, weapons production and design cooled as demand decreased almost overnight. By the early 1930s, the situation changed again; the world began to rearm. Unlike 1914, when France and Germany faced off with essentially similar weapons technology, 1940 demonstrated a noticeable gap in the overall quality and quantity of aircraft and antiaircraft weapons available to France and Germany. This design gap had a noticeable effect on the air battles between France and Germany:

"The French interpreted the technological lessons of the war in light of the overall balance of power between France and interwar Germany. Even after the Treaty of Versailles Germany remained industrially and demographically superior to France, inherently more capable of waging an extended attrition war like World War I. This superiority may actually have increased in the interwar period."[1]

"Even with these problems," wrote historian Barry Posen, "its [France's] aerial capabilities remained superior to that of Germany, since the latter was strictly limited by the Versailles treaty; but in 1935, when Germany revealed the creation of the Luftwaffe, and in subsequent years that organization grew in strength and experience, little was done to alter the confusion that reigned in the French air force."[2] While Posen does not attempt to explain exactly what the "confusion" was or how it came about, his technical read is correct: the French air force (FAF) *should* have entered the Battle of France with a technically superior force.

What were the major differences between aircraft fielded by the FAF and the Luftwaffe in 1940? How did the FAF's equipment differ significantly from its primary ally, the Royal Air Force (RAF)? How did these differences in technology affect the aerial battles? Most directly, why did this technology gap exist in the first place since the Luftwaffe had to start almost from scratch in design and production due to the Treaty of Versailles, while France suffered no such hindrance? This chapter will examine the technical differences between the aircraft fielded by the FAF and the aircraft fielded by the Luftwaffe, and it will explain how this gap contributed to the collapse of the FAF in 1940.

When France and Germany went to war, the outcome was not assured. On a technical level, both sides fought the aerial battle during the so-called Phony War (Sitzkrieg to the Germans or Drôle de guerre to the French) with essentially the same weapons from 3 September 1939 to 10 June 1940. The arms race, which began in earnest when the Luftwaffe sprang into life in 1935, was over. France, Britain, and Germany fought with what their respective industries developed over a period of about seven years, from 1933 to 1940.

Fighters, bombers, and direct support ground attack aircraft saw use in combat roles during the Battle of France. All three types of planes debuted during World War I, although the ground attack aircraft category was a late development by both the Allies and the Central Powers.[3] The British Salamander and the similar aircraft designed in Germany were late additions to the war, but they evolved out of the recognition that the direct support role warranted a purpose-designed aircraft.[4] Although both sides fielded an array of fighter and bomber aircraft, certain types dominated the airspace due to their production numbers. How did these aircraft stack up against each other on a purely technical level? What advantages and disadvantages did each combatant have on a technical level? How did these characteristics play out in the skies over France in May and June 1940?

Technical Data: Fighters

On 1 September 1939, France had the following "new" fighter aircraft in inventory:

TABLE 1

Type	Number On Hand
Morane 405/406	547
Potez 630	85
Potez 631	206
Bloch 151/152	106
Curtiss H.75	165

Source: Andre Van Haute, *Pictorial History of the French Air Force: Volume I 1909–1940*. London: Trinity Press, 1974, 139.

Dewoitine both provided the oldest and the newest type of fighter active in the FAF in the Dewoitine 510 and Dewoitine 520, respectively. Some older types of aircraft were utilized during the Battle of France, but their numbers were so small as to have had little effect on the overall technological comparison.

After months of what can at best be termed "skirmishing" between September 1939 and May 1940, France had a total of 637 *chasseurs* (fighters) in frontline service, meaning theoretically "working" aircraft in active frontline squadrons according to Général Charles Christienne and Général Pierre Lissarrague.[5] Those soldier-historians put Luftwaffe strength at 1,210 fighters on 10 May 1940 out of a total of 2,890 aircraft available.[6] This number is reasonably close to the 2,589 combat aircraft quoted by James Corum.[7] Murray's total of 1,179 fighters on establishment for the Luftwaffe on 2 September 1939, with assumptions regarding losses and replacements, supports the general overall accuracy of the above figures.[8] The performance gap was as noticeable as numbers available to both sides.

A Note on Numbers and the French Air Force

The FAF's numbers conflict more than usual vis-à-vis the RAF, the U.S. Army Air Corps (USAAC), or even the Luftwaffe. The convoluted procurement system, strange methods of acceptance, and the unclear recording of aircraft produced compared to those accepted, those on strength, and those actually flyable has left scholars such as Christienne and Facon, both of whom actually ran the Service Historique de l'Armée de l'Air (SHAA) confounded.

France

The Morane-Saulnier M.S.406 was the backbone of the French fighter arm in 1939–40. In total, 1,098 of the 405/6 series were produced by the armistice in 1940, although some of these (unbelievably, considering the international situation in Europe by the late 1930s) went to foreign contracts.[9] The M.S.406 mounted two 7.5-mm machine guns and a single 20-mm cannon with 60 rounds of ammunition.[10] Its maximum altitude was 31,020 feet and it had a top speed of 303 mph at 16,500 feet.[11] The M.S.406 was very complex requiring more than 16,000 man-hours to build, which was twice that of the Bf 109 or Dewoitine 520.[12] Keeping in mind that production was only fully engaged in 1938, when the Bf 109 was actually receiving product upgrades due in large part to experience in Spain, the ramifications are obvious.[13]

Historian Gaston Botquin noted,

> Even though about one-third of the opposing fighters were Bf 109B and 109D aircraft, and the Aufklarer were lone aircraft, the weaknesses of the M.S.406 were apparent:

1. Lack of armor (partly corrected by the addition of a dorsal shield).
2. Frequent gun jamming at high altitude (corrected in some units by using signal light circuits to feed electric heaters for the gun breeches).
3. Insufficient firepower necessitating a close approach to "kill"—less than fifty yards on some occasions.
4. Pneumatic gun control giving about 2/10 second "dead time" before firing making gun deflection difficult.
5. Malfunctioning of radio sets.
6. Rapid engine wear giving even lower speed and climb rate.
7. Loss of motor and fuselage panels due to deterioration of screws and hinges.
8. Corrosion of rudder parts.
9. Cabin glazing broken by air pressure in high speed maneuvers.
10. Lack of rear view mirror on factory fresh aircraft.[14]

The M.S.406 could barely catch up with German bombers at altitude and often had too little firepower from ineffective guns to bring them down.[15] Almost half of all French pilots killed during the Battle of France were flying the M.S.406.[16] However, the M.S.406 was outfitted with all the equipment of a then–modern fighter including a gun camera.[17] The engineering and design concepts incorporated into the design were sound; on paper, the M.S.406 was an up-to-date fighter. The inherent problem was that its construction and performance were frankly shoddy compared to other models of similar vintage. The German Bf 109, for instance, was as old as the M.S.406. It was not an age issue, neither was it an issue of not having the proper equipment. The M.S.406 had simply been neglected rather than being upgraded and improved.

Interestingly, the media seemed well pleased with the 406 and touted its performance against the Luftwaffe in the Phony War.[18] While the 406 did take its toll on German fighters and bombers, one is left to wonder what results an enthusiastic and genuine upgrade would have yielded.

The Potez 630 and 631 were essentially different variants of the same multi-seat fighter aircraft. They were armed with two forward-firing 30-mm cannon and one 7.5-mm defensive machine gun facing rear; some were fitted with twin 7.5-mm machine guns under each wing.[19] Top speed was 276 mph at 14,850 feet and the ceiling was 29,700 feet.[20] The Potez 630/631 very closely resembled the Bf 110 in appearance, which caused some confusion and unfortunate accidents in combat. It saw service with the Aéronavale (French naval aviation branch) as well.[21] During the entire Battle of France the Potez 630/631 only recorded seventeen kills.[22] Considering the usually inflated nature of reported aerial victories in combat, this is not an impressive combat record.

The Bloch 151/152 was another fighter mainstay of the FAF. "The breed had potential, manifested in the M.B.157, but both the M.B.151 and 152 were rushed into production. The resulting teething troubles wasted precious time and energies which might have been better devoted elsewhere."[23] Like most of the other "new" French aircraft, production began in 1938.[24] "The European political scene had become particularly ominous and it was hoped that the problems would soon be cured—a false hope."[25] Like the M.S.406, the M.B. series was available and it flew; it was better than nothing. Apparently, some subterfuge also lay at the heart of the M.B.151/152's acceptance, an issue that was not discovered until it entered production and service.[26]

Nevertheless, the M.B.151 was a modern design and its complexity was revealed in the official maintenance manuals. There were minute details explaining each of the structural spare parts for the airframe and some of the accessories.[27] Thousands upon thousands of structural spare parts were listed individually over 169 pages.[28] This list did not include spare parts for guns, sights, motor, and so forth.[29] What this reveals is that this new generation of planes was increasingly more complex, which meant that knowledge of each machine would have to be increasingly specialized, thus putting more demand upon the air force.

The M.B.152 carried two 7.5-mm machine guns and two 20-mm cannon with 60 rounds per cannon.[30] Its maximum speed was 301 mph at 16,500 feet and it had a ceiling of 33,990 feet, with a range of 362 miles at 18,150 feet.[31] Pilots complained that it suffered from delicate handling, but it officially racked up 150 kills with 35 probables.[32]

Many of the indigenously produced French aircraft were equipped with the *mitrailleuse M.A.C. modèle 1934*. It was a widely used weapon, and the manual mentions it is quite similar to the 1931 tank-mounted type.[33] It fired a variety of different types of ammunition including ball, tracer, armor piercing, and armor piercing tracer.[34] Further, the French M1929 7.5-mm cartridge was quite modern, with ballistics similar to that of the later 7.62 NATO round. From the outside, this seems again to have been a technically normative gun.

It was an interesting gun that functioned well on the ground and at low altitudes but had some serious problems in the aircraft role. First, it had a very complicated feed system.[35] Second, it was a gas-operated gun that used gas bleed from the fired cartridges to operate a piston that drove the operating mechanisms.[36] This tends to be a reliable operating system, especially for ground-mounted machine guns. When combined, these two weapon systems produced failures at altitudes above 20,000 feet. The manual had four pages of explanations describing how to clear stoppages.[37]

The solution to the most serious of the stoppage problems caused by freezing was to add a heater to the gun. This was somewhat effective, but it did not solve the other fundamental problems with the gun: the limited number that were usually fitted (no more than two) and the low throw weight of the guns relative to the small size of the cartridge.

Germany and the United States had developed an armor-piercing incendiary round, which increased the effectiveness of even smaller aircraft guns, but France had no equivalent. The result was that many French fighters would have to peck away longer at enemy planes or use up their limited cannon ammunition more quickly (if one was mounted). This factor alone might be the reason why so many Luftwaffe airframes were damaged rather than destroyed. The irony is that France could easily have bought or produced under license the American-made Browning guns in .30 caliber that would have solved the reliability problems and the ammunition type problems, even if it would have left the aircraft with an inadequate throw weight vis-à-vis modern metal monoplane design. Although it made more sense from a simple logistic standpoint, even the American-made aircraft, fitted with the better Browning guns, were chambered for the inferior 7.5-mm French round that had less versatile and effective ammunition types.

Why was this rather easy fix never embraced? Although there is no direct evidence, it is likely that the problem lay in the corruption and protectionism built into the procurement and testing process in France that aviation pioneer Alexander de Seversky described with such vitriol.[38]

The FAF was also equipped with the Curtiss Hawk. France purchased the Hawk at an "inflated price" and out of necessity since it was clear by the beginning of 1938 the European situation was rapidly changing and the French aircraft industry could not meet its production goals.[39] The Hawk export version, which France received, carried four or six 7.5-mm machine guns, could reach 304 or 312 mph with slightly different engine variants, and had a ceiling of 33,000 feet.[40]

What makes the Hawk such an interesting choice for France is its history with the USAAC. The Hawk was certainly a giant leap forward for fighter design in 1935, and competed to replace the open cockpit P-36 monoplane in U.S. service. By 1938, when France ordered the Hawk, it was effectively obsolete. The Hawk was comparable to other aircraft in French inventory, but inferior to other aircraft entering foreign air forces from 1938 to 1940. The Hawk was well past its prime.

For aviation and military historians, the 1930s can be something of an enigma and France offers an excellent case study. Many combat aircraft—the F-4, F-15, and F-16—are still found on inventory with modern air forces forty of fifty years after their first flights. Each of these aircraft was upgradable to carry them through the third and fourth generations of aircraft design. This was not possible in the 1930s; technology in airframe and engine design was progressing too rapidly with designs sometimes on the drawing board at the same time rendering each other obsolete. In less than ten years the USAAC went from the P-28 to the P-36 (the Hawk that France purchased) to the P-40—and opted to produce the P-38 in 1937!

In 1942 Pierre Cot testified before the U.S. Senate regarding the performance of the French aircraft industry prior to World War II. The content of the transcript is revealing:

Senator Edwin C. Johnson (D-CO): In 1938 the French and the English were purchasing planes in the United States?

Mr. Cot: Yes, sir.

Senator Johnson: And I recall the French were not very particular: they were taking any kind of plane that we were offering them; and it was not a lend-lease proposition, they were paying good, hard cash for those planes.

Mr. Cot: Yes, sir.

Senator Johnson: They were not at all particular: they were taking any kind of plane that we would offer them, while the British turned most of them down, would not accept them at all, which would indicate the British thought our planes were not good enough in quality while the French were satisfied with the planes.

Mr. Cot: Yes, sir; because the quality of the British planes at that time was much better than the quality of the French planes . . .

Mr. Cot: At the time of the fall of France, Germany was probably producing 1,800 planes a month.

Senator Johnson: 1,800?

Mr. Cot: Yes, sir. France was producing 450 and Germany about 1,800.[41]

American, British, and German aircraft firms were pouring millions of man-hours and dollars, pounds, and marks into design, construction, and development. Unfortunately for France, her aircraft industry was in the throes of desperately needed reorganization, which some argue ruined French chances of winning the air war, and helped keep France behind her competitors. France was buying or building everything possible for its air force, but the overall quality of its aircraft was low in most cases. The good planes were far too few in number, and although German production was overstated, France clearly lagged behind her allies and primary opponent in both quantity and quality.

Foreign military observers inside France also monitored French aircraft performance presumably as much for intelligence purposes as to gain an understanding of potential FAF capabilities. In the final estimate of French combat capabilities, revised and submitted in October, 1939, just over a month into World War II, but before the Phony War became the de facto state of military affairs, the American air attaché in Paris compared the characteristics of various French aircraft in service, including imported American models.[42] While there was no in-depth technical discussion describing the FAF vis-à-vis the Luftwaffe, the data apparent to Colonel Smith was telling. The by-now obsolete Curtiss H-75 (the French variant of the Hawk) was far and away the best performer.[43] None of the D.520s had made it into service by the time of the report. However, the bulk of the matériel with which the FAF would have to fight the Luftwaffe was already on hand. Although Colonel Smith did not give any particularly scathing commentary on the performance data of the French matériel on hand, and he did not compare it directly to the Luftwaffe, one can imagine his reaction internally comparing the data on French aircraft with those entering American service, which were on par or superior to German models.[44]

Germany

Along with the Spitfire, the P-51 Mustang, and the A6M Zero, the Bf 109 is an aerial icon of World War II. "The Design of the 109, originally known as the Bf 109, was begun in 1934, the prototype being flown the following year. The first production version, the Bf 109B, was given an operational try-out in the Spanish Civil War. Many shortcomings were then revealed such as wing flutter and tail buffeting, and although efforts were made to eliminate these failings in subsequent models, it was sometime before they were eradicated."[45] There were multiple versions of the Bf 109 in service by May 1940. The Bf 109E, affectionately known as the "Emil," was the newest variant in service in May 1940. The improvements to the Bf 109E-1 was a "direct result" of experience in Spain.[46]

Germany produced more than fifteen hundred Emils in 1939.[47] The E-1 mounted four 7.92-mm machine guns, two over the engine, and one in each wing.[48] The greatest improvement made to the Emil was the addition of the Daimler Benz DB 601 engine with direct fuel injection giving Emil pilots a constant fuel supply with no engine faltering and better performance in a dive.[49] In combat opposed to the Hurricane and the Spitfire (which occurred frequently in 1940) the Emil was frequently considered an even match at middle altitudes, but superior at high altitudes.[50] Notably, the E-1 still did not provide armor for the pilot.

The E-3 variant, the newest in production and service by the Battle of France, represented yet another series of improvements. The engine was the same as the E-1 giving both a performance of about 350 mph at 13,000 feet.[51] Two 20-mm cannon with 60 rounds each were added to the wings, the canopy was reinforced, and the cockpit was armored.[52]

In 1940, the Bf 110 was still a fighter, which was its primary intended role. It was a long-range multi-seat fighter, fulfilling the same theoretical role as the Potez 631, and again, was physically more than a passing resemblance of the same. Performance wise, both aircraft were similar. The Bf 110 reached 283 mph at 13,120 ft.[53] The Messerschmitt Bf 110 came much more heavily armed, however: two 20-mm cannon and four 7.92-mm machine guns facing forward and one rear-facing defensive 7.92-mm machine gun. It had a range of 1,070 miles.[54]

Great Britain

Like France and Germany, Britain had a hodgepodge of older fighters on strength when the war began, but the Hawker Hurricane was the predominant British fighter for the first year and a half of World War II. It was an excellent fighter in 1940. Although credit for aerial victories should always be taken a bit for granted, the Hurricane was credited with more than 1,500 aerial victories over the Luftwaffe in 1940, which represents more than half of those claimed by the RAF against the Luftwaffe in that year.[55] The Hurricane was potently armed with eight .303 machine guns. The Hurricane I managed 330 mph at 17,500 feet and had a service ceiling of 36,000 feet.[56] It first flew in October 1937.[57]

The Spitfire is probably the most well-known fighter aircraft of all time. However, the Spitfire entered the Battle of France late seeing its first action on the Continent while covering the evacuation from Dunkirk.[58] The Spitfire was initially armed with eight .303 machine guns, just like the Hurricane. The Air Ministry insisted upon the heavy armament for sound reasons in Specification F.5/34 that combat later reinforced:

The speed excess of a modern fighter over that of a contemporary bomber has so reduced the chance of repeated attacks by the same fighters essential to obtain decisive results in the short space of time offered for one attack only. This specification is issued, therefore, to govern the production of a day fighter in which speed in overtaking an enemy at 15,000 ft, combined with rapid climb to this height, is of primary importance. The best speed possible must be aimed for at all heights between 5,000 ft and 15,000 ft. In conjunction with this performance the maximum hitting power must be aimed at, and *eight machine guns are considered advisable*.[59]

Like the Bf 109, the Spitfire was continually upgraded throughout World War II. The Spitfire first flew in 1936, and the prototype reached a speed of 342 mph.[60] Early operational Spitfires, such as those in service in 1940, could operate at 38,000 feet and reach speeds of 367 mph.[61]

Technical Data: Bombers

Bombers were and remain terrifying aircraft. Since before World War I, the bomber captured the popular imagination of the public not because of its glamorous or dashing image like the fighter, but because of what it does; the bomber allows the concept of "total war" to be more than just a phrase. The bomber brought war to the people of opposing nations. Germany attempted to keep pressure on the British populace during World War I by bombing the UK from 1915 onward. Britain attempted to retaliate as much as possible while being restrained by a France that withdrew from its forefront position in bomber development out of a fear that Germany could inflict much more damage on French infrastructure and perceived delicate French morale than France could return in kind.

Bombing results were mixed during World War I, but the interwar period brought the experience and thinking of the bomber advocates to a head. The most famous of these, Giulio Douhet, visualized a graphic Dante-like destruction of civilian targets where the man-made hell created by high explosives, incendiaries, and poison gas made each meter closer to the intended target that much more unbearable, and there were staunch strategic bombing proponents in France. "In fact, the essential features of the doctrine of General Douhet subsist and justly so. Only a few exaggerations in the dialect and certain applications of the thesis, essential to Italy, were modified in France and adapted to the conditions of our national defense."[62]

Bomber technology progressed rapidly during the interwar period, especially in the 1930s. All the major combatants developed improved their bomber designs in the interwar period awaiting the next war, which promised to bring the bomber to the fore. Going into World War II, the French were well aware of how outclassed they truly were in the field of bombers.[63]

― France ―

France entered the war with an assortment of bombers. Of the newer types of bombers available to France, the following were on hand:

TABLE 2

Type of Bomber	Number On Hand
Breguet 691/693	185
LeO 451	350
Douglas DB 7	189
MB 174/5	61
Amiot 351/4	61
GM 167 F	64

According to Christienne and Lissarrague, France had 242 ready bombers on hand versus 1,680 in the Luftwaffe.[64] The authors also note that this "ready" number was fewer than 20 percent of the total number of bombers on the books, which largely agrees with Facon.[65] Murray states the Luftwaffe had approximately 1,726 bombers on hand for the Battle of France, which is also reasonably close to the number derived by Christienne and Lissarrague.[66]

The Breguet 691 series evolved into several different aircraft with different missions. It began life as a multi-seat fighter, but was used much more frequently as a light/medium bomber being far too unwieldy (even by

French standards) to use as a fighter.[67] The 691/3 had a range of 844 miles and cruised at 253 mph although its maximum speed was 300 mph.[68] Its role as a fighter was questionable, its role as a bomber was almost equally so as its maximum bombload was 880 lbs (10 × 100 lbs) carried internally.[69] However, the design did enjoy some success in dive-bombing missions, but it was underpowered and as such took a great deal of punishment when it was used in low level attack; out of 500 sorties in the Battle of France, 100 machines were lost.[70]

The Lioré et Olivier LeO 451 first flew in January 1937, but it did not go into production until February 1939.[71] By 10 May 1940, ninety-four aircraft were in their units.[72] It had a cruising speed of 225 mph, with a maximum speed of 309 mph, and a range of 1,437 miles when loaded with 3,080 lbs of bombs.[73] Defensive armament included four 7.5-mm machine guns or two 7.5-mm machine guns and a potent but awkward 20-mm cannon, which was later replaced by the two 7.5-mm machine guns.[74] The LeO 451 took place on the raid on the BMW factory after France decided to try and conduct a bombing campaign; only two planes managed to find the target.[75]

The Douglas DB-7 was another purchase from the United States. Again, France tried to fulfill expected shortfalls with available American aircraft. "Although it crashed during its trials, the Douglas DB-7 sufficiently impressed the French purchasing delegation."[76] Fourteen were lost during the Battle of France, mostly in low level attacks "in the worst possible conditions imaginable without fighter cover, with heavy Flak [sic] everywhere."[77] The DB-7 carried 1,760 lbs of bombs internally, and it was armed with four forward-firing 7.5-mm machine guns and two defensive 7.5-mm machine guns mounted in the rear. The DB-7's maximum speed was 309 mph at 11,500 feet, and it had a range of 525 miles.[78] It takes little imagination to see the future A/B-26 in the DB-7's lines.

The Bloch M.B.174 was perhaps France's most successful aircraft.[79] It was fairly fast at 331 mph, and it had an impressive ceiling of 36,300 feet, which made it very valuable and successful in the reconnaissance role.[80] The M.B.174 carried fewer bombs than the M.B.175 at 880 lbs, and 1,320 lbs, respectively.[81] The M.B.175 did not enter production until late 1939 and it was intended for use as a bomber. Its speed would have been helpful in the low-level attacks which were so costly to the French in 1940, but for inexplicable reasons, the M.B.175 which were on hand were continually delivered to reconnaissance units![82]

The Amiot 351/4 dated from a 1934 design unveiled in 1936 as a mail carrier.[83] Like most of the other modern aircraft, orders were not placed until 1938, and machines did not begin to leave the factory until 1939, which partially account for the low numbers on hand in May 1940.[84] Thirteen were lost in the Battle of France, and again, a useful if not particularly potent (760 lbs bombload) bomber was used more for reconnaissance duties, although it was slower than other machines at 262 mph cruising speed at 16,500 feet and a top speed of 303 mph.[85]

The Glenn Martin 167F was another light bomber (no French bombers justified the designation "heavy" and in reality, very few would even qualify as "medium") and reconnaissance platform available in 1940. Statistically, it is very similar to all other French aircraft in its class, even though it was an American aircraft. It was armed with four forward-facing 7.5-mm machine guns and two rear-facing 7.5-mm machine guns, and had a very light bombload of 760 lbs, with a maximum speed of 305 mph, but with a cruising speed of only 255 mph and a ceiling of 29,139 feet.[86]

Interestingly, France produced quite a variety of aerial bombs. The standard antipersonnel bomb weighed in at 250 kg.[87] General high explosive bombs came in various weights from 50 to 500 kg.[88] In addition, smoke, illumination, incendiary, and training bombs, along with a wide variety of fuses were available. The fuses included instantaneous, impact, delayed, and those made for special types of bombs such as smoke and incendiary.[89] Thus, in theory, French aircraft had a wide variety of bomb types that would be utilized in a number of specialized roles. However, the problem remained that most French bombers could only carry relatively light bombloads, and at that more slowly than their counterparts. Underpowered engines, and frankly dated airframes not only meant that the bombers carried less, but they did it progressively slower under the weight of the bombs, incrementally decreasing their performance with every kilogram.

Germany

Germany conducted the first large scale attempt in both World War I and World War II to subdue a nation (in both instances Great Britain) by aerial bombardment. During the interwar period, German airmen of the Condor Legion participated in many bombing raids against targets in Spain refining equipment, ideas, and tactics along the way. By 1937, one year before some modern French aircraft were ordered and fully two years before many of them were to be produced, Germany introduced the He 111, the Dornier Do 17, and the Ju 87 in Spain.[90] Germany attempted strategic bombing with a more or less operational air force during the Battle of Britain and was pressuring Britain severely until a shift in bombing priorities occurred. Bomber raids against much less well-armed, organized, and defended targets than Britain, such as Rotterdam and Sarajevo fared much better.

While bomber development was a priority of German aircraft manufacturers in the 1930s, it did not produce the heavy types currently under development in the United States and Great Britain, such as the B-17, the B-24, the Lancaster, and eventually the B-29. Nevertheless, Germany produced several excellent medium bombers that performed very well in the operation role, and in some cases soldiered on until 1945.

Design began on the Heinkel He 111 in 1934; it was in production by 1936.[91] It was not as fast as most of the bombers in the French inventory at only 217 mph, but it carried a very impressive 3,300 lb bombload and had a range of more than 900 miles.[92] The He 111, like the Do 17, the Bf 109, and the Ju 86, were all developed under the guidance of one man, General der Flieger Wilhelm Wimmer, the head of the Luftwaffe technical office from 1933 to 1936.[93] While Wimmer did not oversee production, his guidance produced much of the very successful basic set of aircraft with which Germany fought the first three years of the war, with the Bf 109 and He 111 enduring in one form or another until 1945.

The Ju 87 *Sturzkampfflugzeug* (or Stuka) was in a class all its own in Europe in 1940, but it was not revolutionary. It evolved from the dedicated ground attack/support aircraft of World War I. Ironically, it was the French who put the most emphasis on battlefield support during World War I, not the Germans. The British, not the Germans, also conducted the first dive-bombing attacks during World War I.[94] The Stuka was not particularly fast at 236 mph.[95] Its ceiling was an unimpressive 26,248 feet. It did not have great defensive armament with 1940 variants only having two forward-firing and one rear-firing 7.92-mm machine gun, but occasionally it did win a dogfight. It could however deliver up to a 1,000-kg bomb against a ground target with impressive accuracy for 1940. It also utilized the most effective German weapon of the Battle of France to great effect: the radio. The Stuka was on call aerial artillery made possible by the combined arms concept developed in Germany over the interwar period, which hinged on rapid movement and effective wireless communication. The Allies had no equivalent in 1940. Général Maurice Gamelin, commander in chief, did not even have a radio in his headquarters.

Great Britain

By 1944 Britain and the United States were unleashing almost daily (weather permitting) mass bombing raids against Germany. In 1940 Britain did not have the massive bomber fleets it would later use to pound German cities, industry, and military installations. During the Battle of France, British bomber attacks with light and medium bombers mirrored French attacks coming in unescorted at low- to mid-level and at a very high cost for the attackers.[96]

There were many more types of aircraft used by all three air forces. This discussion has intentionally been limited to the most important aircraft in use by the respective air forces during the Battle of France in 1940 to help clarify the relative technical advantages and disadvantages of each air force.

Analysis: The Facts behind the Data

Pure technical comparisons can be somewhat useful in explaining victory or defeat. Often, however, the proximate causes are lurking behind the data. Technology debates often tend to dominate popular history, especially counterfactual history. For instance, the Tiger I and Tiger II tanks look fantastic on paper. They had very powerful guns and thick armor. Virtually any schoolboy interested in World War II can tell stories of the dreaded

Tiger tank. The back end of the story is how the Tiger actually contributed to Germany's defeat by consuming many times the man-hours and raw materials needed to produce the Panzer IV or *Sturmgeschütz* (assault gun) III. The Tiger was also prone to mechanical breakdown and its great weight meant that in soggy, wet terrain it bogged down easily. German tankers proved in France in 1940, and Russia in 1941 and 1942 that even when tanks were overmatched, they could overcome more powerful adversaries with better tactics; a "supertank" was no guarantee of victory, and in the end the Tiger was far more of a drain than an aid. There is always a story behind the story.

The FAF's equipment during the Battle of France tells both stories—one of an outnumbered, outclassed air force desperately trying to defend the metropole against the Luftwaffe which seemed to be roaming almost at will over the front, and one of civil and military chaos, rivalry, indirection, and incompetence.

Outclassed

"In 1933, Général Victor Denain estimated that French military aviation was five years behind the other great powers."[97] The simple unpleasant fact is that France was woefully outclassed by friend (the RAF) and foe (the Luftwaffe) alike during the six week Battle of France in May and June of 1940.

"Throw weight" is a measure of how much ordnance is delivered on the receiving end of aircraft machine guns to their intended target. Basically, throw weight is a raw measure of the weight of projectiles hurled into an enemy aircraft by an opposing aircraft's guns. Its basic measure does not take into account such factors as the different effectiveness of one incendiary composition over another. It is still a useful yardstick to measure potential damage to enemy aircraft.

There was no significant difference in the ballistic performance the French 7.5-mm, the German 7.92-mm, and British .303 machine guns versus enemy aircraft.[98] Performance of the 20-mm cannon was similar,[99] and French fighters frequently mounted a 20-mm cannon. However, German and British aircraft carried more guns than the average French fighter. The

Bf 109 carried at least four machine guns, sometimes two 20-mm cannon, while the Hurricane and Spitfire carried at least eight .303 machine guns. This meant that in aerial combat, the Bf 109, the Hurricane, or—toward the end of the campaign—the Spitfire, was able to put twice as much ordnance into the intended target.

French aircraft machine guns were notoriously unreliable, having problems with freezing at high altitudes resulting in some of the previously mentioned field modifications such as unit-made heaters being installed on guns.[100] The intricate French procurement system also allowed for many aircraft to be delivered and taken on strength in very incomplete form, ironically often lacking, of all things, guns. Allowing for the fact that different bureaucratic entities find different methods more useful or practical, the French situation is somewhat unusual in that one of the primary reasons aircraft seem to have been delivered without machine guns is the French Army was afraid of letting Communist factory workers handle machine guns.[101] The air force was considered extremely leftist by the army, having been created, and initially controlled and guided by Pierre Cot, a man who was without a doubt vehemently patriotic, but also pushed to align France with the USSR from the early 1930s onward.

Fighters in Combat

French pilots "had been encouraged to cease fire at 200 m when attacking from the rear. This distance was increased to 400 m when attacking from the front, at which distance pilots had to break off their attack for safety reasons. But combat experience showed that at such distances, rifle-caliber machine guns lacked penetration power, and units claimed results were obtained only at distances of about 100 m!"[102] In and of itself, this problem seems easily resolvable, and a normal part of the admittedly painful wartime learning curve. However, French aircraft were slow compared to their German counterparts and were frequently only able to make one pass at German bombers when they could find them. Further, German bombers were not much better armed defensively than French bombers, but they were escorted by fighters into the target, which French bombers generally were not, with predictable results. French fighter pilots had to fight their way through faster, more maneuverable, better-armed Bf 109s to engage the bombers to begin with, only to find they had to completely modify their concepts if they were even able to attack enemy bombers.

Germany sent the Condor Legion to Spain to aid Franco in the Spanish Civil War, a conflict about which the French government and people had passionate feelings, but mostly avoided like a plague. A determined Pierre Cot managed to slip aircraft to Franco's enemies and there were certainly many French who volunteered to fight. However, the government felt that French society and government was dangerously divided to the point that the Spanish Civil War could spill over and start a civil war in France (presumably with Communist factory workers storming the halls of government with aircraft machine guns). At least since the commune in 1870, France was sharply divided socially and politically, with incidents such as the Dreyfus affair, and the mutinies of 1917 bringing to a boil a simmering unrest. While the Luftwaffe, the Italian air force, and the Soviets were using the Spanish Civil War to help formulate tactics and doctrine, and improve aircraft, France stayed away, frequently drawing completely erroneous lessons from what was observed.

The number of types of fighters the French had on establishment created an additional boondoggle. The Luftwaffe fielded one primary fighter, the Bf 109, arguably two if the Bf 110 is counted. The British fielded two types of fighter (although the Hurricane in much greater numbers in 1940). The French counted no fewer than five "modern" fighters discussed herein and still had other types on the books, and indeed in the air in 1940. For an aviation industry that struggled to catch up to its foreign competitors throughout the 1930s, combined with a military logistic system that was at the very least convoluted, this was toxic. Keeping spares on hand for one or two models is difficult enough, not to mentions spares for five types of fighters, some of which had to be shipped from the United States. "One of the most acute problems facing air officials during the May–June 1940 battle was undoubtedly that of supplying front-line units with equipment. How many witnesses to the events of 1939–1940, both among political and military leaders, have not reported the slowness with which the planes, despite being manufactured in large series, were delivered to the front line?"[103]

Bombers in Combat

French bombers did not have much of an effect on the Battle of France. Indeed, France had wrestled internally with the concept of strategic bombing since late November 1914. Cot, the Left, and the FAF had been advocates of bombing as a means to deliver destruction to enemy infrastructure, demoralize the enemy populace, and help create a viable *Petite Entente* strategy. The army pinned its hopes on the Maginot Line. As historian Anthony Cain points out, albeit with a somewhat incomplete analysis, "The airmen and politicians who led the Armée de l'Air as it served the Third Republic worked diligently to create a military institution that they believed met French defense needs. Their efforts reveal the difficulties that arose when airpower theory clashed with established notions of how to employ air forces."[104]

Patrick Facon also alludes to the political-strategic nature of the bomber.[105] Unfortunately for France, the bomber was as much an internal as external question; its development and design in France suffered for it. Although many in the FAF thought "the bombing plane is the real offensive element of the Air Army."[106] This did not translate into effective bomber design and production from 1934 to 1940.

German bombers were not always faster, nor did they bristle with defensive armament like the B-17 and B-24 later in the war. They were simply used more effectively. They were also escorted by fighters. Further, they had useful bombload capacities, something no French bomber possessed in 1940. Additionally, French Défense Contre Aérienne (DCA) or antiaircraft defenses including antiaircraft artillery and just as important, hostile aircraft detection, were grossly underdeveloped compared to those of Great Britain or Germany. "With regard to attacks in the interior of France, the poor warning system and the multiplicity of the attacking formations prevented successful concentration of pursuit in time for interception, although many German units were attacked en route home."[107] Thus, German bombers faced less resistance from the ground. France's problem with air warfare was not simply confined to equipment issues that could have been overcome. France had a "holistic" problem with the air war in general.

Well beyond the arguments over influence and budget in the United States, Great Britain, and even Germany, the arguments over strategic airpower in France had internal security implications that condemned France to an ineffective response to Germany in 1940. When French bombers attempted to bomb targets inside Germany, they were largely ineffective. When unescorted French bombers tried desperately to slow German columns as the battle degraded, they were butchered; if German fighters did not get them, well-developed German flak defenses generally did. French bombers were slow, carried a small bombload, and were underarmed, due not only to problems within the aviation industry, but internal political and military divisions as well.

Conclusions

In summary, French fighters and bombers remained five years behind other air forces in 1940. There were some bright spots—for example, the Dewoitine 520—but they were far too few to make a difference. If one looks at the basic characteristics of French aircraft it is not difficult to come to the conclusion they may have actually lost some ground by 1940 based on the majority of the units available. Many French combat aircraft first flew before their foreign comrades and adversaries, but were still being manufactured as first line aircraft in 1940. Further, while some designs, such as the Bf 109 and Hurricane, were continually refined and lasted throughout the war, designs such as the M.S.406 were overcomplicated, laden with problems, and never significantly improved. Indeed, the pilots and ground crews of the M.S.406 used field expedient methods just to make the plane combat worthy. Additionally, when France went abroad to buy aircraft from the United States, the buyers inexplicably bought aircraft that were already beyond their service life, such as the Curtiss Hawk and the Douglas DB-7. At the same time as France was buying the Hawk, it was being phased out in the United States, and the RAF was buying P-40 Tomahawks, aircraft that were well armored and better armed than any fighter in Europe, carrying six .50-inch machine guns. However, the French viewed the air battle as a numbers game, buying more aircraft from the United States as opposed to better aircraft.

Although it is rare to find, in this instance, a technical comparison of the FAF with the RAF and Luftwaffe reveals more than inferior technology, it reveals social, political, and internal military problems with which France tried to cope and which ultimately led to its defeat. In fairness, once the French realized the German menace would have to be dealt with regardless of internal division, they did try in earnest to introduce better aircraft, and produce or procure aircraft to counter the threat. However, it was too little, too late, and the damage done in the internal conflict between 1934 and 1938 doomed the FAF to fight a lost battle with inferior weapons and little direction.

Again, it is sometimes difficult in 2019 to understand how qualitatively far aircraft technology progressed from 1930 to 1940 and again from 1940 to 1945. However, knowledge of this sort of punctuated equilibrium is an important facet in comprehending the French defeat in 1940. France was simply outclassed in equipment and unable to produce its most modern models fast enough or procure better imported aircraft due to export restrictions and a shortage of funds. As the reassessment of the air battle in 1940 indicates, French pilots performed admirably in their outmoded aircraft. They definitely could have done better. This is not an admonishment of French pilots—far from it. It is rather a condemnation of a system that restrained itself from achieving the best results possible. To understand why and how this happened, it is necessary to explore the history of French doctrine up to 1940 as it relates to all aspects of the air battle.

2

THE FRENCH AND GERMAN AIRCRAFT INDUSTRIES

OF ALL ASPECTS of the French aerial defeat in 1940, the French aircraft industry is the only one to be thoroughly examined, but mostly in French with little appearing in English or German. It is important to reexamine how the industry directly contributed to the overall French defeat in 1940 from a military perspective.

In 1940 German troops frequently overran French airfields before they could be evacuated. As the Germans seized French airfields in their rapid advance, they further crippled the French air force's (FAF's) ability to react effectively.[1] In many cases the Germans were shocked to see the number of complete and seemingly brand-new aircraft sitting on the flight line apparently ready to fight. Although the FAF was putting up a solid fight considering the confusion, lack of coordination, and other problems from which it was suffering, this made a lasting impression on some of the German officers, and later on Allied officers as well. This contributed to the belief that somehow the FAF simply did not show up to fight. If it had, why were so many new aircraft simply left unused, apparently completely so, while the French army screamed about the ravages of the Luftwaffe?

In fact, many of the "new" French aircraft captured on the ground were incomplete, due to persistent and unresolved industrial problems—some lacked vital instrumentation, others were bereft of weapons, and some had no engines.[2] A complex mixture of technical and sociopolitical issues hampered the French aircraft industry until the reality of war with Germany in September 1939 brought France somewhat more together in a genuine spirit of mutual defense against a common and hated enemy.

Unlike the American, British, and even German aircraft industries that seemed to blossom in the 1930s with the advent of new technology and designs, the French aircraft industry struggled throughout the period. While other nations' industries certainly had problems to overcome, the French aircraft industry, the FAF, and ultimately, France itself suffered from a unique set of problems that plagued what was arguably the most effective and influential aircraft industry during World War I.

On the technical side, the French aircraft industry suffered from massive shrinkage after World War I, a lack of orders and funding that led to a significant technology gap between France and its peers that it was never able to rectify. It also experienced a lack of production capacity that it was never able to resolve after partial nationalization and modernization, especially in sub-fields such as engine production, where it was apparent that France was beginning to lag noticeably behind.[3] Further, the French aircraft industry was particularly vulnerable strategically since it was in range of modern German aircraft, whereas German aircraft factories could be based well outside the range of potential French bombing: "Throughout the 1930s, Armée d l'Air leadership tried unsuccessfully to relocate their factories away from the vulnerable Île-de-France area around Paris to locations in the south and southwest that offered better security."[4]

On the sociopolitical side, the stark divisions in French society and politics struck the aircraft industry particularly hard, and the concessions Cot gained from both sides eventually reached a point that defied reconciliation.[5] The division between left and right, labor and management/ownership was persistent. French society and politics were dominated by extreme political poles lacking a powerful center. These problems predated the French Revolution but were grossly exacerbated by the events in France from 1870 forward: "Together and separately, each in its different way, the Siege and the Commune left the structure of the old world fundamentally altered."[6]

The polar extremes were suspicious of each other with good reason, and the machinations of both French Communists, and French ultra-conservatives and fascists, throughout the 1930s and 1940s demonstrated how close France came to civil war multiple times before the outbreak of war with Germany in 1914 and 1940.

Of all of the issues regarding the FAF, the problems inherent in the French aircraft industry have received the most detailed attention. The sociopolitical problems pertaining to the industry have been particularly well covered in three major works: Emmanuel Chadeau's *L'industrie aéronautique en France 1900–1950*, Thierry Vivier's *La politique aéronautique militaire de la France*, and Herrick Chapman's *State Capitalism and Working Class Radicalism in the French Aircraft Industry*. While each source reveals some new information on the topic, the central argument in each regarding the state of the French aircraft industry prior to World War II is valid: the technical, economic, and sociopolitical complications encountered by the industry prevented it from effectively supplying the FAF quickly enough to substantially aid in defeating the Luftwaffe in 1940.

A Proud Industry in Decline

World War I gave birth to the combat aircraft industry. Before World War I military organizations certainly had combat aircraft, but they were few, armament was generally improvised if there was any armament at all: "Besides the occasional bombing mission and the dropping of darts on moving troops (with very poor results), most operations straight observation and reconnaissance [in 1914] for the army in the field ... it was not unusual for German and Allied aircraft to meet in the air, everybody pressing on [because they had no effective way to engage one another] with his main task and not bothering about the chap on the other side."[7]

There were but few manufacturers. By 1918, metal monoplanes appeared, specialized aircraft performing such individualized tasks as bombing, ground attack, reconnaissance, and air superiority dragging the amorphous uncertain world of combat aircraft manufacturing ahead decades in a few years and set the stage for combat aircraft development up to the present.

During this period, the French aircraft industry led and innovated; every Allied military used at least some French aircraft.[8] France lost a major portion of its industrial and natural resource heartland in 1914, which it did not recover until 1918. Yet France managed almost to equal or outproduce its peers.[9] Further, French aircraft and components were excellent during World War I. Although France endured a seesaw technology battle with Germany in aircraft design, Germany never gained a massive technological/design advantage, and France stayed at least competitive with, and was sometimes superior to Germany in this regard.[10]

When the war ended, so did the need for massive numbers of combat aircraft. This was true not only in France, but across the globe. Surplus aircraft were sold inexpensively and served as everything from mail planes to crop dusters, to barnstormers. The French aircraft industry, like other aircraft industries, naturally downsized as a result.

The German aircraft industry was almost eradicated because of Versailles, but a small civilian aircraft industry, combined with covert development in Russia, kept it on life support until the early 1930s when it began to expand in earnest.[11] In both the United States and Britain, the potential role of strategic airpower kept combat aircraft industries alive, and indeed progressing in the interwar years. By December 1941, although both Britain and the United States were on their heels somewhat strategically, their combined air fleets were the most modern on the planet and already producing war winning designs such as the Spitfire, Lancaster, Flying Fortress, and the Mustang (probably the best fighter of the war, combining an American airframe and armament design with a British power plant). The Soviet Union was least idle of all, producing tens of thousands of combat aircraft in the 1920s and 1930s. Although it began World War II with a largely obsolescent air fleet, its new Yak and MiG fighters, and the legendary Il-2 Sturmovik ground-attack aircraft eventually proved an overwhelming challenge for the Wehrmacht.

Unfortunately for France, there was no major effort until the mid-1930s to prop up or modernize the aircraft industry. Throughout the 1920s firm after firm closed shop while others consolidated. The steady, although never all that brisk procurement, combined with subsidies enjoyed by U.S. and British aircraft firms materialized too late in France; while their British and American peers received larger and larger apportionments for their air arms, the FAF remained a secondary consideration.[12] In the late 1920s and early 1930s when aircraft design underwent some fundamental changes, France lagged. Instead of impressive and daunting airpower, France backed the Maginot Line as the ultimate security policy. The move away from the offensive mentality in 1928 toward a land-based defensive firepower mentality signaled that for France, the salient memories of World War I were those of 1914–17 and not those of the very different battlefields of 1918, when the deadlock finally broke with movement restored to the battlefield. This resulted in a "Maginot mentality" with understanding of fire and maneuver fundamentally different from other armies.[13] If the proximate cause of this shift toward defensive firepower was the horrendous casualty rate of 1914–17, the direct effect was the Maginot Line, which began construction in 1928 as the result of the shift. The Maginot Line was a monumental project with an astronomical price tag. Although its concept proved to be fundamentally flawed, the product was state of the art. It was supplied with every modern convenience and technology from a tram system to ultra-modern telephonic communications (although it lacked in radio equipment) to water treatment, gas protection, and ventilation. However, the Maginot Line came at a cost—other programs fell by the wayside as funding only went so far. One can only speculate how World War II or the events leading up to it might have tuned out differently had France invested the money dedicated to the Maginot Line in airpower.

The French aircraft industry fell behind in the early 1930s across the board. There was no single specific weakness that had to be overcome (as in Germany's case, where power plant design was problematic), rather the fault was general. During the 1930s French designs lagged behind across the board compared to their peers.

The lack of fiscal stimulus meant that money for research and development, expanded workforce (including more engineers), modernization, and expansion were curtailed in the aircraft industry. While the United

States and Britain prepared to take massive leaps forward in design, often rendering new aircraft outmoded within a few months of their release, French industry seemingly wallowed in the late 1920s.

Part of the problem was an obsession with the Bombardement, Combat, Reconnaissance (BCR) project that took the FAF some time to finally shelve.[14] The BCR program devoted precious time and money to a concept that was unsolvable until after World War II: designing an aircraft that could perform multiple roles reasonably well. This was not solely a French failure. Other countries attempted to create a similar aircraft with more or less similar results. For instance, the German Bf 110 enjoyed little success overall at anything beyond a specialized role as a night fighter, though its original design concept was much the same as the French BCR.

Thus, the French aircraft industry approached World War II understaffed, underdeveloped, and under the shadow of the Maginot Line.

A Beautiful Anachronism

The most important issues with the French aircraft industry up to nationalization were the respective states of its production facilities and techniques, and foreign observations were not generally positive, as when Lawrence Bell of the Bell Aircraft Corporation toured the Amiot factory and noted "very poor, low headroom, inadequate light, untidy and most of the equipment is obsolete, no really modern production methods. . . . The employees did not look industrious, discipline was poor, and morale appeared to be low."[15]

In short, the industry still operated as an atelier or workshop industry where planes and even engines were still made in a workshop, often by hand. In an age when technology was leaping forward, the French aircraft industry to an extent held to its roots from World War I, when ad hoc workshops in barns and vacant rural or industrial areas were set up to create planes in any environment possible. The further foreign industries progressed in an age of rapid technological advancement, the further French industry fell behind.

While this method worked well during most of World War I when aircraft were largely wood and fabric, by the mid-1930s the lack of modern equipment and techniques began to show as exemplified by aircraft such as the M.S.406, which was often more dangerous to the Frenchmen flying it than the Germans flying against it.[16] However, a major part of the problem was the airframe and skin, which had a nasty habit of simply coming apart mid-flight, as did other components such as the cockpit canopy.[17] What was in fact happening is that although the design was airworthy and comparable in most ways to early 1930s monoplane fighters, the plane itself was not well built, despite being assembled by craftsmen who were experts in the production of handmade aircraft. The inherent problem was that the materials had overtaken the extant state of tools and craftsmanship, and a new generation of tooling, manufacturing processes, and facilities were required.

Strategic Vulnerability

Aside from the antiquated processes that largely defined the French aircraft industry up to 1935, another major weakness was the industry's strategic vulnerability in light of its close proximity to Germany. Most of the industry was either within the regional confines of Paris or in the traditional industrial heartland; the need to relocate these factories was obvious as early as 1934, and discussions about how to do so date from at least that period.[18] The inherent problem with this was that it put the French aircraft industry in the range of German bombers. As time progressed, aircraft ranges extended farther and farther, especially those of multi-engine bombers that struck fear into the hearts of virtually every politician, soldier, and civilian in the interwar period. While strategic bombing did not yield overly impressive results during World War I, it certainly promised them in the long term. The fear of the possibilities was not only generated by theorists such as Douhet, but by novelists as well, who regaled the public with imaginative and dystopian scenarios regarding the almost godlike destructive forces airpower portended.[19]

While airpower had yet to realize this theoretical potential, the increasing range and payload of bombers meant that any vital target—such as the aircraft industry—within range of German bombers could expect to be hit in the event of war. Thus, the industry was precariously positioned to be put out of action by German bombers.

In the postwar analysis, Germany may be seen as a minor player in strategic bombing, especially in comparison to its opponents, the RAF and the USAAF. However, the Luftwaffe was extremely interested in strategic bombing prior to World War II.[20] German officers digested prolific amounts of theoretical information, added their own ideas, and were well prepared to act on the results.[21] Recall how close run the Battle of Britain was when the Luftwaffe switched its strategic efforts from RAF targets to civilian targets.

Thus, in addition to the industry being unable to match real potential peer production by 1935–36, French industry was already recognized as being particularly vulnerable. It must be recalled that France planned for a long war, not entirely unlike that witnessed during World War I. If the French were obsessed with Verdun, their endgame envisioned an eventual counteroffensive that pushed the exhausted and depleted Germans back into their homeland. In the ensuing period, there would be plenty of time for both air forces to attack vulnerable targets inside each other's homelands. Although the French were always reluctant to pursue bombing campaigns, there was nothing in the Nazi psyche before or during the war that mitigated against it; Luftwaffe bombing throughout the war on virtually every front verifies this. Although German strategic bombing of French targets was light during May and June of 1940, it was because the tempo of ground operations required the Luftwaffe to commit its assets to assisting the army. Considering German actions following the French Campaign, there is absolutely no reason to assume the Germans would not have engaged in strategic bombing in France. In fact, alternate German plans that would have gone into effect in a protracted ground war in France planned for it, and Wehrmacht leadership did not anticipate being able to initiate "a promising breakthrough offensive against the strong French-Belgian fortifications until the Spring of 1942."[22]

Thus, French industry was not only less productive, but what productive capacity it did have was more vulnerable to potential German air attacks than the other way around. These problems alone were enough to put France in a very awkward position, but this was not the end of the air industry's woes by far. French politics and social culture also greatly complicated the aircraft industry's problems.

Labor versus Management: France's Perennial Struggle

There are people who still await the outcome of the French Revolution; Mao's comment on waiting for the French Revolution to "be settled" may be anecdotal, but the sentiment is legitimate. In some respects, the events of the French Revolution are yet to be decided. France has never really had a happy middle ground where the bulk of the country functioned on a normative basis compared to countries such as the United States and Britain. Whereas the United States endured four years of civil war from 1861 to 1865, after which it was in some ways stronger than before, France has been in a state of relative flux since 1789.

The social upheaval in Europe from the 1830s to the 1850s shook France again in the wake of the French Revolution. The Franco-Prussian War, the Paris Commune, and the associated events sank the wedge even deeper into French society, and "nothing would ever be quite the same."[23] Combined with the Dreyfus affair, this century of instability permanently divided the French army from its government. While the army remained loyal to France, it maintained its position as a paragon of conservative French values and was often morally divided from its civilian masters. This division persisted into the interwar years.[24]

It was also a problem for the French aircraft industry. As the Left grew increasingly militant, so did the attitude of French workers. The French Communist Party usually operated in a grass roots movement through "factory cells."[25] While all concerned French workers were definitely not communists, the fact that the government and the owners knew that communist cells were involved in the movement meant that the threat was more viable, and that it was more difficult for either to figure out exactly who just wanted a "better deal" and who was a communist with deeper and more sinister motives.

To make matters worse, in France the French Communist Party was strong within the Left compared to other Western countries, and it was very active in the interwar period.[26] It was also a tangible part of the French Popular Front. The threat of communism and the specter of Soviet-style communism (via the Comintern, which communicated and worked with the French Communist Party) loomed over any negotiations. To be certain, the French Communist Party embraced broad aims, and it looked to restructure its movement from the ground up with extensive youth movements wrapped in the banner of anti-fascism.[27] While effort was clearly designed to appeal broadly to the center (who would openly support fascism?), the underlying motives were at least suspected and later made clear, when communists sabotaged equipment in aircraft and armaments factories.[28]

Following the Popular Front's victory in 1936, a wave of strikes hit France described by owners/management as a "contagion."[29] Ultimately, the Popular Front victory, combined with the strikes, led to individual concessions on the part of ownership, and eventually to labor laws designed to curtail the disruption and appeal to labor. The theory was that this approach would take some of the momentum out of the more radical factions, specifically the communists, inside the labor movement. However, the motives of the French Communist Party were deeper, as their deliberate acts of sabotage proved.

It is also fundamentally important to remember how critical 1936 was to France. Not only did the Popular Front come to power radically changing the internal perspective in France, but the Spanish Civil War began, and Germany reoccupied the Rhineland. France was thus under incredible political and indeed security pressure from within and without. Speculatively, part of the inability of the anglophone world to understand the French position immediately before World War II, stems from the lack of direct threat both events presented to Britain, much less the United States, but how much of a threat these events presented to a France struggling, often violently, for some internal dominance and stability.

— Nationalization —

Pierre Cot, the on-again, off-again air minister during the 1930s, led the movement to nationalize France's aircraft industry.[30] Any assessment of the nationalization process and its results must consider the social and political environment in which it occurred, and specifically Pierre Cot himself, whose politics moved ever leftward throughout his career. To be objective, nationalization must be viewed from two points: first, France's sociopolitical environment and the nationalization process, and second, the technical outcome of nationalization. This leads to the fundamental questions: what were the technical (production) results of the nationalization process? Subsequently, what were the faults inherent in nationalization, and what was the true overall outcome?

The evidence proves that although production capacity in airframes did noticeably improve following modernization, fundamental flaws remained in the French aircraft industry. The bizarre assembly process that involved mounting different parts at different places due to internal fears lasted right up to the armistice, and contributed to the number of aircraft that might have appeared complete from outward appearances, but were missing significant pieces of necessary equipment.[31] Many of the subsidiary industries (engines, radios, etc.) were not modernized and there were multiple problems due to poor quality and reliability.[32] Further, during the time the nationalization/modernization process occurred, there was a gap in research and development, putting French designs further behind those of their German adversaries; the focus was on moving the factories and improving the machinery and production.

The simplest and most direct way to analyze the results of the nationalization and modernization process is to examine the numerical output of the French aircraft industry before and after nationalization. Compare also, the various production plans envisaged by the air force and ministry, vis-à-vis the number of aircraft available in 1940.

TABLE 3

Plan	Aircraft Desired
Plan I 1933–1936	1,365
Plan II 1936–1938	2,851
Plan V 1938–1941	4,739
Plan V Modified 1939–1941	5,133
Plan V Strengthened 1939–1941	8,094

Total airframe production increased noticeably from the mid-1930s until the defeat in 1940. Pre-nationalization figures versus post-nationalization figures are telling. In 1936, the air force took delivery of 569 planes, and 418 were delivered in 1937.[33] However, by the declaration of war on Germany in 1939, the industry was cranking out almost as many aircraft per month as it had delivered in previous years: 284 were produced in September 1939, 358 were produced in January 1940, 364 were produced in March 1940, and amazingly, 434 were produced in the chaos of June 1940.[34]

Thus, the nationalization and modernization process did result—after much effort, stress, and controversy—in a greater number of airframes produced than before. The rather monolithic goal of producing more aircraft (airframes) was thus achieved. However, two critical flaws in the nationalization persisted. First, critical subindustries such as power plant, armament, and optics production, design, and development were not modernized at the same rate, nor did they witness the same progress as airframe production. The end result was that a revamped and modern airframe industry found itself mated to subindustries still experiencing those same problems. Second, almost all research and development ceased while many of the aircraft companies focused their efforts on moving their operations and updating their manufacturing machinery and processes.

The result of nationalization was that the French aircraft industry was more able to meet the projected needs of the air force on a limited basis. Some problems were greatly resolved, while other problems were seemingly neglected or ignored. The true overall outcome was an industry more able than it was before, but largely imperfect due to critical flaws, and behind not only in numerical production, but in technological development as well.

These basic facts being stated, the assumption that the nationalization and modernization process somehow impeded the FAF, and ultimately the defense of France must be rejected. There is no evidence suggesting that not attempting to modernize aircraft production would have somehow aided France. In fact, not modernizing it certainly would have created a greater burden not only on the FAF, but France as a whole. Labor disputes aside, there is no comparison between the gross production of 1939 and 1940 (up until capitulation) and that of the mid-1930s when aircraft production was just a trickle.

The obvious major controversy regarding nationalization was determining what the actual overall goal was. Much of this had to do with the sometime air minister Pierre Cot. Cot's machinations in the air force had a very disturbing extremely leftist (read communist) feel to them among people on the Right and in the conservative army. Cot's radical shake-up of the air force and his egalitarianism, combined with his desire to create close ties with the Soviet Union, created this intense distrust.[35] His support of the labor movement, with its direct ties to communists, and at least indirect association with the Comintern, exacerbated these feelings.

The View from the Outside

The state of the French aircraft industry did not go unnoticed by France's peers. The sentiments ranged from the rather specific to the general. German intelligence had a relatively low opinion of France's aircraft industry before the war, if rather general: "The strength, equipment, and striking force of FAF, insofar as it was supposed to support the ground forces, had been correctly evaluated down to individual figures. This fact was confirmed after the campaign by the former air attaché, Stehlin."[36] Further: "The French aircraft industry was even worse organized and had a lower capacity than the Germans estimated."[37]

The United States received regular reports on the progress of the FAF and the French air industry, especially when it came to technical issues. These reports came from various sources.[38]

As early as 1936, the military attaché in Paris reported on specific problems with engine design and production: "The temperature of the cylinder heads and walls [of the Gnome-Rhone K14 motor] was much too high. It costs 90,000 fcs to modify the K-14 and turn it into a NO-14. As the Air Ministry has ordered 2000 of them, it would cost the French taxpayers Fcs: 180,000,000 ($8,571,429)."[39]

By 1938 when war was on the horizon and the French aircraft industry was clearly not going to be able to meet the anticipated needs, the attaché reported,

> The increasing importance that the FAF has attached to the single-seat pursuit plane is evidenced in its desire to increase the production of this type as well as its decided interest of foreign types.[40]
>
> This plane [Potez-63] has been under production for many months but as yet none are in the tactical units. As of this date 50 or 60 are complete but are awaiting engines.[41]
>
> This office feels that a large order will be given for the Nieuport 161 in that it seems to be comparable to both the Morane and Bloch and it is constructed in a factory capable of increasing production. Another reason is that it is powered by a well tried and proven engine, the Hispano-Suiza 12 Y.[42]
>
> From the above, it will be seen that none of the new program planes is [sic] in the tactical units.[43]
>
> France's problem is to get new aircraft equipment to the tactical units and get it there as quickly as possible.[44]
>
> It is reported that the French government is purchasing ten (10) Pratt & Whitney Twin Wasp Juniors for experimental purposes in the Potez-63 and possibly other types.[45]

Thus, the American attaché was aware of two of the French aircraft industries critical flaws, engine design and production, and airframe production. A slightly earlier report dated 18 March 1938 indicated: "The Air war of both Spain and China have influenced France to the importance of the single-seater pursuit and the present Air Ministry program is for the rapid development of pursuit aviation."[46]

While this may retrospectively seem logical, keep in mind that FAF doctrine continually evolved into a more strategic bombing-oriented doctrine, and the revamped aircraft industry was using that as a focus. Switching gears to fighter production created another difficulty in an industry attempting to modernize, relocate, and deal with complicated labor problems simultaneously.

Bizarrely, a confidential unsigned report from May 1938 stated,

> My informant (an engineer-pilot of the Hispano-Suiza Company) further informed me that the 12 Y—31 engine has been run at full

throttle for five hours at 1200 H.P.; that the Morane 406 airplane can be given a service top speed of 550 kms/hr at any time by installing a high-compression engine with increased supercharging, but the Air Ministry is keeping to the 860 H.P. engine because of its increased engine durability, *and particularly because an increase in speed of the 406 will push the Germans into higher fighter needs.*[47]

It appears that the Air Ministry (if this report is viable) may have intentionally kept a more powerful engine out of the Morane 406 out of fear Germany would then fear the plane. It is difficult to understand exactly how the Air Ministry, expecting nothing less than open combat with the Luftwaffe in the short term, wanted anything less than every advantage possible. This attitude smacks of the rather naive idea that if the French refrained from bombing the Germans, the Germans would reciprocate.

Another interesting twist in this same report indicates: "My informant states that the Morane 405 and 406 fighters have been dived vertically to a speed of 700 kms/hr [467 mph] with as sharp a pull out as the pilot could stand; that it is *a very solid fighter; in fact too much so.*"[48]

Considering all the reported problems with the Morane 405/6 in service, and the above report, one has to wonder how this is possible. It at least presents the possibility that the saboteurs inside the various French industries might have been working hard to make certain the aircraft was as poorly built as possible.

— *Summary* —

Compared to its peers, the French aircraft industry failed to provide France with enough quality aircraft in enough time to meet a technically and operationally superior opponent. While peer industries in allied states and in Germany certainly suffered technical and production difficulties, the depth and nature of the problems experienced by the French aircraft industry were fundamentally different, and challenging.

From an airframe production standpoint, nationalization and modernization, contrary to previous arguments, has to be judged as a success. The massive jump in late 1938 through June of 1940, when each month the French aircraft industry produced almost as many planes as it did during a year from 1934 to 1937, is simple proof. Further, removing the industry from its geographically vulnerable position was a sound and reasonable decision. In the event the war bogged down (which all parties involved agreed was a possibility), the increased range, speed, and payload of German bombers would have put the French aircraft industry within easy range, whereas counterpart German industries could have remained well insulated from similar French attacks.

However, the nationalization and modernization process failed to successfully encompass subsidiary industries that were vital to the overall functioning of the aircraft. Engines, gauges, armament, and radios were all necessary for modern combat aircraft to perform their roles; they could not reasonably fly without them. Whether it was technical problems with the matériel provided or simply the lack of it, the result was the same, and worse for France, its peers seemed to be highly aware of the problems.

Further, the technology gap is important to note. In the modern world, aircraft such as the F-15 and F-16 have survived and thrived over four decades primarily due to improvements in avionics. In the 1930s this was not possible and looking objectively at the performance improvements from 1928 or 1929 through the 1930s, the obsolescence rate was measured in months. Fighters were often outmoded shortly after production began. The Curtiss Hawk and the M.S.406 were produced simultaneously alongside the P-38 Lightning, the P-40 Warhawk, The newest marks of Bf 109, the Spitfire, and the first of the P-51s. The time lost to research and development as the French aircraft industry moved, reorganized, and retooled, put French aircraft behind those of the best of the Luftwaffe by a vital two to five years. While this might not seem like a great time gap in the modern world, it was fatal in the 1930s.

The aircraft production plans touted and continually revised by the Air Ministry and the air force were totally farcical, at least until late 1938, after nationalization. While the idea was certainly admirable, the production goals did not approach attainability until war was imminent. Funding was simply not made available considering austerity measures and the massive funding required to complete the Maginot Line. Although the government did approve substantial increased spending on the air force from 1938 to

1940, with the increase in production as the obvious result, it was too little too late when combined with the myriad of problems the industry faced.

The one problem unique to the French aircraft industry was the intense sociopolitical turmoil between the left and the right, between labor and management. While the United States and other countries witnessed similar problems in the 1920s and 1930s, they managed, even after extreme violence in some cases, to resolve them. This was complicated by a political process that allowed for frequent changes of government that resulted in France shifting from left to right so frequently and so rapidly that no one group could get enough momentum to create and maintain a legacy policy. Further, the extreme distrust between the poles was not without merit. Communists on the left deliberately sabotaged vital war industries before the war and during the Battle of France. Afterward, fascists and others on the extreme right cooperated, and indeed participated, in the Nazi purges of "political undesirables" during the Vichy regime. The idea that France might actually have engaged in a civil war if the Germans had not beaten them to it is well within reason, and in the view of the present author, likely to have happened.

The entire process was complicated by the one man who made the nationalization process and the independence of the air force possible—Pierre Cot.

The German Aircraft Industry: Endgame 1918

The German aircraft industry was in its infancy in 1914. The aircraft were simple, often carrying no more than a single pilot in a relatively slow plane with no armament. Germany invested heavily in dirigibles prior to World War I and was dominant in that field. As the war progressed, it became rapidly obvious that the fixed wing airplane was dominant. Large airships, although mobile, were under-armed and extremely vulnerable. Observation balloons were almost a suicide duty by early 1916. The airplane, still very much in its infancy in 1914, was fully matured by 1918.

In November 1918 Germany produced every type of standard combat aircraft and offered many innovative designs as well. Germany fielded all-metal monoplane fighters in addition to dedicated ground attack aircraft and heavy bombers; the future was present at the armistice. Further,

Germany continued to produce aircraft under adverse conditions to the very end.[49] In an odd echo, this trend repeated itself in 1945.

The armistice and Versailles treaty imposed terms upon Germany that are debated to this day. Whether or not these terms contributed directly to the outbreak (or according to some points of view resumption) of hostilities in 1939, is debatable. What is beyond debate is that the terms (that included total emasculation of German airpower) were cited both directly and indirectly within and outside Germany as a reason to justify resurgence and radicalism. Regardless of the restrictions that gutted the German aircraft industry more surely than any economic downturn, the German aircraft industry managed to not only maintain a pulse in the interwar period but recover and grow to an extent that when open rearmament resumed under Hitler, modern, mass producible, and improvable designs were readily to be tested and fielded.

Dodging Versailles

The German aircraft industry had inherently different problems than those of France between 1918 and 1934. Whereas France ordered few combat aircraft in the interwar period, Germany could not order combat aircraft openly until it was in such a position under Hitler to ignore the terms. From the development and production standpoint, the German aircraft industry creatively dodged Versailles and its inspectors through two methods. First, the Reichswehr, along with German engineers and producers, worked clandestinely deep in the Soviet interior to develop modern aircraft while aiding Soviet aircraft industry development. Second, eventual permission from the Allies to allow German civil aviation permitted the German aircraft industry to design and create modern "dual purpose" aircraft.[50]

Clandestine cooperation with the Soviet Union was productive for both states. The Soviet Union, burdened with many of the traditional technical deficiencies it inherited from Russia, wanted to change. Germany wanted to continue development. Both countries were drawn together not only due to necessity, but perhaps because both were to an extent pariah states.

The technical developments and manufacturing know-how, coupled with tactical, strategic, and doctrinal discussions benefited both sides prior to World War II.[51]

Civilian aviation developments in Germany were popular and overt. Both airlines and civil air clubs did not need to hide their activities so long as they did not commit any particularly grievous sins (e.g., camouflaging and arming their planes). While both organizations developed new pilots and kept the skills of established pilots (including military pilots) sharp, they also allowed open development and production. Many of the models were theoretically and functionally dual-purpose aircraft, and thus excellent platforms for fighter and bomber development.

The Junkers Ju 52 (later known as the Tante Ju) is the most readily recognized product of this effort. The Ju 52 was a successful airliner before it dropped bombs on Spain or Poland. While the design was rapidly superseded by dedicated bomber designs, its production, the staff maintained for production and design, and the continual modernization of the facilities were the big wins for Junkers and Germany, especially vis-à-vis France.[52]

Sport clubs were popular throughout Germany. Several organizations existed to promote aviation under the Weimar government and more obviously to most under the Nazis. Much like Lufthansa, the erstwhile national German airline, these civil air clubs helped keep former military pilots sharp. These clubs also clandestinely trained a small crop of new military pilots and spurred interest among the youth, providing a fertile breeding ground for future military pilots.

Sport clubs also provided a legitimate market for aircraft. Just as the airlines provided a legitimate market for thinly veiled bomber designs. The Ju 52 served as a potential and actual bomber, and planes such as the Messerschmitt 104 paved the way for future designs, most specifically the Messerschmitt Bf 109. The Bf 109 was a direct descendant of earlier Messerschmitt designs, and its prototype was available as a modern, easy to improve and modify airframe that was ready to produce in the early 1930s.[53]

Modern mass production facilities were not universal in the German industry just before open German rearmament; only Junkers and Heinkel were prepared for mass production in 1934. Other aircraft firms such as Messerschmitt, Focke Wulf, and Henschel were largely atelier-style workshops much like the French firms.[54]

The key difference between France and Germany in this regard was the relationship between the government, society, and the aircraft firms and the speed of modernization, especially in production methods. This is not to state that there were no problems in standing up the German aircraft industry for mass production. In fact, Germany and its aircraft industry had to resolve several serious problems before they were prepared for mass production and ultimately war.

Open Rearmament: Expansion and Labor

While Germany added aircraft producers as rearmament was followed by war, many well-known firms benefited from rapid expansion of Germany's arms industry under the Nazis in the 1930s. Only Junkers and Heinkel had modern enough facilities, well established supply chains, and enough skilled personnel to begin mass production on demand (in the early days this was perhaps as few as a few dozen aircraft per month). Firms such as Messerschmitt, Henschel, Focke Wulf, and Dornier, needed to build modern mass production facilities before they could initiate meaningful production. In addition, these firms needed to expand skilled personnel to run the factories. This was an additional complication as the more technical jobs required considerable training before the worker could be considered proficient. Engineers were also a limited commodity and could not be trained in short order. From sheet metal workers to airframe designers, the will to expand the industry was present, but the process was still time consuming. Given time, German firms managed impressive production numbers and enabled the Luftwaffe to face all its early war foes with equal, if not superior, designs. Although the Luftwaffe was frequently outnumbered from 1940 to 1941, its planes were superior on average with planes such as the Supermarine Spitfire and Dewoitine D.520 always being in the (sometimes significant) minority.[55]

One of the most distinct contrasts between the French and German aircraft industries was the timing in expansion and modernization. While

French aircraft producers modernized and expanded only after a grueling sociopolitical spat beginning with partial nationalization in 1936 and ending in 1938, German expansion was smoother, less controversial, better organized, and concluded far earlier. As French industries were just preparing to modernize, most of the German manufacturers were finished or very near it. Further, German firms were in some cases expanding their initial production facilities and did so through 1940, and in most cases later into the war.[56]

The German aircraft industry did not suffer from the vitriolic labor relations problems that plagued France. Although there were issues, German economic recovery and the jobs associated with the growth of the aircraft industry were seen as positive instead of an owner/management/labor debate that went from the factory floor all the way to the highest reaches of national politics. French labor relations were almost universally poor, and the core arguments behind the strife between labor and management/ownership dated at least to 1870, if not all the way back to the French Revolution. Further, after the declaration of war, the French military pulled many skilled French workers from the aircraft assembly lines as they had not taken such matters into account as Germany had. Nevertheless, Germany had its share of difficulties.

Shortages

The Nazis certainly had the will to rearm at flank speed, but the means were another issue. Germany in the 1930s was not the Germany of 1914; although economic conditions were improving, they were far from ideal. Germany was short on currency, and it needed to create funds through export to purchase the critical resources required for rearmament. While the public (and even academia to some extent) tend to overlook Germany's financial woes, they were serious concerns for the Nazis. Hitler was extremely cognizant of the need to maintain popular support of the German people, primarily through prosperity. In fact, the Nazis prioritized consumed production for far too long, and only switched to a total war footing well after they should have. This juggling act certainly kept the German populace happier longer, but it was also a distinct factor in the ultimate German defeat.

Germany had few natural resources from which to draw. While it had abundant coal, it had very little oil, iron, aluminum, copper, nickel, tungsten, chromium, and other natural resources required for modern war. Unlike Britain and France, Germany had no colonies from which to draw such material at reduced or beneficial prices. Unlike the United States and the Soviet Union, Germany suffered from the absence of those resources from the soil and substrata. Without conquest of lands containing these precious materials (which became a later goal) Germany simply had to buy them.[57]

Further, there were three branches competing for scarce materials. The Luftwaffe was arguably the showpiece of German rearmament propaganda during the late 1930s; it certainly caused more hand wringing than any other German service prior to the outbreak of hostilities. However, it had to draw from the same resource pool as the Heer, which was clearly the predominant concern of a Wehrmacht bent on continental conquests, and a Kriegsmarine that although smaller, required massive quantities of such scare materials for even the smallest ship.

The competition for resources was predictable in the environment, but leadership issues exacerbated production stresses.[58]

Leadership and the Aircraft Industry

German leadership played mixed roles in aircraft design and production during the war. As with all organizations, some of these decisions were beneficial while others were detrimental. German leadership's effects on the aircraft industry prior to 1940 can be broken down into two significant categories: effects on design and effects on production numbers. Like other air forces, the Luftwaffe and its leadership was concerned with theoretical impact of new weapons. Unlike France most importantly in this case, the Spanish Civil War provided practical, hands-on experience for Germany.

Design generally follows purpose, and for the most part, prewar German designs were specialized, with the idea that some dual-purpose missions were appropriate. For instance, the Bf 109 was designed to be a fighter. It performed the fighter-bomber role reasonably well, but it was not as effective in close air support and point target battlefield strike as the Ju 87.

The Bf 110 took heavy losses in the Battle of France, and suffered even greater losses later in the Battle of Britain, had to find a purpose for which it was well suited. Prior to the outbreak of World War II, the Luftwaffe generally requested a design based on a specific purpose, and the various design firms responded in kind.[59]

On occasion, the Luftwaffe's vision was a bit too complicated or irrational, but not nearly to the extent of the late-war period. In fact, the one salient example was the insistence upon trying to make medium and heavy bombers perform as dive bombers. This was due to the insistence of one man, Ernst Udet. This requirement created considerable strife, especially in the Junkers firm that set out to fix a plane that was fine the way it was, the Ju 88. Although the feat was accomplished, it was done by adding five tons to the airframe, making a very effective plane with a specific purpose (*Schnellbomber*, or fast bomber) less capable at its primary mission for the luxury of having an mediocre to poor dive-bombing capability. Udet also insisted the He 177, a heavy bomber that was developmentally problematic for a multitude of reasons, be outfitted with multiple capabilities. To give the reader not familiar with obscure Luftwaffe aircraft a conceptual reference, imagine outfitting an American B-17 or a B-24 with dive-bombing capability, and expecting it to successfully fulfill that role.[60]

Overall, the results of this tampering were limited where the Battle of France was concerned. However, production numbers fluctuated wildly primarily due to the resource shortcomings compounded by Hitler's close control of assets and the continued jockeying by the various services for these precious materials. Although industry responded well to the constant seesaw resource distribution, it was difficult to juggle asset allocation along with continuous expansion and the drive for modernization.

One glaring difference between France and Germany concerned leadership and partial nationalization of both countries' industries. While France had a stark sociopolitical divide that defined the multitude of problems it experienced with its process, Germany did not. The German aircraft industrialists who resisted partial nationalization found no allies in other political parties to support them; they eventually succumbed the pressure to play by the Nazis' rules. Further, there were no strikes or disruptive labor disputes, sabotage, slowdowns, or any of the other multitude of problems from which the French aircraft industry—and ultimately the FAF and the nation itself—suffered.

Conclusions

The German aircraft industry profited from willing national and military leadership that interfered less with its operations than was the case in France. Once Germany became a one-party system, it did not have to contend with the more serious issues that hindered the French aircraft industry and ultimately the FAF through the Battle of France. It is important to separate Germany's later problems from its earlier successes in this field. While the French aircraft industry was in some ways the center of the stark sociopolitical struggle in France, the few hindrances in the German aircraft industry were more easily removed by a unified and strong central government, sinister though it may have been.

Unlike Britain, the United States, and the Soviet Union, the French and German aircraft industries both basically started from scratch in 1934. Both industries produced some solid designs following World War I. However, Germany's edge in being more easily switched to mass production, and in more modern, easily modifiable designs was significant. No single French firm was able to enter mass production before the partial nationalization and modernization program initiated two to two and a half years after Germany's start. France was not able to mass produce any aircraft until the latter part of 1937 or early 1938, and the results were not truly viable until 1939. At that, the airframes produced were generally inferior. The M.S.406 was not equal to the Bf 109, and no French bomber could truly be called modern and competitive. Only toward the end of 1939 did France begin to produce modern competitive designs such as the D.520, a plane that was still not quite a match for the Bf 109, but good enough in the hands of a skilled pilot. Although France had talented engineers who were equal to their German counterparts, and there were some tentative designs that would theoretically have surpassed German designs, none or extremely few of these were produced before mid-June 1940.

France's persistent issues with labor conflicts directly impacted its aircraft industry and France's preparation for war. German expansion went smoothly in comparison. Government instability in France, rapid and frequent power shifts, and spending patterns leftover from the 1920s that did not address the period's rapid modernization in both technology and doctrine left France critically behind. While German leadership did interfere with engineering to a limited extent before the war, it was in a mostly technical fashion. French leadership problems went much deeper and negatively influenced the industry from top to bottom.

Germany's significant shortage of raw materials did not disadvantage it as much as it should have vis-à-vis France. Although the FAF and the Luftwaffe had to compete for money and resources, with other branches, France had fewer problems with raw materials. At the risk of being stereotypical, the outcome was reversed until almost the end; Germany made more out of far less, while France seemingly dithered. One cannot help but think of the joke about the French farmer with a leak in his roof on the second floor: He moves his bed to avoid the leak. When the leak finally works its way downstairs into the kitchen and starts dripping on the table, he moves the table.

3

FRENCH AND GERMAN INTELLIGENCE, 1934 TO 1940

INTELLIGENCE ASSETS have operated to inform military leaders of enemy capabilities and intent since time out of memory. As an organization, bureaucracy, or structure within both governments and militaries, the field of intelligence has only been formalized and professionalized for less than two centuries. The depth to which these intelligence agencies have evolved is now staggering, consuming vast sums of money, and with the advent of modern technology, gathering more information than can arguably ever be analyzed by the people assigned the task.

France's defeat, and that of the French air force (FAF), must include an assessment of the accuracy, scope, and utility of French intelligence before 10 May 1940. Was French intelligence somehow culpable in the defeat? This is a fundamental question.

Unlike many glaring deficiencies in the French military, French intelligence actually performed admirably. Primary documents from French military archives, as well as books and journals from the period demonstrate that French intelligence had a clear picture not only of the Wehrmacht's technical capabilities, but of its doctrine as well—and this long before Poland's defeat that launched France into last-minute overdrive to remedy the imbalance. France was aware of how Germany intended to conduct the next war when in 1939, before France went to war with Germany, Pierre Cot wrote: "What is a brief war? The Germans have studied a special technique of brief (short) war called *Blitzkrieg*."[1]

Four key aspects support this conclusion. First, French intelligence, especially concerning Germany and the Wehrmacht, was generally accurate, timely, and thorough, though it did grossly overestimate German production capacity. French intelligence kept a close eye on Germany from the end of World War I through the outbreak of World War II. Further, information provided by French intelligence was not properly utilized by leadership; therefore, it could not remedy structural problems inside the military, specifically the FAF and French army, to avoid the mismatch in May and June 1940. Additionally, persistent sociocultural issues in the structure of France's military relegated intelligence to a lesser status, much like the engineers and gunners in early modern armies. This class structure led not only to intelligence being neglected and to some extent ignored, but it was a dead end for career officers that ultimately led to underrepresentation of intelligence officers at higher levels where its voice was most needed. Last, French intelligence did not fail, but it failed to be used properly. Specifically, regarding the FAF, intelligence efforts and assets were grossly misdirected and wasted on pursuit of infrastructure intelligence for a strategic bombing doctrine that was never within the realm of reality for military, industrial, social, and political reasons.

A Note on Organization

There were two primary intelligence groups or organizations in the French military. The first was the Deuxième Bureau. This was the primary source of conventional military intelligence on a national level. The second agency, the Service de Renseignement handled the bulk of France's clandestine spy network and management of foreign agents. The evidence indicates that the Service de Renseignement operated well inside Germany up until the defeat, and it had some well-placed high-level agents and sources inside the Wehrmacht.[2] The FAF also operated its own Deuxième Bureau that focused primarily on issues directly related to the FAF.

The Accuracy of French Intelligence

An analysis of the evidence reveals that three key components confirm the overall accuracy of French intelligence prior to May 1940. First, the technical information provided regarding German capabilities was accurate. Second, the information provided on German doctrine was accurate. Third, the information provided on German performance up to May 1940 was accurate. These details combine to demonstrate that French intelligence provided a functional overall picture of the Wehrmacht in advance.

Assessment of Wehrmacht Technical Capabilities

French intelligence kept a close eye on German developments virtually from the cessation of hostilities in November 1918, until the invasion of France on 10 May 1940. Although the Treaty of Versailles forbade Germany an air force, or even combat aircraft, French intelligence watched developments in Germany closely. Even in the 1920s, when there was no real threat of immediate German resurgence, the intelligence apparatus regularly reported on military developments, and perhaps more importantly for that time period, military thinking inside Germany.

From a technical standpoint French intelligence performed admirably well in keeping up with two aspects of German technological developments that had a dramatic impact on the battles of 1940. First, French intelligence kept a close eye on the development of the German aircraft industry when it existed strictly as a "peaceful" enterprise in the 1920s and early 1930s, before open rearmament. It then followed German aircraft design and production closely up until 10 May 1940. Second, French intelligence created an accurate picture of the development and capabilities of German ground-based antiaircraft defenses.

Air forces tended to consider the airborne threat, that is to say enemy aircraft, as the primary hostile concern. Therefore, accurate information on their relative capabilities was essential. In general, French intelligence provided a quality overview of the capabilities of various German aircraft, especially the Bf 109. Additionally, French intelligence followed the development of German transport aircraft closely as they recognized that it would and did take very little modification to convert a civilian transport into a bomber. Finally, French intelligence also monitored the development, production, and capabilities of purpose-built German bomber and attack aircraft.

Technical Assessment of German Aircraft

Much of France's technical intelligence regarding German aircraft came from the rather open way in which foreign observers of missions were allowed to watch the Spanish Civil War from the sidelines. Data on German aircraft (and German doctrine) was readily available from the press in France and Germany or the German propaganda industry.

French observers followed the Spanish Civil War closely as it developed. Information being fed into the intelligence system was in many cases summarized into accurate technical reports. One document, "L'aviation de chasse en Espagne" (Fighter Aircraft Aviation in Spain) was accurate and revealing.[3]

The technical assessment of the Messerschmitt Bf 109 was accurate, and in light of later testimony, the threat it presented was taken quite seriously. The Bf 109's introduction initiated the "third phase" of the Spanish Civil War for French analysts, and they quickly pointed out that the Bf 109 was vastly superior to anything else being flown in Spain.[4] "The Messerschmidt [sic] is actually the most modern aircraft being used in Spain."[5]

Detailed technical information regarding the models being used in Spain (mostly C and D variants) was fairly precise. The report indicated that the Bf 109 was equipped with a Jumo 210 engine of 19.7 L, enabling it to attain speeds of up to 460 kph.[6] Further, the report discussed the Bf 109s armament, apparently being quite impressed by its effectiveness. While the number of guns (2 x 7.92-mm machine guns) on the variants being used on the variants in Spain was accurate, there was apparently some mystery regarding the ammunition being utilized by the Condor Legion.[7] The report notes that the explosive ammunition being used in the guns was quite effective, although it was a mystery as to exactly what type of ammunition it was.[8]

In a revealing statement, the report indicates that the armament and the ammunition was still being "kept quite secret by the Germans."[9] On the surface, this is a direct and easy to understand statement. However, it reveals that in fact much of the information in the report is open source, meaning that the Germans were not keeping much of their information secret, and that as is true today, a certain amount of overt bragging regarding one's capabilities was a useful tool for the Germans. However, this seems to be combined with the firsthand experience of witnessing the effects of the armament in Spain. What appears to be occurring in this report (which does not list detailed sources) is that the report is being compiled and analyzed from various pieces of information to provide a more cohesive whole.

Although the effectiveness of the Bf 109's armament was clearly respected, other reports indicated that large-caliber armament (presumably cannons or heavy machine guns, not 7.92-mm machine guns) was superior to many small-caliber guns on a fighter.[10] Thus, French intelligence was not just regurgitating, but analyzing the information available before the war, and presenting various points of view to those with access to the compiled information.

Both of these reports were ultimately shown to be correct. The early Bf 109's armament was impressive when used against its less modern and less robust opponents in Spain. However, the Germans themselves also saw the same shortcoming with small-caliber machine guns against more modern machines, as they continually improved the quantity of guns on their fighters and increased the overall caliber of same as the war went on. By the time of the Battle of France, Bf 109's rolled off the assembly line with not only more 7.92-mm machine guns, but with a 20-mm cannon as well.

One salient, and shocking, conclusion was also drawn by French intelligence regarding the Bf 109: the properties inherent to the design were difficult to achieve with the existing state of technology at the time.[11] In reality, aircraft designs that were already in production or in the last phases of design in the United States and Britain exceeded the Bf 109's capabilities, sometimes considerably so, in speed, armor, and firepower measured in throw weight. However, from a French point of view considering the technological state of French aviation shortly before World War II, this is not an unreasonable statement. Whether or not the author was trying to imply the state of French technology was not up to par is speculative, but by no means entirely unreasonable.

French reports also considered general observations about overall fighter design on the modern battlefield. In general terms they stressed the importance of firepower in fighter design.[12] Further, one report indicated that armor for both the aircraft and the pilot was critical, based on the assessment of battle-damaged aircraft.[13] Foretelling the tragedy that befell French and British aircraft attacking German ground targets at low level in 1940, the report noted that armor is as important to protect the pilot against ground fire as fire from enemy aircraft.[14]

Fighter design and production dominated French thinking shortly before the war, as Pierre Cot testified to the U.S. Congress in 1942. The French assessed the overall performance of their fighters as compared to German fighters (really just the Bf 109) as a set of percentages.[15] The dialogue between Cot and Senator Edwin C. Johnson is particularly revealing. When asked why France accepted planes the British refused, Cot stated that the quality of the British and German fighter planes was on par at the time:

> The Germans and the British were at about the same level. The British had their Spitfire, and the Germans had their Messerschmitt 109, and both the Spitfire and the Messerschmitt were to my mind the best planes in the air; our best fighter at the time was the Moraine 405, which was about 15 percent behind; and so we bought your planes which were at the same level [as the French]. Our obsolete planes were at about the same level when we bought your obsolete planes [primarily the Curtiss P-35 Hawk]. We did not therefore improve the quality of our aircraft; we improved quantity first; and second we improved the quality of our planes in an indirect way because your engines were better than ours.[16]

Cot's testimony clearly indicates that as far as fighter aircraft went, French assessments were quite accurate in their information regarding the Bf 109. This testimony dates from 1942, but Cot was discussing decisions and information dating from 1938 to 1940 when France purchased aircraft from the United States.

German bomber design and construction received less attention overall than the Bf 109. There are relatively few specific design notes on German bombers. The bulk of the technical information relates to bomber design in general. Although France never managed to assemble anything resembling a strategic bomber force, reports derived from information in Spain are quite clear about the best protection for bombers—that is, no amount of defensive firepower festooned on a bomber can match the efficacy of an aggressive fighter escort, and that "all the pilots questioned estimated that this was absolutely necessary."[17] The United States would later learn this lesson the hard way when unescorted B-17 Flying Fortresses presumed to be invulnerable due to their defensive firepower were heavily attritted over Germany when they had no fighter escort.

However, there were French dissenters to these ideas, and their views did make it into professional journals. One article in 1936 suggested that aircraft engines would eventually become so powerful that bombers would simply outpace their single engine counterparts (as indeed they had for a while before the fighter engine revolution in the early 1930s) and maybe even become so powerful that they outran projectiles.[18] Admittedly this article was speculative and hopeful, not indicative of the present state of reality in 1936 or 1940 (or 1945, for that matter).

French reports also indicate that bombers should be designed to carry as much of a payload as technology and power allow because "effective" bombardment required the application of massive quantities of explosives.[19] Although this report did not elaborate (indeed one is left to wonder if what it left unsaid is important as what it said) beyond this generality, another report was quite clear about why payload was so important. Bombs did much less irreversible damage than interwar theorists suggested they should do, perhaps except for employment against personnel *in the open*, and therefore it was difficult to have the effects desired without the massive and overwhelming application of tremendous amounts of explosives to basically guarantee flattening a target.[20] Again, this lesson was prescient, as the United States and Britain later discovered.

In short, very little had fundamentally changed concerning aerial bombing since the end of World War I, even though interwar air theorists suggested technology had brought the ideas into the scope of reality. During the Battle of France, the aerial bombing of French troops had less physical affect than morale.[21] Thus in 1923 when Commandant Marcel Jauneaud commented that successive and methodical airstrikes against ground troops would have much greater moral effect than physical, but nonetheless decisive, he might have been describing the effects of German bombing on the poorly trained and prepared French units defending Sedan in 1940.[22]

Additionally, French open-source articles commented on the dominance of the fighter over the bomber in actual combat.[23] This illustrates that information from multiple sources and groups was finding its way into the professional journals as well as secret or classified documents. The big secret regarding the supremacy of the fighter over the bomber, especially when the latter was unescorted, and the value of air superiority in any area of operations was thus no secret at all before the war began.

One interesting note is that the reports derived from information incoming from Spain say virtually nothing about the Ju 87 Stuka. This indicates that French intelligence (at least until Poland was invaded in 1939) did not always have a clear view of German technical development or capacity. Recalling the reports indicating that the Germans kept close tabs on some technical information, they seem to have done an exemplary job testing the Ju 87 in Spain while revealing almost nothing about it. In fact, the Ju 87 arrived very late in the conflict and the Germans were exceptionally careful in its operational usage leaving no physical examples behind for the Nationalists to study.[24] The fact that French intelligence had little to say about its use in Spain is likely because there was so little experience with it. The perception that it was somehow an important facet of the Spanish Civil War likely has more to do with a recasting of the Spanish Civil War as a test bed for blitzkrieg.

In summary, French intelligence's technical assessments—not only on the specifics of German capabilities in aircraft design, but in general concepts as well—proved to be accurate, not only pertaining to the Battle of France, but as they applied to World War II as a whole. From the intelligence perspective, the information about the state of aircraft technology writ large was valid, and some of the excellent early analysis by French intelligence proved amazingly accurate and predictive of many problems encountered by the Allies long after France fell in 1940.

Technical Assessment of German Ground-Based Antiaircraft Defenses

The severe drubbing dealt to French and British aircraft attacking German units from low to middle altitudes during the Battle of France might reasonably lead one to believe that French intelligence provided woefully little warning as to the German capabilities before the initiation of hostilities. Surely, had the Allied aviators had any inkling of the efficacy of German flak (*Fliegerabwehrkanonen*) they would have approached their attacks differently. Unfortunately, the evidence does not support this conclusion. Throughout the 1930s, French intelligence provided reliable technical information on German flak. From the mid-1930s and especially during the Spanish Civil War, French intelligence presented a clear picture of German ground-based antiaircraft armament and its development, as well as a solid overall assessment of the efficacy of modern ground-based antiaircraft defenses.

By the 1930s, ground-based antiaircraft defenses made great strides over the largely improvised or immature defenses of World War I. French intelligence accurately advocated that the best defense against attacking enemy aircraft (again, short of friendly aircraft) was for ground forces to put up a "veritable wall" of fire to dissuade, disrupt or destroy the attacker.[25] Further, French analysis also indicated the need for "layered" antiaircraft defenses.[26] The suggested short-, medium-, and long-range air defenses were deemed crucial not only for defense of ground units in general, but specifically for sensitive targets such as airfields.[27] What French intelligence effectively described was the existing state and practice of German antiaircraft defenses from 88-mm guns for long range, to 37-mm guns for medium range, and 20-mm and 7.92-mm weapons for close range.

French Intelligence Assessment of German Doctrine

Again, French intelligence regarding German doctrine was quite accurate in the years leading up to World War II. This information can be divided roughly into two parts. The first part is "closed" intelligence, information compiled by French intelligence services for internal use from various sources including but not limited to French observers, French agents, and foreign agents in French service. The second source of information available to French intelligence and French military personnel as a whole, indeed virtually any literate person in France, was open-source information available on the market in the form of journals, books, and so on.

The closed source information indicates that French intelligence was aware of developments in German doctrine concerning both the employment of airpower as a part of *Bewegungskrieg* and ground-based air defenses acting in conjunction with same.

Further, the French followed other important aspects of Luftwaffe development, such as communications, closely.[28] The opening notes indicate: "The radio communication troops constitute the nervous system of the air force."[29]

While the document is brief, it is quite detailed. For instance, it details the relative rank of personnel for various positions and their training and deployment cycles.[30] The document details how such troops were recruited.[31] The interesting aspect of this document is how it mirrors French personnel needs and problems in highly technical areas for reasons political, technical, and military, the FAF fell short in 1940.

Open sources of information in the 1940s, just like today are some of the very best sources for intelligence information concerning the thinking and intentions of potential adversaries. In fact, the 1930s was an especially rich time for publishing from a military point of view. The various ideas culminating after a decade of peace and perspective on the potential battlefield evolution that started to germinate in the last year of World War I led to a rash of publishing on future war. During the relatively peaceful 1930s (with the notable exception of the Spanish Civil War) military writers and thinkers were active in every country. Many of their works were even translated into various languages. However, even those works that were not translated from one language to the next were still available on the open market and available for purchase by anybody with a few francs, marks, or pounds to spare. "The lion's share of all intelligence, it appears comes from the public domain . . . [and] accounted for at least 80 percent of French military intelligence."[32]

An Obsession with Numbers

French decision-making was driven by data on German production. Unfortunately, most of the reports on German production were inaccurate; French intelligence overestimated German production capacity and extant numbers.

Pierre Cot's testimony before Congress reveals how the numbers influenced French decision-making. Cot testified that Germany produced 1,800 planes per month by May 1940 and stood firmly behind this estimate.[33] In reality, Germany produced only 156 fighter aircraft, 24 twin-engine aircraft, and 3 four-engine aircraft per month.[34] Germany did not reach a total combined output of 1,550 aircraft per month until the second half of 1943, and this number was still well short of the 1,800 Cot attributed to them in May 1940.[35]

Cot's figures were far off from reality, but the error was positive in a sense. Overestimating German production gave more fodder to the FAF to demand more funding for more production. The negative aspect of this gross overestimation of German production is that it contributed to France's and Britain's decisions to concede Austria and Czechoslovakia to Hitler without a fight.[36] Interestingly, French overestimations of German strength seem to have been the cause for British overestimations.[37]

At some point during the war, however, Cot's numbers became far more accurate. Cot's estimates on German airpower were quite close to reality in *Triumph of Treason*, published in 1944.[38] While Cot does not specifically mention the source of his apparently revised statistics, the source is certainly interesting. Without a concrete source, one can only conclude that either a) Cot was brought in on what was still highly confidential information, assuming the Allies even had that information by around 1943 when this book was being written or b) Cot had access to accurate information all along that the French possessed, but that did not make it into official reports because it made the imbalance seem less severe before the war.

French plans for another long attritional war dominated by firepower and production (which is ironically what World War II turned out to be, but with more movement and maneuver than imagined by leadership) meant that a production imbalance in Germany's favor added to the already impressive manpower advantage Germany enjoyed. France was aware of these disadvantages—especially in manpower—but France was confident of winning a long war with the military it had. Most of the rest of the world was convinced France could hold its own as well; France's rapid defeat shocked not only France, but the rest of the world—including the Germans, who had plans to fight just the sort of long attritional war France expected.[39]

A Waste of Excellent Resources

Retrospectively much of the good information provided by French intelligence services regarding the Wehrmacht was underappreciated. There were two related reasons for this failure. French leadership was genuinely convinced of the soundness of its doctrine, training, and technology, at least until 1938 when cracks began to appear in the foundation, and more overtly after the collapse of Poland, which started a panicked effort to reform and refit to meet the German threat well after it was too late to do so. Some of the ideas and concepts proposed and endorsed in the face of evidence to the contrary were remarkable in their inability to grasp what was being developed and what would ultimately befall France. When Gamelin tried to defend French prewar doctrine in light of the defeat, he rightfully explained exactly how complicated it was to create usable doctrine and how it had to fit with the military one has and the enemy one potentially faces.[40] While this was undoubtedly an excuse of sorts, Gamelin did not shy away from the fact that tactical/operational airpower had become of primary, if not ultimate, importance on the modern battlefield.[41] Gamelin reserved special attention for the Ju 87, which if the invasion of Poland rendered important, the Battle of France turned into something of an undeserved legend. However, Gamelin did not hesitate to place massive blame on the FAF as being primary in France's defeat: "The characteristic inferiority of our aviation played a critical role in the defeat."[42]

In essence, Gamelin blamed the FAF for not being the Luftwaffe. Although the story is deeper, the summary was essentially accurate; the FAF was not the Luftwaffe. Its doctrine and equipment created a fundamentally different air arm. Even though intelligence provided good information about how the Germans were viewing the nature of the next war, it did not create a major shift in doctrine.

The French obsession with numbers and what was in their eyes going to be a long war of grinding attrition focused too much on the parts that French intelligence got wrong. Taken as a whole, the French military establishment, including senior leadership in the air force and Air Ministry, accepted what reinforced their preconceived notions and ignored what challenged their operational paradigms. The French commitment to its own doctrine meant that intelligence reports and information were acknowledged, but they had no fundamental effect on doctrine.

French faith in their doctrine was underscored by a culture of compliance. The French military was its own worst enemy: "Discussion in the classroom was not encouraged; individual thought and initiative were not rewarded; dissent was frowned upon."[43]

The inherent problem with this attitude, of course, is that any thinking that did not fit was not given voice. If the officers and men of a military organization are silenced internally, what real chance does intelligence have of making meaningful inroads in warning of an external threat that has very different ideas regarding warfare? Even generals were not immune:

> General Lucien Loizeau was carpeted in 1935 for too positive a report on the Russian army maneuvers, [this was before the purges when the Soviets were doing an excellent job moving forward with combined arms theory] a mistake his successor, General Schweisguth carefully

avoided much to the delight of the Army Staff and War Ministry which had already concluded that the Russian army was a paper tiger. In autumn of 1938 Colonel Palasse, the military attaché in Moscow made the mistake of Loizeau and was reprimanded for exaggerating Russian military capacity.[44]

As late as 1938 Général Alphonse Georges was assuring a group of French and foreign officers that "in the opinion of the French War Council, no new method of warfare had evolved since the termination of the Great War."[45]

With closed ears and minds at the top of the structure, there was little chance any sort of warning from intelligence would make significant inroads. An internal intelligence report that suggested the high command was not paying enough attention to modern developments in warfare was not likely to make any significant inroads.[46]

French Society and Culture and Its Impact on Intelligence

Society and culture have a direct impact on the militaries they create. Some examples, such as the Spartans or the Cossacks, have been well studied. Although many World War I and World War II histories give a superficial nod to the divisions in French society and suggest that somehow there was a military impact, few give any details worth mentioning. At most a superficial understanding of such issues as the Dreyfus affair are offered as a tantalizing surface scraping of what is a very deep subject. The politics of the FAF, Pierre Cot, and the Popular Front aside, French society in relation to the military had a series of peculiar effects upon French intelligence services that impacted the way intelligence was viewed, staffed, and represented in the military. This sociomilitary interaction led to a shunning of the intelligence branch by many career-minded officers, and a lack of forceful and effective representation of the intelligence services at higher echelons where they might have had greater effect on the decision-making process.

Deep socioeconomic-political divides in France showed themselves in the military, and these were felt in the intelligence branch: "Interestingly, we are told that the Intelligence Bureau was considered the least attractive of the Army Staff departments, for promotion was perceived to be slower than anywhere else. This may well have meant that those who served there did so either because of their genuine interest in the bureau or because they had been judged insufficiently orthodox [compliant] for work in operations or mobilization."[47]

In essence, military intelligence was a dumping ground for the noncompliant. This clearly indicates a deep sense of mistrust between not only the command and intelligence, but the military as a whole and intelligence. This sense of mistrust must ultimately be blamed for the information provided by intelligence not being taken seriously enough.

Not a Failure, Just a Failure to Be Used Properly

Ironically, the FAF itself was responsible for wasting much of the efforts of its intelligence services. While it is debatable whether greater focus on German technology and doctrine would have had any effect at higher levels (and there is no overt evidence to suggest that would have been the case), FAF intelligence spent countless hours focused on gathering information for a French strategic bombing campaign against Germany that never had even the dimmest flicker of hope of becoming a reality: "The broad strategic possibilities of air action have never received very adequate attention in France."[48] When Air Commodore Colyer sent this report on 30 May 1940, both France and Britain were on their heels in the battle with Germany. While Colyer was correct on a national level, the FAF did officially take a serious interest in the strategic application of airpower. In fact, intelligence spent some time examining and collating quite an impressive list of potential strategic targets inside Germany.

A rather impressive document titled *Géographie aérienne de l'Allemagne*, produced by the air force's Deuxième Bureau, began keeping track of German industrial production, statistics, and specifics of location and types of German aircraft inside Germany.[49] Additionally, detailed maps were updated with some regularity illustrating sensitive targets such as fuel and munitions depots vital to not only the Luftwaffe, but the Wehrmacht as a whole.[50] Further, these same maps were used in exercises combined with actual industrial targets inside Germany, such as engine and munitions factories, in preparations for war with Germany.[51] To state that the FAF has no concept of strategic air operations is thus, inaccurate. Further, intelligence provided the air force with target sets of not only Luftwaffe airfields, but sensitive industrial and logistics sites, which in form and content very much resemble the targets the Allies later bombed.

Again, the information intelligence provided regarding potential targets for strategic airpower was compelling and accurate. However, it was never put to any use. Although the FAF internally at least on paper tried to view itself as an independent arm with an important strategic mission, which if properly executed could hinder the German war effort, it was never put to use because of fears of reprisals. The quality intelligence work that created these target packages thus went for naught, and their efforts were wasted.

Internal Enemies and French Intelligence

Military intelligence organizations probably get too much credit for a win and take too much blame for a loss. Like the quarterback, they are supposed to act as the brain, providing and analyzing information and then suggesting courses of action. However, the coaches ultimately call the play. This was certainly the case for French intelligence prior to World War II.

French intelligence was timely and accurate regarding German technology and doctrine prior to World War II. The primary inaccuracy found in prewar French intelligence estimates concerns German production, and in light of Cot's remarkably accurate numbers in his mid-war work, one must question how much French intelligence actually knew before the war and how much was altered or suppressed.[52] Since prewar French intelligence files are still being sorted following their return from Russia, this may come to light at some point.

The ultimate failure then does not lay at the feet of French intelligence; there is little that can be found to be inaccurate in their reports and assessments. French leadership was provided with accurate information regarding German intentions. The problem was what was done—or in this case, not done—with the information provided.

The reasons are far more complex. While the data was technical and factual, it was being assessed by emotive people devoted to one side or another of complex sociopolitical-military squabble inside France itself. The levels of distrust were epidemic. Consider this exchange:

"Your report is incomplete; you have forgotten to point out the 'revolutionary propaganda' of the Communist workers."

"But I have no such propaganda in my regiment . . . the morale of my men could not be better."

"I want you to understand . . . that there is always some revolutionary agitation to report."

"Even if there are none?"

"There always are. Look at what is going on in Spain. Don't be stubborn, take your report and return it to us amended."[53]

It is difficult to imagine this discussion taking place in either Britain or the United States. Such were the ingrained internal fears, divisions, and prejudices that they interfered directly, and in fundamental ways, to include altering what was an objective assessment, turning it instead into a subjective, politically charged document. Outside of the Soviet Union, there was no direct parallel. It is vital for anybody studying the French military prior to World War II to understand how deeply this affected the internal machinations of French national defense. Unfortunately, this is rarely if ever discussed in analyses of French military performance in 1940.

Intelligence reports were thus assessed in this environment. Conservative French leadership at the highest levels plainly refused to accept until it was far too late that their doctrine was going to prove grossly insufficient in the coming conflict. In essence, if it was out of touch with the accepted dogma, it was immediately discarded. It is difficult to imagine intelligence reports being assessed honestly and objectively in this environment.

Further, the relatively poor light in which French intelligence was viewed did not help. If the closed minds at the top were not bad enough, a generally low opinion of the intelligence corps grossly exacerbated the problem. While there is no specific information that suggests the intelligence services were politically unreliable, the way in which officers were often farmed out to intelligence rather than a more desirable post suggests that the branch would not be taken that seriously anyway.

Bluntly, if it was not something the command wanted to hear, read, or see, it was ignored. Anything that went against the established norm was increasingly suppressed as time went on. By 1938 outside opinions were being suppressed to the point that politicians were summarily expelled from their positions and military journals were shut down and nothing other than established and accepted versions of the "truth" were accepted.

It is difficult from a non-French perspective to assess the misuse of French intelligence at all levels. The pervasive political thread that seemed to permeate all levels of French politics and society, had thus taken root in French intelligence. On one hand, Cot's desire to diplomatically shift France toward the Soviet Union using strategic airpower permanently reoriented a great deal of FAF intelligence toward identifying and analyzing potential infrastructure targets inside Germany that were never to be targeted by nonexistent French bomber fleets. On the other, conservative officers and command demanded intelligence be revised to conform with "official" opinions. Considering the generally low regard in which intelligence was held in the French military structure, it is difficult to imagine it making a significant impact on decision-makers whose rather monolithic decision-making processes were seemingly inviolable.

German Intelligence from 1934 to 1940

German military intelligence produced mixed results during World War II. While tactical and operational level battlefield intelligence was often excellent, strategic intelligence was often poor, especially in reference to the Soviet Union. Conversely, policies, procedures, operations, and special operations conceived and developed by German military intelligence during the war was sometimes superlative, and there are successful aspects of these developments that were key to developing NATO intelligence during the Cold War.

German intelligence on France's preparations for war was decent in general. There are many reasons for this, but primary among these was the relatively "open book" that France represented (not unlike Germany) in the prewar years. As with France, much German intelligence regarding such things as industry and infrastructure came from open-source intelligence as diverse as Michelin guides and snapshots from "tourists." Debates and developments inside the French military were barely concealed from the public eye (if at all), and Germany frequently had to do little more than read French books and newspapers, watch French newsreels, and listen to French radio broadcasts to gain a reasonably accurate understanding of developments. Even after the French relocated military airfields, Luftwaffe attacks were effective because the movements were so-noted.[54]

The Germans had a clear picture of the FAF's strengths and weaknesses. Much like its French counterpart, the German intelligence efforts can be discussed in three parts: technical intelligence (aircraft type, quality, numbers, etc.), doctrinal intelligence related to use of airpower, and intelligence related to antiaircraft operations.

German technical intelligence related to French airpower was well-informed. As with other intelligence-related issues, much of the technical accuracy came from a lack of secrecy in France. Unlike modern aircraft with advanced avionics that can fundamentally transform performance, period aircraft were judged according to speed, firepower, range, reliability, and maneuverability, and most countries were all too happy to brag about them.[55] A plane could be faster, more maneuverable, carry more bombs, drop those bombs more accurately, or have more throw weight. Other than perhaps the Norden bomb sight and the German *Knickebein* (crooked leg) beam navigation system, however, there were few sensitive technological "wonders" that would equate to the secret or top-secret features found in modern military aircraft. A plane was often very much just a plane that was faster or had more guns or bombs; all very straightforward and familiar features. Thus, the state of technical intelligence on either side was generally easier to get right considering the state of technology and the openness of all parties involved.

The Germans also had accurate intelligence regarding French capabilities and numbers. Germany was familiar with current French aircraft, including the M.S.406; its assessment of the 406 vis-à-vis the Bf 109 was also accurate; the Germans understood that French fighter aircraft were inferior and less capable in general. Germany understood that France had fewer modern fighters than Germany, but recognized that France had large quantities of older aircraft, many of which would be of little utility in a modern war.

German intelligence also understood that France had serious problems with bomber development even though it was clear that the French air force was interested in bombers and strategic bombing. Germany recognized that most French bombers were outmoded, and that the bombers that France had on establishment were inferior. Further, Germany saw that France had serious production capacity problems in bombers as well as fighter aircraft.[56]

Having read French material on airpower and theory, German intelligence operatives understood that France was literate in the basic general theories and professional ideas. Germany saw the FAF become independent.[57] However, there seems to be little direct evidence that Germany understood how deep the FAF's organizational problems were and how those problems were exacerbated in the critical year before the war by sociopolitical disruptions that reformatted, and in a sense jumbled, French operational capabilities on the brink of war. Postwar assessments, based on good primary sources, offered indications that at least internally some in the Luftwaffe argued the picture of the FAF was quite muddled and unclear.[58]

German intelligence tried to keep close tabs on where French aircraft were positioned. This became more difficult after mid-1938 when French airpower was dispersed in penny packets among the army.[59] Although the Luftwaffe regarded French airfields as priority targets, it found it difficult to hit them all meaningfully in the opening days of the campaign. Ironically, the dispersion, although not to the liking of the FAF, likely preserved some its airpower. The major French airfields were well known before the reversion to army control and those were treated to increased Luftwaffe attention as range and availability permitted.

The array of French aircraft on hand was also well known to German intelligence. The Luftwaffe well understood that most French aircraft were dated or at least aging and that a large portion of the French air fleet was completely obsolete, and it had a good read on the likely tactics and doctrine to be employed (which was dissimilar to that developed by the Luftwaffe), but more directly because of practical experience in Spain and Poland.[60]

However, German intelligence, especially it seems air intelligence, suffered from many deficiencies (as did the French intelligence section), but not to the dysfunctional depth suffered in France. According to Horst Boog, "Intelligence work was quite incomplete, and it was the quick success of the fighting troops that saved the Intelligence Branch from exposure."[61] At the highest levels, the Abwehr spent much time gauging the tone and morale of the French and British people before the war (often inaccurately), but also spent a great deal of time considering what specific internal demographics, especially Jews, might think of a war, shortages, etc., and this ideological component, driven by Nazi ideology, was time very questionably utilized.[62]

One aspect where France and Germany were remarkably similar was in the way the services felt about intelligence work, and the way it was treated. Inside the Wehrmacht, just like in French service, intelligence was not a glamorous job. Although it is perhaps not fair to rate the German assessment of intelligence work as low as that of France, Germany had few if any real intelligence specialists outside the Abwehr, and staff trained offers could find themselves stuck in an intelligence job with little or no training.[63] There was often a lack of intelligence reporting at various planning levels, which seems to have been an intentional pattern of neglect.[64] What emerges is a picture of nonprofessional intelligence officers up to at least the operational level proffering improvised intelligence to various levels of command, if they were asked for an assessment at all. In short, intelligence in Germany was a humdrum field with few if any true specialists outside very small offices and organizations. This did little damage to the German war effort in France due to the campaign's brief duration, but the neglect had devastating consequences later when trying to assess the capacity of both the Soviet Union and the United States to wage war. The academically interesting, but factually flawed, focus on the assessment of Germany's "racial enemies" as a part of active intelligence work also points to a dysfunctional environment driven more by internal politics than the realities of strategically operable intelligence during wartime.

Conclusions

Both sides had a rather clear picture of each other in terms of armament and doctrine before May 1940. The key difference is that German intelligence was not presumed to be inundated with spies like the Deuxième Bureau. Even though France had a clear picture of the Wehrmacht, it ignored it. The Luftwaffe changed little other than targeting data simply because it did not have to; its model worked for the campaign. The tragedy is that France had enough information from both open-source intelligence and espionage to understand that it needed to adjust, but these reports and data were ignored. As a result, Germany was much better prepared to fight France than vice-versa.

To be fair, solid German intelligence on France and French airpower did not instantly equate to victory. Recall that many German officers, especially those who were veterans of World War I on the western front, were quite nervous on 10 May 1940. While German intelligence identified problems, shortages, and technical deficiencies, none of the newer German concepts up to that point had been tested against a near-peer adversary. Further, the reader must keep in mind that even though the Luftwaffe emerged victorious in June 1940, it was at considerable cost in personnel and aircraft, even given the tremendous perceived advantages from equipment, doctrine, and intelligence. Although it worked *well enough*, it failed immediately thereafter in the Battle of Britain, and catastrophically beginning in 1941 to the point of being unable to meet its duty requirements by 1944.

This was not the last time that good intelligence was ignored during World War II. Consider the many times that Stalin in a paranoia not entirely dissimilar to that of certain French officers toward the Deuxième Bureau, ignored solid intelligence that he could have potentially dramatically turned to his advantage, and this trend dates demonstrably to before the war.[65] Distrust of intelligence was nothing new, and although Germany did not seemingly distrust its intelligence branches, specialists (what few there seem to have been), and officers, it also did not place a very high value on them. While this worked from 1939 to 1941, the lack of bolstering strong and long-term intelligence capability with dedicated specialists producing high-quality information was key in Germany's ultimate defeat. In 1940 Germany and the Luftwaffe were simply more able to cope with their intelligence flaws than France proved to be.

4

THE FRENCH AIR FORCE, THE LUFTWAFFE, AND THE SPANISH CIVIL WAR

HISTORICAL ANALYSIS pertaining to the lessons learned, not learned, or unlearned by past military organizations is useful. It not only establishes some baseline as to the quality and content of information available to decision-makers, it allows for sometimes excellent insight into their mindsets. The decisions made based upon information at hand during the period can be revealing. Further, the disputes in analysis during the period frequently reveal the divisions in thought, the figures and "schools" prominently involved in the process of military thought and establishment of military doctrine, and reveal how the final decisions affected the outcome of later military operations.

Prewar France was no different. While much has been made of the theorists in Britain and Germany during the interwar period, little time has been devoted to understanding how the French interpreted military actions in smaller conflicts during the interwar period, especially as they related to the deployment and use of airpower. The lack of serious study of French airpower and airpower theory is indicative of the negligent treatment of the topic as a whole. Even those anglophone authors who devote some effort to seriously examining the French air force (FAF) often give this subject superficial treatment.

The French observed the Spanish Civil War and other minor conflicts in the interwar period even though they did not participate in most of them. From 1936 to 1939 the Spanish Civil War figures not only in French intelligence reports, but in articles and books as well that were in open circulation. Sometimes important figures weighed in on the matter, such as Général Maurice Duval's work *Les leçons de la guerre d'Espagne*, which included a forward by a figure no less prominent than Général Maxime Weygand.[1]

The important point is that these small wars were being prominently discussed and debated in French military circles. Regardless of the problems inherent in the French military system that led to the defeat in 1940, there was active debate before the war regarding the lessons to be learned from small wars, especially when it came to airpower.

There was a robust flow of information arriving in France from Spain. It was a mix of open-source material and classified reports as reflected in the SHAA files.[2] The information was accurate and proved to portend not only some of the events of the Battle of France, but World War II as a whole. The reports and information were particularly revealing in the areas of technical analysis, strategic bombing, the fighter versus the bomber, and battlefield air attack. The information derived from these reports often had mixed results on decision-making as similar reports did in other countries.

France, however, is unique again in its interpretation of the Spanish Civil War. French interpretations were influenced by the politico-military conflict occurring inside France. All the above observations must finally be viewed through that particular filter before conclusions can be drawn about French information and interpretations. Further, internal French angst over the Spanish Civil War directly affected France's decision to abstain from the conflict.

Flow of Information

The Spanish Civil War caught the world's attention almost immediately. In many ways it was a microcosm of struggle between fascism and communism, though each side often viewed its own actions and motivations in a softer light. Hemingway wrote about it and Picasso painted it. It was an emotive war, and it was a brutal war (if any war can be anything but), often defined by atrocities.

From a strictly military point of view, it was also an informative war. The direct involvement of Germany, Italy, and the Soviet Union made it more so. While each country's experience yielded different results, the world's other militaries observed from a distance as many concepts and technologies that had emerged during World War I were tested on a more modern battlefield. Viewed in the light of the entirety of World War II, the Spanish Civil War was instructive, though it was definitely not a blueprint for blitzkrieg as it was to some extent made out to be in World War II's immediate aftermath.

The flow of information into France was strong from the beginning. From shortly after the beginning of the war until the outbreak of World War II on 1 September 1939, the Spanish Civil War was a dominant subject. There were three major outlets for information and analysis coming from Spain. These were intelligence reports kept internally, journal articles, and to a lesser extent, books. The intelligence reports were generally kept classified, but the journal articles and books were an open source and available on the market.

The bulk of the FAF intelligence reports still extant can be found at Historical Service of the FAF at Vincennes.[3] These reports include technical data and interpretation of the effectiveness not only of technology, but of doctrinal issues as well, and are largely derived from reports of observers on the ground in Spain.[4] The journal *Revue de l'Armée de l'Air* featured a number of articles about the Spanish Civil War from 1937 to 1939. Finally, books such as *Les leçons de la guerre d'Espagne* provided readers with further information and analysis.[5]

These resources represented the serious attempts at analyzing the military picture in Spain. There were of course other articles and books written on the war during the period, but many if not most of them were more emotive and political in nature and designed to elicit a response from a receptive and sympathetic audience on the left or right.

Quality of Information and Analysis

Retrospectively, the quality of the information and the analysis provided in many of the intelligence reports and articles in professional military spheres was quite good. There are four areas in particular where the information provided was later reinforced by actual battlefield experiences during World War II. These include technical analysis, analysis of strategic bombing, analysis of the fighter versus the bomber, and the analysis of battlefield air attack.

French technical analysis of the equipment being used in the air war in Spain was not only thorough, but accurate. It gave the men and officers of the FAF an objective view of technology likely to be used in the immediate future, especially by the air force's presumed adversary, the Luftwaffe.

The only head-to-head comparison of French and German aircraft was in 1936, the first year of the Spanish Civil War. French analysts determined that the Dewoitine D.371 was superior to its primary Nationalist adversaries, especially the Fiat F.32.[6] It was also reckoned to be superior to the Heinkel He 51 that was also beginning to appear in theater.[7] The D.371 was a transitionary monoplane that first flew in 1932. While American and British designs moved away from the wing fixed above the fuselage and supported by struts to an under- or mid-fuselage wing attachment with an enclosed canopy, the D.371 resembled a late-1920s biplane with the bottom wing removed. French intelligence described this as the "first phase" of air operations in Spain.[8] In realistic terms, this phase represents the escalation of the war without a firm or established supply chain from any of the outside powers.

During the "second phase," French intelligence followed the deployment of Soviet aircraft and pilots sent to aid the Republicans and compared them with their Nationalist (including German and Italian) adversaries.[9] This Soviet aid arrived just as the little French aid provided by the government disappeared. Again, the assessment indicates that the Republicans still maintained the edge with the Polikarpov I-15 and I-16 provided by the Soviets.[10] Retrospectively, these reports were accurate; in general, all of the above aircraft were superior to those of their Nationalist adversaries.

The "third phase" (and notably the final phase) according to French intelligence was delineated by the Messerschmitt Bf 109's deployment.[11] French intelligence quickly acknowledged the superiority of the Bf 109 to all other aircraft in Spain: "The Messerschmidt [sic] 109 is in reality the most modern aircraft in use in Spain. It is equipped with a Jumo 210 engine of 670 cu. Its armament is only composed of two machine guns. It can reach speeds of 460 km/h at altitude."[12]

This report reflects that French intelligence was ignorant of some of the Bf 109's technical features, and to a greater or lesser extent would be until after 3 September 1939. French intelligence noted that the Bf 109 was "only" armed with two 7.92 x 5-mm machine guns, but that the effects of the guns combined with their ammunition were impressive, and the exact technical capabilities of the guns and their explosive ammunition were closely guarded by the Germans.[13] It is interesting to note that while French designers were adamant about mounting 20-mm or larger cannon to combat aircraft in the mid-1930s, really even before the Spanish Civil War. The fact that the Germans were, in French eyes, achieving impressive results with only two machine guns and some sort of new ammunition is especially ironic considering the French consistently had problems with aircraft-mounted machine guns right up to June 1940, but the Germans found the two machine guns, even with the new ammunition, unimpressive enough on the C models deployed in Spain during the Spanish Civil War, that an upgrade including a 20-mm cannon on the D mark of Bf 109 and later models.[14] Additionally, ammunition capacity was drastically increased with the D-forward.[15]

In general terms, French discourse on fighter design in the Spanish Civil War concerned power, speed, and maneuverability, with particular emphasis on the importance of speed and maneuverability.[16] Shockingly, the same report indicates that the characteristics of the Bf 109 were difficult to achieve with the existing technology.[17] While the Bf 109 was certainly an excellent plane for its time, other planes such as the Hurricane and Spitfire were meeting or exceeding the 109's capabilities, as were new designs in the United States, including the P-38 and P-40. What made the Bf 109 different is that although it was older than any of the above designs, it continued to be effectively updated and at least competitive up until late 1944.

One is left to speculate exactly why the author of this report came to this conclusion. One rational possibility is that the state of French aircraft design was basically five years or so behind that of Germany. This conclusion could be the result of an insular idea that if it was difficult for France, it might be difficult for everybody else as well. However, it could have been an attempt to save face, obscuring an embarrassing inferiority.

Interestingly, the Germans seem to have been aware of the overall inferiority of modern French aircraft in both numbers and quality. In a postwar study by Generalleutnant a.D. Andreas Nielsen, written for the Allies (probably while he was in captivity), Nielsen stated that before the war in the West began: "The combined British and FAFs were considered as numerically and qualitatively inferior to the *Luftwaffe* in Western Europe."[18]

What seems to be clear is that the FAF (and probably everybody else), knew that the data from the Spanish Civil War onward indicated that French aircraft were remarkably inferior to their German counterparts. The reports indicated that French intelligence certainly understood what made a good plane, as their unvarnished praise for the Bf 109 demonstrates.

The French intelligence reports did not focus too much on bomber design. It is unclear why this was the case, but little was said about German bomber design. This seems strange considering that if anything, French bomber design was further behind German bomber design than fighter design. This is even more interesting when one considers that the FAF was officially and doctrinally (on paper) edging closer and closer to pursuing strategic airpower to its own effects.

One thing is certain: the French focused on the effects of bombing, and the duel between the fighter and the bomber.

The Effects of Strategic Bombing

The overall effects of strategic bombing during World War II are to an extent an unresolved debate. The promise of new technology before World War II, which was felt by some at the time to be maturing into the capacity that theory thought it should have, seemed to offer the possibility of strategic or even grand strategic dominance over all other considerations. The inability of World War I aircraft to carry significant bombloads over long distances and drop them accurately was reckoned by many to have been resolved with a new generation of bombers before World War II.[19] As early as the Spanish Civil War, this new generation of bombers still had not proved the problems solved, nor the doctrine sound, and French intelligence caught on.

Prewar French intelligence reports indicate that regardless of the currently achievable payloads, increasing the payload seemed to be the only solution for effective bombing. In short, regardless of the improvements in capacity and accuracy, more payload was always desirable, and bombing still had not reached the level of maturity described by theorists.[20] Even though planes were noticeably improved as were bombsights and payloads, bombing built-up areas in Spain was not proving as productive as arguments indicated they should be.[21] What this hints at is the conclusion ultimately reached much later in the war by the Allies that area bombing (mass saturation bombing by as many bombers as possible repeatedly over an area) was the only way to approach the effects bomber advocates sought to reach.

The French were also clearly interested in how morale was affected under heavy aerial bombardment. Under the intermittent guidance of Cot and his circle of officers, the FAF gravitated, at least on paper, toward a more strategic role: "Over the course of the past few years there have been a great number of vague enough theoretical discussions on the character and probable effects of aerial [strategic] bombardment on future war . . . it is the purpose of this study to examine the effects of these attacks as well as the effects produced by them on the nerves and morale of the [civilian] population."[22]

Spain did not change the fundamental quotient of World War I: strategic bombing did not have that great an effect upon civilian morale. Sandys pointed out that over a period of forty-one hours, Barcelona was bombed twelve times.[23] Further, he noted that the population "was not discouraged [by the bombing]."[24] The population did not cower in houses and basements. Indeed, Sandys noted that while there were some shaken nerves, the population remained constantly active, and worked to repair buildings, aid the injured, and prepare for the next raid.[25] This was clearly not the screaming mass of demoralized humanity that Douhet prophesized and to which Sandys alluded.

The Bomber versus the Fighter

One other area that received attention in prewar French literature pertaining to the Spanish Civil War was the duel between fighter and the bomber. The bomber could use three possible defenses against the fighter: speed, defensive firepower, and escort fighters. As engine technology and fighter design improved rapidly from the early 1930s onward, speed became less of a possibility. The idea that speed could eventually become a defensive factor again for bombers was explored as early as 1936.[26] The United States fully embraced the second possibility of inherent defensive firepower until costly raids over Germany proved that theory incorrect in 1943. Finally, the French understood the value of fighter escort in the Spanish Civil War well before World War II: "The vulnerability of bombers is great ... it is advisable during daytime to have an escort of *six or seven fighters per bomber.*"[27]

This assessment of the bomber versus the fighter shortly before World War II indicates the French had information that ran counter to notions of the time that the bomber would be able to fend for itself. In fact, this idea was constantly reinforced. In June 1938, an author writing under the pseudonym of "P. E." remarked regarding aerial bombing in Spain: "The superiority of the fighter [air superiority] is of great importance in these [bombing] operations."[28]

As late as June 1939 an article originally appearing in the Italian *Le vie dell' aria* was translated for the *Revue de l'Armée de l'Air* illustrating the points of view of two Italian airmen who participated in the Spanish Civil War. The pro-fighter argument by Fucini basically reflected much of what the French already observed that the lessons in Spain proved that the speed of the fighter, its maneuverability (combined with the bombers' need to stay on target) easily kept a bomber from hitting its intended target if the fighter did not destroy the bomber outright.[29]

An Italian bomber advocate made some interesting points: "The probability of contact with fighters is minimal, and in that case, the contact only endures a few seconds."[30] "It is true that the fire of the fighters is more precise, but the fire of a formation of bombers is greater and can establish a barrage."[31]

These arguments probably would have seemed familiar and logical to American airmen before their experiences over Germany from 1943 onward.

Further, the Italian commentator argued, "The Nationalist bombers [presumably including Italian and German] execute extremely precise bomb runs at 6500m . . . at 6500m one can place sixty large caliber bombs in a zone of 100 to 200m; it is a question of lead [aim]."[32]

These arguments must have seemed a little hollow: if the fighters only encountered the bombers for a few seconds, the danger was minimal, but what if they engaged longer? Yes, the fighters were more able to concentrate their fire on bombers, but why had this barrage of fire seemingly not done much good before (or indeed afterward). The Italian airmen's testimony also had to be taken in the context of the war at the time: by 1938 into 1939, the Nationalists were largely having their way in the air war, thus Fucini likely saw what Nationalist fighters did to lightly or unescorted Republican bombers, whereas the other Italian source probably encountered little overall resistance.[33] Context mattered and what was overtly argued by Fucini was grudgingly and half-heartedly admitted to by the other Italian commentator: the fighter was a serious threat to the bomber, and likely its best protection.[34] Further, 100 meters to 200 meters represented quite a spread (and this likely under optimal conditions of little resistance if we read through the context), numbers of which reinforces the earlier French assessments that lots of bombs are the only real solution to destroying a target; aerial bombing just is not that accurate or effective.[35] The "trail of folly" from Spain to France and Britain, then to the United States presuming the precision of bombers and their invulnerability to fighters was at least argued against repeatedly in French literature before the war began.

Battlefield Air Attack

Battlefield air attack was both effective and destructive during World War II. The Luftwaffe played a key role in dismembering and destroying an ill-prepared French defense in 1940, and as the war went on Allied airpower proved increasingly destructive to German ground units in northwest Europe and on the eastern front. Battlefield air attack was not new to World War II. During World War I, the increasing utility of airpower in the tactical role eventually led to specialization. "By 1918, the major powers were producing large numbers of aircraft with reliable 250-horsepower engines, bombers capable of dropping one-ton bombs, and armored ground attack aircraft. Some German units were flying all-metal aircraft into battle."[36]

The ground attack role was nothing new. However, improvements in technology, specifically in airplane design, and communication resulted in a maturation of battlefield air attack to what could be considered decisive levels during World War II. Again, the Spanish Civil War hinted at the realities and possibilities. The French were paying attention. What is remarkable is again how little was actually "new." One writer noted that "10 to 20 aircraft, Heinkel, or others, attack a certain point with machine guns and small bombs. Before this attack, the infantry prepares themselves for the assault. When the demoralization effect is expected, the enemy initiates the attack protected by their air force."[37]

This model was essentially the same as the World War I model. The aircraft in use at the time (notably the Heinkels) had improved performance over their World War I predecessors, but their payloads and other attributes were not drastically different. Germany developed its battlefield air attack tactics toward the end of World War I, especially after their experiences with British attacks at the Somme.[38] Although the system was tweaked and developed until the end of World War I, the above model was essentially the same, although on a much smaller scale in Spain than occurred especially in the later phases of World War I, most notably the battles of 1918.

These observations of Nationalist (read: German) battlefield air attacks date from a very early point in the Spanish Civil War. The author was not terribly concerned about specific amounts of casualties caused by specific weapons. The author does, however, extend the description of the battlefield air attacks upon crushing ground troop morale when they are unable to defend themselves adequately from the ground in the absence of antiaircraft defense, since infantry weapons did not yield optimal results in the defense role.[39] Further, the author suggested that air–ground cooperation is as effective in defense as it is in offense; in other words, the best defense against battlefield air attack is an integrated battlefield air defense.[40]

The Battle of Guadalajara in March 1937 (the month after the above article was printed) was indicative of how effective battlefield air attack was under the right conditions and when it was unrestrained. Briefly, the

Nationalist troops involved were Italian and not adequately protected by air cover or ground-based antiaircraft defenses, they were driving on Madrid and a relentless series of Republican air attacks savaged the Italians and kept Madrid from being surrounded. An author calling himself "H. B." described the battle and its effects and concluded that during the period up to and including 12 March, the battle was won by government [Republican] aviation.[41] On 12 March 1937, mostly Soviet aircraft immobilized the bulk of the Italian troops on the move. The Italians, lacking air cover or adequate ground-based air defenses, were savaged by a series of air attacks consisting of "over 500 bombs dropped and 200,000 rounds fired" by Republican aviation.[42] Thereafter, Republican troops conducted a ground attack capturing large quantities of Italian equipment and meeting little resistance.

H. B. concluded the discussion of the Battle of Guadalajara with an interesting observation: "The air-cavalry is a redoubtable weapon. By the end of 1918 one observed the disarray of the German troops in retreat when the Allied pursuit monoplanes, especially on the Northern Front, harassed them without respite . . . specialized ground attack units tend to make this new instrument of battle eventually an instrument of pursuit."[43]

What is clear is that the author was not writing about some new sort of battlefield alchemy. He described the situation in Spain as basically resembling the situation of airpower during World War I. He expanded upon the possibility of battlefield air attack becoming even more decisive and influential by becoming a weapon of persistent pursuit whereby it was not only effective in breaking an enemy, but pursuing the defeated enemy as "air cavalry" replacing the destructive horse cavalry pursuits with airpower, much the same as he noted it clearly did during World War I. There was nothing essentially new about anything going on in Spain, nor was there anything to come later during World War II, which was fundamentally different. The Luftwaffe was not doing anything new in Spain, it was picking up where World War I left off and enhancing them with better technology.[44]

Although researchers generally point to the defeat of Poland as the tipping point in France, the wakeup call that came too late, there is strong evidence that some of this information coming primarily from Spain had an effect well before the world became transfixed on the screaming Stuka sirens of September 1939. By 1937 to 1938, there is evidence that France began to take the threat of battlefield air attack seriously.

In his book *L'Armée de l'Air*, first published in early 1939, Pierre Cot mentions the need to increase attention to antiaircraft defenses.[45] Cot specifically mentions both Spain and China as providing valuable lessons about the state and the execution of modern war, especially as it relates to the role of airpower in combat.[46] Following the fall of France, Cot revisited his earlier warnings in *Triumph of Treason*, where he specifically mentions (in addition to the above) his prewar request for a purpose-built ground attack aircraft.[47]

Beyond this, in *Triumph of Treason* Cot launched into his adversaries for their shortsighted assessments of the Spanish Civil War:

> Even the Spanish war brought no change in ideas; the General Staff refused to be dragged out of its torpor ... the French military authorities tried to find confirmation of their theses in the Spanish war, which they interpreted as a defeat for the massed action of armored divisions [which of course did not happen], as a defeat for the intervention of air power in land battle, and as proof of the inefficacy of anti-aircraft artillery.... General Duval in *The Lessons of the Spanish War* (1938) and General Chauvineau, in *Is an Invasion Still Possible* expressed exactly that interpretation.[48]

Cot wrote *Triumph of Treason* as a direct rebuke to his critics, and the Riom Trial. While he certainly glazes over some areas, he did hit his mark almost perfectly regarding the conservative assessments of the Spanish Civil War inside the French military establishment. Those who backed a continuation of the army's established doctrine, including both Gamelin and Weygand, were also a part of the conservative right in French politics, and opponents of Cot and his allies in the Popular Front with its leftist agenda. Weygand was once accused by Clemenceau as being "knee deep in priests."[49] This staunch Catholicism was a trademark of the French Right, and the army in particular.

France had very similar internal political divisions. Spain and France had closely related and communicative Popular Fronts, and similar conservative movements. Thus, France was hesitant to become involved with the Spanish Civil War throughout a series of political administrations with widely varying alignments, but similar concerns. While this does not overtly suggest that politics bound the French Right to double down on the conservative army's strategy, it does so obliquely considering that the FAF was openly more leftist under Cot. Of course Cot did not hold back in implying that many army officers were outright fascists.[50] Further, Cot suggested that this fascism directly influenced France's "neutrality" in the Spanish Civil War, an act he judged a grave error that enticed Hitler to become more aggressive.[51]

What the internal French discussion reveals is that even doctrine was politicized through the lens of the Spanish Civil War. Only when it was far too late, after the air force was firmly under army command, and after Poland had been decisively overrun, did army leadership try at the last minute to reform, an act the evidence suggests it could not do as it would have aligned too closely with the ideas of arch political enemies.

Similar Interpretations

Reports from other observers in other countries largely reflected those being transmitted to France. For instance, an article written by P. Mikhailow for *Krasnaya Zvezda* in Moscow made a number of points very similar to those above.[52] Mikhailow stresses that good communications are vital to the effective employment of fighter aircraft in defense.[53] He also mentions that a combination of ground-based antiaircraft fire and fighters are a vital combination for aerial defense.[54] In a very similar vein to several French sources, he states that fighters are absolutely vital to defend bombers that cannot effectively defend themselves.[55] Portending British and later American bomber losses, Mikhailow also mentions that night bombing, although difficult, greatly curtails bomber losses.[56] Perhaps most importantly in predicting the events of the French Campaign in 1940, Mikhailow argues that aircraft are very effective in attacking ground targets, especially those targets that are unprepared to deal with aerial threats.[57]

A slightly later article in *Krasnaya Zvezda*, by G. Gagarin reinforces Mikhailow and much of what was being disseminated in France.[58] Gagarin argues for the concentration of defensive aircraft.[59] Very predictively for France he mentions that aircraft responding to raids are almost always too late to prevent the bombers from reaching their targets, and he reinforces thus the need for ground-based antiaircraft defenses to cooperate.[60] Finally, in harmony with many observations being printed in France, and again foreshadowing events that occurred in 1940, especially at Sedan, Gagarin warned, "The effect produced on the morale of the enemy by bombardment operations is very great."[61]

Thus, it can be demonstrated that the information arriving and being printed and subsequently disseminated in France regarding the Spanish Civil War was not unique or different. These observations were sound and were in fact reflected by other experienced airmen and officers who were often witnesses to the same or similar events and arrived at similar conclusions. There was no attempt to push an agenda outside of what the data and analysis were demonstrating.

These were not amateur conclusions derived from inexperienced ad hoc amateur officers, but from professionals from many countries, whose eyewitness and professional analyses brought them to eerily identical conclusions.

Conclusions Regarding France

France had solid information about airpower, its use, and its efficacy during the Spanish Civil War. While France played nothing but an extremely minor direct and indirect role in the war, it had observers on the ground during the war and observing its effects. The literature in France clearly indicates that the French went to foreign sources as well to get different perspectives on the air war in Spain, its developments, technology, and its effects. The FAF, and indeed the French establishment, cannot be said to have operated in a bubble or a vacuum. It cannot be sustainably argued that France was not exposed to some of the portents offered by the Spanish Civil War.

Why did the French not pay more heed to the lessons being provided by Spain? Martin Alexander argued that the dominant argument was that offered by works such as Duval's *Les leçons de la guerre d'Espagne*, that suggested that there was not enough airpower deployed in Spain to create meaningful enough data on which to predicate the actual effects of strategic airpower in a future war between major combatants.[62] This was not an alien argument elsewhere. However, as the evidence from Cot suggests, there was a political motive to these findings.[63] Whether Cot considered that this sword cut both ways is questionable; his unceasing vitriol for fascism was in vogue due to the conflict with Germany and support for Soviet Russia was popular in 1944.

The sense that the Spanish Civil War was somehow amateurish, or a sideshow was not unique to France. The same data (especially regarding strategic bombing) was in some form reaching other air forces around the world and it was having the same non-effect. For instance, years after the war, John Slessor wrote off the misread of the Spanish Civil War in Britain as a product of the environment and the times.[64] Objectively, the strategic airpower theorists put so much on the line, including vast sums of money in research and development into an argument that sounded excellent on paper, they did not want to be diverted from their cause by inconvenient data they could play off as "minor" due to its circumstances. However, the information on the Spanish Civil War did not focus solely on strategic bombing.

The war France thought it would get with Germany, one of some duration, consuming vast quantities of matériel and men and mimicking in no small part World War I, never occurred. What did occur is that the Wehrmacht attacked and scattered a French defense force in no small part because of its use of tactical and operational airpower against an unprepared French army and air force.

If one could argue to an extent that the airpower applied against civil targets in Spain was not enough ordnance applied professionally enough, and in enough volume to approach the theoretical possibilities envisioned, what should not have been ignored were lessons such as those provided by Guadalajara. After all, the devastating aerial attacks that saved Madrid for the Republicans were executed mostly by professional aviators from the Soviet Union upon professional soldiers from Italy.

Additionally, much of the other data was purely technical and did not require theoretical application to be valid. Everything from the dominance of the fighter over the unescorted bomber to the need for armor for pilots in modern aircraft did not require mass application to prove its point.

Thus, the French could not retrospectively state that the information they had in hand from the Spanish Civil War was flawed and it led them to make poor decisions in preparing for an eventual war with Germany, but these decisions were later reversed in a flurry of activity after Poland fell. The primary literature at the time, although reflecting different points of view, provided access to data from professionals in major military establishments. Although there were large numbers of amateurs involved in the fighting in Spain, professionals made the assessments, and many times the actions taken into consideration directly involved professional elements of both sides in conflict with each other, *especially when it came to the application of airpower.*

What can be firmly concluded about French information available concerning airpower in the Spanish Civil War is that it was accurate. The information did not cause France to fail during World War II because the reality of the only modern war in Europe was fundamentally different from that encountered in May and June 1940 or still in 1945, or arguably even today. After Iraq's air defense network was dismantled in 1991, the inability of Iraqi ground forces to meaningfully defend themselves against Coalition airpower did a great deal to contribute to the sundering of morale and the collapse of resistance.

It must also be remembered that Britain and the United States had the luxury of continuing World War II from some degree of safety, especially in the case of the United States. U.S. Army operations planning was based on the French model and only completely revised to appear more like German methodology after France fell in 1940. If the French were confident that they were correct and that the information they received did not apply to them for whatever reason, they were ultimately in good company.

Thus, the Spanish Civil War provided a formidable amount of information to be digested in France. Regular reports and articles in open sources were clearly available to everybody from the man on the street to officers and officials who had the ability to implement and impact French policy. The internal French arguments also impacted the analysis of the information.

The Luftwaffe and the Spanish Civil War: Laboratory

Unlike France, Germany actively participated in the Spanish Civil War. When the Spanish Civil War began, General Franco—and what became the core of this Nationalist army—was stationed in Morocco. The Nationalists thus had a dilemma; there was no practical way they could reach Spain quickly with the mass of their forces. They had access to some transport aircraft and some ships, but not enough of either to get the job done quickly.[65]

Adolf Hitler intervened almost immediately. In a very short time, the Luftwaffe whose existence was officially acknowledged barely a year before, was dispatched to shuttle Nationalist forces rapidly from Morocco to Spain, giving Franco and his right-wing forces an opportunity to mass and march against their Republican adversaries. This simultaneously afforded the Luftwaffe its first of many meaningful aerial laboratories during the Spanish Civil War.[66]

Following World War II, Germany's efforts in Spain were turned into something they were not: a training ground for blitzkrieg. This transformation was directly linked to the mass of memoirs and analyses generated by both former Wehrmacht officers and their erstwhile admirers trying to both understand the course of World War II, and to no small extent sanitize the German experience therein.[67] This was a fundamental part of the reordering the world was undergoing in a bipolar world where Germany was divided into free and communist poles. NATO quickly rehabilitated the German armed forces. Bundesheer and Luftwaffe leadership for the newly formed Bundeswehr came directly from former Wehrmacht officers and former Waffen SS members whose records were (at least apparently) clean enough to be palatable less than ten years following World War II's end.

The Spanish Civil War was not fought as *Bewegungskrieg* (maneuver warfare). German volunteers in the Condor Legion were controlled by Nationalist leadership although they advised Franco and his officers; they planned for and controlled their forces during the conflict. In essence, the Condor Legion maintained tactical control, especially in the air.

German ground forces were, out of necessity, more directly influenced by Spanish tactical needs, and a simple examination reveals that the panzer soldiers were often committed piecemeal in the infantry support role. In fact, observers on the ground quickly pointed out that tank performance during the Spanish Civil War was unimpressive; there was no horde of tracked hussars rampaging through rear areas after a massive hole was blasted in enemy lines.[68]

The aerial battlefield was quite different. Government, civilian, and military fears of airpower were exacerbated (often erroneously). The Luftwaffe was at the core of that fear, and its actions during the Spanish Civil War were closely followed by a nervous Europe that feared airpower's potential even before it became a viable weapon.[69]

While not a dry run for blitzkrieg, the Spanish Civil War provided the Wehrmacht—and most especially the Luftwaffe—with a laboratory. The Luftwaffe generated considerable direct data and feedback in five critical areas: air transport, battlefield air attack (including air–ground coordination), aerial combat, strategic bombing, and aircraft design and improvement. Unlike the FAF that was relegated to an observational role, the Luftwaffe used its direct experience to formulate ideas that when further refined in action between September 1939 and May 1940 allowed it to dominate the airspace over France.

German Aircraft Design and Improvement

When asked about Germany's involvement in the Spanish Civil War, Hermann Göring was quoted as saying "Where else were we supposed to test our planes?" Prior to the Nazi ascension to power, the answer was Russia. However, that sort of technical and doctrinal cooperation was not possible with the Nazi's "racial enemies" regardless of how productive it was, and how productive it could have been. Aerial combat in Spain helped the Luftwaffe with doctrinal development; it helped reveal what had changed since 1918 and how those changes might affect the outcomes of a future war.

The Luftwaffe fielded a variety of aircraft in Spain from 1936 to 1938. Many of these aircraft became famous during World War II. The Ju 52 was the first to make an appearance and was largely responsible for transporting

Franco's army from Africa to Spain.[70] Once combat aircraft were committed to provide direct aid to the Nationalists, aircraft such as the Messerschmitt Bf 109, Heinkel He 111, and the He 51 appeared in Spanish airspace. Toward the end of the conflict, the Junkers Ju 87 Stuka made its initial appearance.

The Luftwaffe's experience in Spain not only allowed the world to see how far the German aircraft industry progressed in combat aircraft design in a short amount of time, but it also more importantly allowed the Luftwaffe to experiment and make important changes before major combat with its future adversaries in Europe. These changes were rapidly implemented, and by the time of the French Campaign, the Luftwaffe was flying planes that were individually and collective superior to those of their adversaries.

German Aircraft Testing and Development in Spain

The Bf 109 is one of the most iconic and recognizable aircraft of World War II. It served in continually improved variants from the Spanish Civil War until the end of the war. In 1936 it represented the pinnacle of fighter aircraft in production. The early models flown in Spain were faster, more maneuverable, and as well if not better armed than their adversaries. The Bf 109 was dominant in Spanish skies, but continually improved. By the end of the Spanish Civil War, the airframes were almost identical, but the internals could not have been more different: "In mid 1937, Messerschmitt initiate development of a version of the Bf 109 powered by the Daimler-Benz DB 601 A Engine. Compared to the horsepower of the Jumo 210G, the DB 601 A produced 1,100 horsepower . . . the E-3 was armed with two MG-17 machine guns above the engine and two 20 mm MG FF cannon in the wings."[71]

The Bf 109, which entered the conflict dominant, thus gained speed and firepower as a direct result of action in Spain as the war continued. Compare this with the French officer who worried that making the M.S.406 faster would unnecessarily increase tensions with Germany and lead to an arms race he apparently did not know he was already in. By 1940, the latest Bf 109s were far superior to virtually any fighter the French had, again largely due to the "Spanish laboratory."

Most of the improvements in the Bf 109s that saw service in France in 1940 and over Britain later that year were the result of experiences in Spain. While the 109 dominated all aerial comers, that did not result in German engineers, pilots, and technicians simply stating "Good enough" and calling it a day. The two primary improvements to the 109 included a better power plant offering more speed and better performance at all altitudes and increased armament. Both modifications required some stretching or modifications of the airframe or components to accommodate. The genius of the design and the designers was that this plane was able to be consistently modified to remain viable until almost the end of the war. The greater speed and firepower in the form of a 20-mm cannon with which most 109s went to war in France, were the direct results of aerial combat in Spain.

Bombers and ground attack aircraft were also tested and improved in Spain. While the Heinkel He 111 is often compared unfavorably with American and British bombers such as the B-17, B-24, and Lancaster, in 1936 the He 111 was a peak performer, much like the Bf 109. Although the He 111 was marginal as a strategic bomber after 1940 due to its range and bombload, it was an efficient and effective medium bomber throughout World War II; during the Spanish Civil War, it was dominant. The He 111 was effective in both strategic bombing missions and to some extent battlefield support. Although improvements continued with speed, payload, and accuracy, the Germans did not have as bad an experience with bomber losses in Spain as did the Republicans. As a result, defensive armament was not noticeably improved and the He 111 suffered accordingly later during World War II. While engineers were already at work in Germany and other places trying to improve bombing accuracy, especially at height, Spain again revealed that bombing was not as accurate as previously imagined it might be and the experiences therein pushed the development and adoption of systems such as *Knickebein* that increased bombing accuracy.

The Ju 87 Stuka is as evocative an icon of *Bewegungskrieg* as any other. In fact, it was the Stuka more so than the panzer that provoked images of terror among allied soldiers and civilians. It was an effective psychological weapon with its built-in siren. As a dive bomber in the attack, it seemed as if it were coming right for an individual soldier regardless of its target. Already slow and vulnerable by the Battle of Britain, it lost little of its psychological value, and it served throughout World War II as did many of its compatriots in Spain. Later variants were modified as specialized tank busters predating such aircraft as the American A-10 Warthog.

Although the Stuka is frequently associated with the Spanish Civil War, it was a late arrival.[72] It was also a top-secret aircraft. Although the Allies knew of it, they knew little about it until at least September 1939, and it was not a "showcase" aircraft in Spain. However, the limited time it saw service in Spain aided in improvements later put to good use in 1940.

Why it became so directly associated with the Spanish Civil War in the postwar environment is difficult to state. It saw very limited service in Spain, and the Condor Legion went to great lengths to keep it concealed when it was not operating. The Ju 87s in Spain were little different from those that operated in Poland in 1939 and France in 1940, which objectively served as far more of a testing ground than did Spain.

The Luftwaffe and Battlefield Air Attack in Spain

Operation Michael looked promising when it began in 1918. The Germans created significant breakthroughs and sowed panic in the Allied lines. Ultimately, the offensive fell short. The Allied offensive beginning in September 1918 did not fall short. When it began, no one knew the Allied offensive would be the war's last. While the German *Stoßtrupp* (storm troop) tactics were indeed impressive and effective in the spring, it was the final Allied offensive beginning with the Second Marne that set the scene for *Bewegungskrieg* in World War II.

The model was primitive. Radio communication was sketchy, there was no effective motorized artillery (often cited as one of the reasons the Operation Michael failed), tanks were employed, but mostly at walking speed only occasionally wreaking havoc in rear areas. After four years of experiment and expedient, however, Allied airpower played a critical role in direct battlefield support, interdiction, and on a much more limited basis, strategic bombing. The Allied battlefield air attacks were extremely effective, and these lessons were not lost on the Germans. Even though Versailles forbade Germany military airpower in the interwar period, the army under Hans von Seeckt did not sit idly by; experienced airmen and covert operation kept the Germans in the thought process even if they were limited in their ability to apply practical, physical lessons off the sand table.

Spain offered the Luftwaffe a good laboratory to make up for lost time, especially when it came to experimenting with battlefield air attack and coordinating operations between ground and air units. Between 1936 and 1938, the Condor Legion refined air–ground operational concepts in a combat environment against a comparably equipped enemy offering lessons no domestic training situation could simulate. This was arguably the most useful, practical, and profitable experience gained by the Condor Legion during its time in Spain.

The Luftwaffe's experiences with battlefield air attack generally mirrored the information available to the FAF. During combat in Spain, the Condor Legion reported multiple times that air attack against unprepared or undefended ground targets and ground troops resulted not only in higher casualties, but panic and loss of morale. Unfortunately for the Condor Legion, the Republicans, and most specifically their Italian allies, this proof did not always come at the expense of the Nationalists.

As the war progressed, the Condor Legion continually refined its air–ground cooperation and its battlefield air attack procedures. By the time the war ended, the Condor Legion developed procedures for battlefield air attack that became standardized for the Luftwaffe prior to World War II and was the foundation for *Bewegungskrieg*.[73] While the Condor Legion improvised greatly up until the end of German involvement, the paramount importance of near-time or real-time communication with Heer units was stressed and developed to a truly impressive degree for the period. As a result of the Condor Legion's experiences, the Luftwaffe deployed air liaison officers with designated divisions to provide closely coordinated air support down to the tactical level. These *Fliegerverbingundsoffiziere* (shortened to *Flivos*) became the Luftwaffe eyes and ears on the ground that operated directly with the ground units to coordinate air support throughout World

War II. Although not every division was staffed and equipped to cooperate intimately down to the tactical level, the Wehrmacht was able to cooperate closely at the operational level to the extent forces were available at almost all points until the closing weeks of the war at the corps (mostly), army, and army group level. While the Allies in part eventually developed similar procedures, it was this ability to utilize modern communications technology to coordinate air and ground operations that perhaps more than any other factor contributed to the rapid operational victories from 1939 to 1941.[74] This innovation saw its murky origins in 1918, but came to full fruition and became doctrine as a result of experiences in Spain.

The Luftwaffe learned another key lesson in Spain that it utilized before 1940: ground fire can cause immense losses to aircraft if properly directed.[75] This was understood and acted upon very quickly in Spain. Germany had a fully integrated air defense system by 1918 and ground-based antiaircraft defenses were a part of this if somewhat primitive. Technology advanced greatly in the interwar years, and the volume and effectiveness of ground-based antiaircraft ordnance had duly increased and the experiences in Spain contributed to the strengthening and broadening of already solid ideas in Germany that produced devastating results for Allied airpower in 1940.

Although the French noted the effectiveness of air defense, air training, and armament, the Germans took the lesson to heart. The experiences in Spain played a role in this. The structure of German air defenses—generally divided between heavy, medium, and light, even before the Spanish Civil War—was reinforced as viable. The experiences in Spain indicated that air defense working at every level, from the division or higher down to training foot soldiers on how to effectively engage enemy aircraft with an MG34, paid future dividends, especially in Poland and France. The experiences in Spain reinforced the idea of airfield and ground troop antiaircraft defenses understood as vital to success. Even later in the war, when the combined efforts of the Allies made effective air defense seriously challenging for Germany, the ability of German ground troops to defend themselves against enemy aircraft was notable. Unlike German troops, unprepared French troops withered under the aerial assault.

The Luftwaffe and Strategic Bombing in Spain

German experiences with strategic bombing during World War I were a mixed bag; zeppelins and bombers were terrifying, but the results were questionable. The promise was there and writers such as Douhet extended, at least in theory, the possibility of strategic bombing. Combined with an inherent fear of the potential, something that predated the reality of aerial bombardment, civilians, governments, and militaries genuinely dreaded the next generation of strategic bombings. Spain gave the Luftwaffe a chance to not only practice strategic bombing but assess the realities of its physical and moral destructiveness on a modern, Western population.

Interestingly, in the Condor Legion's case the outside assessments of strategic bombing (especially those of press and politicians) were dramatically different from the internal lessons. The Condor Legion conducted many bombing raids on population centers during the Spanish Civil War. Most of these raids had a military purpose, even if it was limited. Some of them were designed to disrupt Republican operations by interfering with communications, logistics, or transportation, and thereby can be classified as strategic interdiction even though from a purist standpoint, the effort and the intended effect never exceeded what most would reasonably view as the operational spectrum. During World War II the Luftwaffe excelled for a time at operational air warfare in general, and the Spanish experience helped hone that ability.

While the Luftwaffe's experiences in Spain helped craft its bombing doctrine, the various bombing raids on population centers, whatever the desired effect, broadly reinforced conclusions derived from the first decades of attempted strategic bombing. The real shock effects on civilian morale were short term and often led to adaptation, improvisation, and a spirit of defiance rather than the predicted eminent moral collapse.

Two raids in general illustrate the Luftwaffe's conclusions and provide interesting parallels to popular reactions in the media and populace abroad: Madrid and Guernica.

Strategic bombing in Spain received an inordinate amount of attention from the international press. This was most likely due to the interest in the topic prior to the war and the human-interest story it provided. During World War I, fighting had real, direct impact on the civilian population, but the potential, especially of the casualties theoretically possible through strategic bombing, kept the interest of politicians, airmen, and civilians, even though the results were universally extremely disappointing. The bombing of Madrid and especially Guernica received considerable coverage as a result.

However, the Luftwaffe was unimpressed with the results. In the case of Madrid, which seems to have been taken more seriously than Guernica, the assessment was the same as that of the French, and largely reflective of the results of strategic bombing during World War I: lots of bombs did little real damage to cities in relation to the effort expended, and although civilian morale might slump a little in the beginning, it quickly recovered. The bombing had no legitimate and visible long-term effects, and without a committed campaign, it certainly would not. The other issue was trying to consider how much of a campaign over how long a period of time would be required to begin to achieve the potential that proponents of strategic bombing argued was possible. [76]

Guernica was a total public relations disaster for Germany from the outside. From inside Nazi Germany, it hardly mattered. The raid itself is discussed elsewhere in this work, and in considerable detail in other sources. It was not meant to result in the conflagration that resulted, and frankly, it received relatively little attention ex post facto in German sources other than to reflect that the results were not that stellar. In fact, German reports indicated that bombing civilians in Spain sometimes had quite the opposite effect desired by Douhet in that it strengthened civilian resolve.[77]

In the end, strategic bombing in the Spanish Civil War reinforced the idea with the Luftwaffe, that although it might yield some long-term effects when wielded against civilians. However, these benefits were minimal when compared to the direct and observable effects of utilizing bombers against military targets, especially in the interdiction role and in degrading military bases and facilities. This reflects the results observed during World War I, where bombing raids on military infrastructure had an observable and immediate effect, whereas raids on civilian centers were costly and ineffective.

As a result of both the German experiences in World War I and the Spanish Civil War, the Luftwaffe did not neglect the bomber force, but it gave it a different fundamental mission than that of Britain and the United States later in the war. In fact, the bomber force received the best pilots in the Luftwaffe, and the excellent pilots who had their hearts set on flying fighters sometimes found it necessary to tweak their results to get bumped down to fighters. Germany simply saw observable objective evidence that suggested that bombers had a much greater effect when used directly against military targets than civilian targets, especially considering efforts versus outcomes.

No better example of this exists that the eventual Luftwaffe effort during the Battle of Britain. When the Germans pressed the Royal Air Force (RAF) by concentrating on RAF facilities and the industry directly related to aircraft production, the RAF was hard pressed to win. Once Hitler decided to switch the effort to bombing London and other almost pointless civilian targets, the RAF turned the tide and presented the Luftwaffe and Germany with its first defeat.

The Luftwaffe did not neglect strategic bombing as a result of the Spanish Civil War and previous experiences, it used the evidence to design a force and doctrine that yielded good results on the operational level to achieve overwhelming defeats of local forces in conjunction with Heer cooperation. Criticizing the Luftwaffe for failing to develop a long-range strategic bombing force comparable to that of the RAF or U.S. Army Air Forces (USAAF) in postwar literature often had more to do with trying to justify an extremely costly and sometimes questionable Allied strategic bombing effort, the best result of which, arguably, was not the damage it did to meaningful targets or civilian morale in Germany, but using the bomber force as a chum line to draw up the remnants of an increasingly overstretched and diminished Luftwaffe and administer what amounted to a coup de grâce in 1944.

However, from both the offensive and defensive side, the Luftwaffe came to understand (much as French sources reported) that the bomber was very vulnerable if left unescorted, and it drew lessons from aerial combat in Spain that it later put to good use.

The Luftwaffe and Aerial Combat in Spain

If the potential lessons of armored warfare were misleading in Spain, the conclusions regarding aerial combat most certainly were not; in fact, the broad conclusions regarding aerial combat in Spain were accurate. The Luftwaffe benefited from two years of air combat experience in fighter versus fighter duels and fighter versus bomber duels on more than a technical level. While the lessons led to serious improvements in design it also led to tactical improvements in aircraft employment that paid dividends especially early in World War II. Although Italy and the Soviet Union participated in the air war in Spain, each drew limited utility from its lessons. The Soviet Union purged too many of its best thinkers and labeled their thinking heresy, airpower in Italy under Mussolini was simply never able to benefit to the extent the Luftwaffe did. France, Britain, and the other allied powers did not actively participate in aerial operations, and sometimes ignored otherwise solid analysis.

During the Luftwaffe's involvement during the Spanish Civil War, it refined its aerial combat doctrine and methods, and emerged with some remarkably effective ideas such as deploying fighter aircraft in the "finger four" formation that is still in use today more than eighty years after it was introduced. Thus, the Luftwaffe emerged from Spain with not only better aircraft, and better ideas regarding how to improve them, but better ideas as to how to utilize them as well. Although many of these ideas were reflected in the reports and articles read in France, they were not acted upon as they were in Germany. The result being that although France and later Britain certainly produced or purchased good enough planes and put them in the hands of some extremely skilled and brave pilots, Germany acted upon its firsthand experience in the Spanish Civil War to give the Luftwaffe tactical advantages that yielded operational advantages that were difficult to overcome. This was especially true over the short duration of the French Campaign. While Germany's advantages in 1939 to 1941 were often devastating, the Allies were able to observe patterns of strikes and maneuvers and to survive long enough to overcome them and develop effective countermeasures. Unfortunately, France did not have time to make these adjustments. Both French and German doctrine reflect the advantages and deficiencies in greater detail as World War II emerged and evolved.

5

FRENCH DOCTRINE AND TRAINING, 1934 TO 1940

FRENCH AIR FORCE (FAF) DOCTRINE remains poorly understood, especially compared to air forces of the other major powers during World War II. Very few authors have written about FAF doctrine, and most of those have limited their efforts to a line or two while discussing the fall of France. Alistair Horne afforded a few pages to his discussion of the prewar FAF in the classic *To Lose a Battle*.[1] Authors such as Barry R. Posen, who have concerned themselves mostly with doctrinal issues, frequently give the FAF some attention, but with the admission, "The doctrine of the FAF in 1940 remains something of a mystery."[2] Only one author, Anthony Cain, has devoted an entire book to the topic in English, *The Forgotten Air Force*.[3] While Cain does an admirable job of explaining how the FAF genuinely strived to produce a workable strategic airpower doctrine, he did not evaluate its suitability in the overall French national strategic framework, or deep-seated French concerns regarding French civilian morale and the threat of strategic bombing, a complex sociopolitical problem that haunted France from World War I onward. Most newer works such as *Case Red: The Collapse of France* by Robert Forczyk tend to gloss over the fallibilities of French doctrine and training, preferring to reduce the defeat of the FAF to more of an issue of technological and numerical inferiority, but sometimes giving French pilots their due for bravery and effectiveness at long odds.[4]

All the approaches to studying FAF doctrine before World War II fall short pertaining to the government, national strategy, and unrealized possibilities. This misunderstanding is partially the result of traditional anglophone views of French military effectiveness and character in 1940, and an overall lack of research and interest in the topic.

FAF doctrine from 1934 to 1940 demonstrated continuity and evolution, which was consistent with overall FAF strategy.[5] Political ramblings, a lack of time, finances, and industrial difficulties in a critical period kept doctrine from becoming reality. The FAF created a workable framework on paper for strategic airpower, both offensive and defensive, but the problems kept that "paper vision" from becoming a physical reality.

Doctrine and training are vital to cohesion in a military organization. When combined, training and doctrine create the mindset for a military organization that should assure that members think and act similarly enough that their combined actions are fluid and effective. However, doctrine is a lockstep process, and training does not prepare every member for every conceivable outcome. Doctrine and training must be in step with reality. They must also be in step with a nation's national strategic outlook, and its capacities. If doctrine and training do not fuse well with everything from industrial output to the educational levels of troops, it can fail—often miserably.

Doctrine and training in the FAF were critical weaknesses that greatly contributed to its ultimate failure in 1940.[6] FAF doctrine and training failed on multiple levels and the problems range from the simple to the complex. Further, the problems were spread across every possible spectrum, and they left the FAF unable to cope effectively with the Wehrmacht in 1940.

The FAF's gradual evolution of doctrine toward a strategic airpower doctrine not unlike the concepts of the Royal air force (RAF) and the U.S. Army Air Corps (USAAC) was a failure. There were inherent problems with this approach to airpower doctrine. It was not in line with French national strategic outlook and policy. Although France had maintained a bomber force since 1914, it was always reluctant to use it even when there was little chance of effective German retaliation.[7] French leadership was afraid not only of potential physical damage, but morale damage as well; France was a deeply divided country since at least 1870 (arguably since 1789), and these divisions frequently threatened France with collapse or revolution. Additionally, the French industrial base was never in a position to design, develop, and supply modern bombers in the numbers needed to pursue strategic airpower on the scale required; although the French aircraft industry made some amazing strides in airframe production from 1939 to 1940, it was too little, too late.[8] Strategic airpower doctrine gradually pushed the FAF away from the army support role making it less operationally effective in what was arguably the most vital role it needed to play in 1940.

For France, strategic airpower doctrine only made sense in the case of a long war of attrition against Germany. While both France and Germany planned for the potential of a long war before 1940, this movement toward strategic airpower meant that operational-level airpower was neglected, and this contributed to the FAF's defeat.

As strategic airpower doctrine continued to develop, it pushed the air force further away from the army support role. Considering relations between the air force and the army were not superb anyway, this exacerbated the problems experienced in 1940. The FAF's attitude toward technology, especially radio technology, and that of the army, were quite different. This combination led not only to communications problems during 1940, but a virtually complete lack of understanding between the services that proved fatal for France. Pierre Cot pointed out this difference between German and French operational models in *Triumph of Treason*, a work published in 1944.[9]

French organizational doctrine and concepts for national strategic air defense began to evolve into a pattern that could have potentially proven effective against the Luftwaffe if not the Wehrmacht before 1940, but these concepts were almost inexplicably abandoned in 1938 when the air force was returned mostly to army control. Unfortunately, the army had no idea how to effectively employ the airpower at its disposal.

Finally, French pilot training, although undeniably effective considering the combat record of French fighter pilots in 1939 and 1940 was inexplicably and systematically neglected from 1933 to 1940, and when French industry finally began to produce greater numbers of aircraft for the air force, there were not enough pilots to man the aircraft.

Strategic Airpower: Out of Touch with Needs and Reality

One thing for which the French cannot be faulted before World War II is an inactive military press. During the 1930s much military theory was put into print worldwide. There were two fundamental reasons for this. First, the experiences from World War I were being digested and assessed to future use. Second, international tension that seemed to indicate the probability of a war in the not-so-distant future produced a large mass of interested leaders from civilians to politicians, and most predictably military professionals. In France, native works were published alongside translations of foreign works regarding every possible topic from airpower to armored warfare. These books were readily available through the traditionally large number of booksellers with which France has been and continues to be graced. Strategic airpower was a quite popular topic. Books such as *La doctrine de guerre du Général Douhet* were published as early as 1935.[10] Many of the French works were also translated into German, such as *Das Bombenflugwesen* (originally *L'aviation du bombardement*) by Camille Rougeron, published simultaneously in French and German in 1938.[11]

The professionals in the FAF read them much like the professionals in other air forces at the time; even the Soviets had lively prewar debates over the best utilization of airpower.[12] Airpower was a new branch of service. The 1930s witnessed a large output in airpower literature not as much concerning its history (which at the time was brief) but with its future possibilities; this was digested much more by the public and politicians than it seems to be today. Perhaps because of the seemingly ever-present underlying threat of war that permeated the 1930s, and the fascination with the possibilities of airpower that imagination delivered leaving many people stuck somewhere between terror and wonder.

Regardless of the effect this literature had or did not have on the public and politicians, most of it argued toward one point: airpower has an independent strategic role to play in strategy and war. The RAF and the USAAC to an extent built themselves and maintained their independence (the USAAC's was virtual if not in reality quite physical) on this point. However, these were also carryovers from World War I. The RAF and the USAAC continued to build on strategic airpower concepts that both began to embrace (the RAF more fully) in combat during World War I. Strategic airpower also made sense for both Britain and the United States as it gave both the ability to project power well beyond their watery isolation, and it seemed prudent for both to defend against as the only realistic and likely source of aggression against their respective homelands.

In Germany, the Luftwaffe also carried over its missions and concepts from its predecessor, the Luftstreitkräfte from World War I.[13] The Luftwaffe was formatted as a multi-role air force. Whereas the RAF and USAAC almost ignored battlefield airpower and close air support prior to World War II in favor of strategic attack and air defense, the Luftwaffe tried to play all positions equally well. This gave the Luftwaffe an advantage in the early years of the war before the full weight of Allied manpower and industrial power could come into play.

Not surprisingly, France also carried over its World War I airpower policies into the 1930s. On a national strategic level, there was little differentiation from World War I policies; French high command and the government in general did nothing to prevent the air force from developing bombers of strategic airpower theory, but there is no indication that either the government or the military had any inclination to allow the air force to use its bombers in an aggressive manner against Germany. Throughout the entirety of World War I the French demonstrated extreme reluctance to bomb German targets that were not in the front lines or the immediate support area behind the German lines.[14] French command made it abundantly clear that bombing German cities was only permissible as retaliation for bombing French cities: "Since German planes had bombed some French open cities, the Commanding General approached the war minister a second time . . . a new decision once more authorized attacks on

factories, stations, and military establishments in open German cities. ...
These bombardments were not to be carried out except as reprisals. Furthermore, let us note the care that French High Command took, by the very wording of the decision."[15]

Even late in 1918, during the Allied offensives when the German military was in full retreat, the government and the high command not only restrained French strategic airpower, but they were concerned about Allied bombing as well. Valid reasons existed for this concern. First, during both World War I and World War II there were more important French targets within range of German airfields than there were German targets within reach of French airfields. This was exceptionally frustrating to the British, who again, before World War II tried to overcome French objections to these concerns with little to no progress; the French were still insisting on tit for tat bombing exchanges with nothing that could even be remotely construed as an attack on the German population.[16]

Philippe Pétain suggested guidelines in 1918 regarding all strategic bombing, the last of which was to make it clear that any Allied bombing operations should be reprisals.[17] Pétain did not consider German morale to be vulnerable to "morale bombing" at the time.[18] Pétain was also fully cognizant of the real and potential problems of French morale, having personally dealt with the mutinies of 1917.[19]

However, the FAF looked at the potential of strategic bombing during World War I, reflectively and with purpose toward their new doctrine. One report suggested that France recognized the importance of strategic bombing from the very beginning of World War I (the report specifically suggests November 1914), and that although neither Allied or German strategic bombing in the war was particularly effective, the potential was indeed there.[20] The report contends that raids deeper than those typical of World War I could yield results.[21] Obviously bombing could cut both ways.

The bulk of French industry and important natural resources such as coal and iron were in the northeast; areas occupied by Germany during World War I. Moreover, the area around Paris contained not only the bulk of France's manufacturing, but a significant portion of its population as well. Interestingly, Pierre Cot made a rather strong argument for the relocation of French industries based upon their strategic vulnerability during the nationalization argument, which was valid, but virtually ignored this relative success when vindicating his polices in the immediate wake of defeat.[22] However, so many vital defense targets spread throughout France's most populous area meant that German bombing, especially over the long term, was likely to inflict serious casualties on the civilian population.

Concerns about political and social divisions, some of which stem from the Revolution, but most of which were focused on the events of 1870 and later (such as the Paris Commune and the Dreyfus Affair) left France in a state of division so severe, the possibility of civil war seemed likely to many at almost any given point. Indeed, Gamelin was so concerned about the communist elements inherent to the army and the military as a whole as part of the levée en masse that he articulated the fear that he may actually defeat the Germans in the field only to find a million communists under arms who would then overthrow the country. Many French officers felt that the Soviet Union through the Parti communiste français would step up its attempts to destabilize France if the country in any way proposed a strategic relationship.[23] It was this justified fear, the fear of the stark divisions inside France itself, that made the prospect of strategic bombing so frightful to French leadership. This fear even led French leadership to disbanding promising units, namely airborne infantry, for fear of their communist sympathy and what they might do if the communist influence was real.[24] It was not that France had an inherent objection to using bombers otherwise.

The Rif War in North Africa is proof that France did not spurn the possibilities of strategic bombing when it did not fear similar reprisals. The Rif War is little known in North America, but it represented a serious challenge to Spain, and later France when it stepped in to help Spain not simply eliminate the Rif (a coalition of tribal groups in North Africa), but to maintain a toehold in Africa after a series of embarrassing defeats that saw the Spanish almost driven off the continent.[25] The struggle was severe, and little restraint was shown against the tribes. The Spanish government even went so far as to hire German engineers to set up clandestine chemical weapons factories to help defeat the Rif.[26]

France used airpower freely against the Rif, and did not hesitate to bomb villages, Rif military concentrations, or any other target that seemed viable. The results were mixed. In the beginning, the bombing seemed to have a significant effect on Rif morale, but as has shown to be the case in virtually every case of strategic bombing against civil populations, the Rif population eventually adjusted to the attacks, and even adapted by digging slit trenches outside their homes in which to shelter. Interestingly, the French also experimented with a sort of air mobility and resupply during the war (as did the RAF in Iraq during the same period) and perhaps more interestingly, they experimented with air casualty evacuation.[27]

French aviators conducted objective research regarding strategic bombing from both a historical and modern perspective. Colonel Hebrard clearly illustrated that at least some members of the air force were well aware of the challenges of modern bombing.[28] For instance, he pointed out that the fundamental problem facing bombing remains inaccuracy.[29] After an overview of bombing during World War I, the author goes on to explain that inaccuracy remains one of the great risks, even though technology had improved, and that fighters and antiaircraft defenses are tangible threats to the modern bomber.[30] In fact, Hebrard later points out that better technology has increased the threat posed by antiaircraft guns, and that these improvements represent a fundamental and serious threat to any bombing campaign.[31] Perhaps most importantly, Hebrard's research illustrates that the FAF was not operating in a bubble; they were very well aware of developments elsewhere. Hebrard filtered much of his research through the lens of experiments and concepts in the United States, the Soviet Union, and Italy.[32] He also mentions that many proponents of strategic airpower are convinced that even relatively small-scale bombing can result in morale effects on the ground.[33]

Others expressed similar frustrations ex post facto. Colonel Pierre Paquier, a French bomber officer, detailed a litany of causes for the failure of French bombing efforts during the campaign, but focused on bad communication, poor understanding of the possibilities of bombing, and bad handling by army command.[34] It is interesting to note, however, that although prewar proponents of French strategic bombing stressed the same general targeting packages as expressed elsewhere, by late 1939 and 1940 the new change of command altered the literature presented to the public stressing that bombing raids against German cities were possibilities only as reprisals.[35]

Thus, it is exceedingly difficult to condemn the French for lack of imagination, research, or foresight; indeed, it was probably overactive imagination, and a very real concern for what could happen under the right circumstances that pushed French leadership to fear the possibilities. Instead of denying the possibilities of strategic bombing when it came to its effects on civil populations, French leadership endorsed it by showing so much fear of it. Even if they did see some possibility in doing so, their overall fear of its effects on fragile French morale indicates that they thought France much more vulnerable.

France was thus opposed to bombing Germany on an official level. No better evidence reinforces this fact than French leadership's outright refusal to bomb not only German infrastructure targets from September 1939 to June 1940, but also vulnerable German troop concentrations—this was in spite of clear indications that there was a massive buildup of German troops in the Ardennes early on in the 1940 offensive.[36] The fear of potential German reprisals was so great that France missed an opportunity to severely disrupt German operational timetables that might have proved decisive in giving France enough time to react and create an effective defense. While this is admittedly a counterfactual argument, it must be seriously considered in light of the overall hesitation exhibited by the Oberkommando der Wehrmacht later in the French Campaign after French defenses had effectively become degraded and were crumbling.

The air force was finally allowed to try bombing German targets in the interior only after the campaign was effectively slipping away from France, and the results were laughable.[37] Sadly, it is clear France had good intelligence on such vital targets as German airfields and aircraft-related industrial targets.[38] These documents, and other valuable intelligence were used in map exercises as late as 1939 to evaluate a potential air war.[39] French leadership thus let what could have been a potentially decisive opportunity slip away because of fear of what *might* happen. In fact, this fear does much to explain French strategic outlook overall from 1928 forward and the "Maginot mentality" in particular. The shift to an emphasis on defensive firepower in 1928 and the doctrinal overhaul instituted as a result were designed in theory to inflict crippling casualties on an invading German army, while preserving French manpower, and presumably France's dubious morale.

Verdun more than any other battle penetrated and enveloped French thinking regarding World War I. Germany's intent from the beginning was to force France to expend more men than it could afford in Verdun's defense while minimizing German losses. French strategic doctrine, centered on the Maginot Line after 1928 was in effect a reversal of this concept meant to put Germany in the situation it was trying to create for France at Verdun. While Verdun might well have been the graveyard of both armies, German doctrinal thinking after the war looked more toward the battles of 1918 and the restoration of mobility, as did that of the British, who experimented with armor and mobility operations in the 1920s and 1930s but failed to continue in development. France in effect became gun-shy because of its World War I experience to the point of undermining its own strategic security, although it did so unwittingly: "[French planners] saw no reason to abandon or modify [their strategic aims] without careful thought, thorough analysis, and challenging tests. None of them foresaw the disastrous defeat of 1940 that would inflict fewer casualties but greater damage to the ideals, institutions, and international stature of France than the Great War."[40]

Again, it is important to recall that the rapid defeat in 1940 was as much if not more of a shock to the Wehrmacht, which was exceedingly nervous about the campaign to begin with. While France can be condemned retrospectively for being shortsighted, it is not necessarily fair considering its peers and near-peers were convinced that France's doctrine and military establishment were sound. Indeed, so much so that the Germans were nervous, and the rest of the world expected a prolonged fight, likely ending in a French–Allied victory. This sentiment was clearly expressed in the Wehrmacht's war diary.[41] However, there were progressive French thinkers who did embrace concepts that developed into what is now commonly referred to as blitzkrieg, no matter how inaccurate the moniker. Shortly after the defeat, their voices became even louder as expressed by

Paul Reynaud in 1942: "Does anyone believe that Frenchmen will always be ignorant of the fact that our high military authorities declared that a continuous front running from the North Sea to Switzerland is impregnable ... that General de Gaulle has declared on the contrary that an armored corps ... would be capable of breaking that continuous front at a selected point ... and that on March 31, 1935 ... I laid before the Chamber counterproposals for creating such a corps?"[42]

Regardless, the doctrinal path the FAF drifted toward in the 1930s was increasingly out of touch with the realities of prescribed and accepted French national strategic thought, planning, and French industrial capacity. While the army, command, and political leadership never averred from its reluctance to conduct strategic bombing operations against Germany, from 1933 onward the FAF progressively shifted its emphasis from more of an army support role to more of an independent strategic role somewhat similar to that of the RAF or U.S. Army Air Corps. This is demonstrated by following the official manuals delineating air force operations/role priorities from 1933 right up until the outbreak of war in 1939. The evidence clearly shows that the air force, at least internally, envisioned its primary role as strategically independent, which was not in line with collective thought.

If one examines the evolution of FAF doctrine from 1934 to 1940, it becomes obvious that the FAF continually kept its role in the overall French strategic structure in mind. Beginning with the 4 October 1933 *Instructions provisoire sur l'aviation légère de defense au combat*, an outline of FAF intent of operations is apparent: "The role of light defense aviation is to cover national territory in conjunction with land forces and naval air forces against the enemy air reconnaissance and attack."[43]

Before World War II and throughout the war, this statement clearly defines the role of fighter aviation (light aviation did include some light bombers at the time, which would be redefined later as fighter bombers by the remaining combatants during World War II), not only for France, but for most air forces throughout the world. Fighter aviation was the national shield against enemy air attack whether it be from fighters or bombers. This demonstrates that the FAF clearly understood its role in national defense, particularly in the defense of national air space.

Continuing, the document defines light aviation as having two roles: normal (or regular) missions and *exceptionnelle* (special) missions.[44] Regular missions included the following:

> Defense of land objectives
> Defense of aerial objectives
> General attack
> Independent attack [strategic bombing]

Defense of land objectives is self-explanatory. Defense of aerial objectives equates to defense of airspace. General attack is best defined in English as close air support to defend land objectives. Independent attack is best defined as attack missions of opportunity and by plan determined independently by the air force.[45]

There is absolutely nothing in this list of operating principles which suggests that the FAF had a cognitively differentiated understanding of the role of light aviation in the prewar environment. In fact, it would be easy to mistake a more nuanced translation of these principles as Luftwaffe, RAF, or USAAF light aviation doctrine in 1941 or later if viewed in a vacuum with the reader being unaware of the source.

The principles of employment were defined as follows:[46]

> Concentration
> Surprise
> Economy of force

These require little explanation. This is not incoherent doctrine. In fact, it is difficult to imagine anybody in the prewar environment (or even in the modern world) disagreeing with these concepts. This then begs the question, did this clarity of understanding change as the 1930s progressed and did FAF doctrine remain idle?

A mere eighteen days after the above document was issued, *Circulaire confidentielle pour les cadres de l'Armée de l'Air* was published. It indicates the FAF was immediately concerned upon its foundation with continual development of thinking and doctrine.[47] The general concept is defined as follows: "To judiciously employ the materials currently in service, conceive and prepare a new doctrine based upon modern materials and techniques to prepare for the future and the years to come."[48]

Again, the reader is left to ask if this sounds regressive or progressive. The answer is obvious. The document goes on to say, "Further, at the beginning of a war, their [the army and navy] role is no less important than the responsibility of the air force."[49]

This suggests that the air force was not only adhering to the principle of combined operations, but it was also fully cognizant of its own importance in an independent role. The document continues to demonstrate that not only was the FAF thinking clearly, but it was also in line with the formulas that ultimately created victory for the Allies during World War II: "In effect, we want to inflict upon the enemy from the beginning the bombardment of military centers, interdict troops and supplies, disrupt industrial production, and disorganize [demoralize] the civilian population."[50]

One might wonder: how was the overarching doctrinal concept failing as early as 1933? In simple truth, it was not. This is not to suggest, however, that all was perfect. There were some blind alleys in FAF doctrine in the early to mid-1930s.

France embraced the possibility of a multipurpose aircraft that could do every job the air force needed; in theory, a fighter-bomber with reconnaissance capabilities, or as the French termed it, the BCR (*bombardement, combat, reconnaissance*).[51] The concept was compelling from economic, technical, and military points of view. If one aircraft could do everything reasonably well, there would be little need to develop continuing series of purpose-built aircraft.

It is tempting to attribute this project to the influence of Giulio Douhet, and *Command of the Air*, but the BCR was considered before the time the work had any traction in France. In theory, the BCR idea was sound, and when viewed from a strictly theoretical point of view, it was reasonable, but the technology simply did not exist to create the sort of plane envisioned. Arguably, no aircraft until the American F-4 Phantom met the rough all-around requirements of this theoretical aircraft. France finally gave up on the BCR concept in 1935, however U.S. attaché reports indicate that apparently the French continued to manufacture the BCR well into 1936, and the language being used to describe them indicates that the aircraft and the program was still considered modern and viable.[52]

In 1935 FAF doctrine readdressed seemingly army-specific (but again best defined as strategic) needs by defining the role of airpower in reconnaissance duties.[53] This is sometimes tied in with the army's need for observation aircraft to plot artillery fires, and so forth. However, this is inaccurate. Aerial reconnaissance was and indeed remains a vital airpower role. Even after the advent of reconnaissance satellites, aerial reconnaissance via aircraft remains vital. It is difficult to argue that aerial reconnaissance was a diversion from useful and effective air force roles. This must then be considered a logical progression of FAF doctrine, and not a diversion from useful airpower roles.

Much criticism has been leveled against the FAF for not covering and coordinating with the army in 1940. Gamelin chastised the air force as early as 1942 for failing to support the army. This suggests that the FAF simply did not consider coordination with army prior to the war, which doctrine has already shown to be patently false. Further, FAF doctrine prior to World War II bluntly stated that air defense was a job that required coordination directly with the army, specifically with antiaircraft artillery.[54]

France had a well-integrated system of antiaircraft defenses during World War I, and by 1918, these defenses were quite dense.[55] The concept of mutual integration of air defense was nothing new. It developed during World War I, and every nation from France to Britain to Germany expected their airspace to be protected with a combination of both.

> Light defence aviation will initially ensure in conjunction with land based anti-aircraft defence the following missions in order of importance:
> Covering territory against enemy bombardment.
> Covering transport, logistics, and troop concentrations against enemy bombardment.
> Cover of aerodromes and eventually strike missions.
> Cover of aerial observation.

> It is particularly necessary to ensure at the outbreak of conflict that unity of action be as complete as possible.[56]

Regardless of the virtual total failure of coordination of the army and air force in 1940, the written evidence clearly indicates the intent (which is all doctrine is until put into action) was to coordinate air defense with ground-based units as demonstrated in this document.

Moving forward, in 1937, the FAF defined doctrine as "the basis of all decisions concerning national defense."[57] From 1918 to 1937 there is clear evidence indicating that the air force viewed its role in national defense as integrated, not independent, and aloof as could be suggested some strategic airpower proponents. It is, however, indeed true that the language and "order of operations" did undergo subtle changes if one pays close attention to the written FAF doctrine. Thus by 1937, one reads the following:

> The adaptation of war doctrine and military structure of different powers in new concepts is a universally observable phenomenon today . . . the decree that created the air force . . . defines these missions: The air force should be capable of:
> Aerial operations.
> Operations combined with the army and navy.
> Defense of national territory.[58]

Superficially, this seems identical to earlier doctrine. However, the order of missions subtly suggests a shift in air force thinking. In the above, the air force mentions independent aerial operations first, then combined operations, then defense of national territory, which is a departure from prior doctrine. This clearly indicates a gradual shift in the way the air force thought of itself and its role. Later in this same document, one reads, "The air force is a strategic air unit."[59] Again, this is a shift in language indicating the air force's changing view of itself in the French strategic paradigm. Further on in the document, the air force suggests that airpower should be concentrated under the command of an overall air commander and guided by air force officers.[60] What this document does not suggest, nor does any document available ever suggest, is that the FAF should view its role as completely independent from that of the army and the navy. The FAF never forgot its role as a "team player" in national defense, nor should it have. After all, Germany was always viewed as the primary threat to national sovereignty. France is and was primarily a continental power, and its primary threat (Germany) needed cross no oceans to reach France as it would have had to do to reach Great Britain or the United States.

Regarding the offensive, the air force, again, takes a modern (for the 1930s) view of airpower, not unlike the RAF and the USAAF before and even during World War II:

> On the offensive, the air army should operate in the following manner with its formations:
> Against enemy aviation in flight or at their bases.
> Against ground based enemy air defenses.
> Against political and economic objectives.
> Against enemy objectives in combination with the army and navy.[61]

Note again the reprioritizing of missions, not the omission of missions. For all intents and purposes, this is a logical order of operations from an air force point of view. The greatest threat to an air force is generally the enemy air force. As such, the first objective is to gain air superiority, as mentioned above. The best way to keep enemy air formations from being a threat to ground forces is to eliminate them in the first place. At no point does this revised doctrine, printed just short of two years before the outbreak of war, suggest that cooperation with land forces is not a vital mission of the air force. At no point did the FAF ever walk away from its support roles required by the army.

For contrast, examine the Luftwaffe Luftkriegsführung (aerial warfare doctrine) from 1935, divided into six major missions: "1) Combat action to achieve and maintain air superiority; 2) combat and other action in support of ground troops; 3) combat and other action in support of the navy; 4) action to interdict routes of enemy communication and supply; 5) strategic operations against sources of enemy power; and 6) attacks against targets in cities."[62]

French force doctrine was at least for a time like that of the Luftwaffe. The primary difference is that the Luftwaffe put greater emphasis on operational support than it did strategic bombing.[63]

The French army did not embrace close cooperation of air and ground forces as delineated by German combined arms doctrine. The prewar French armor proponents hardly described what would later be deemed blitzkrieg—an operational air force acting in conjunction with tanks and mechanized infantry and artillery connected by wireless communication on a highly mobile battlefield with the end goal of out-maneuvering as much or more so than physically overpowering and destroying the enemy. "On the whole, studying German doctrine reinforced French confidence in their own methods."[64] The French adherence to central control and methodical battle predicated upon closely coordinated and tightly controlled movements was almost completely removed from the German concept of *Auftragstaktik*, or generalized mission goals with planning and execution largely left up to subordinates.

However, there is ample evidence that the FAF contemplated the ground attack role and how it could be implemented. An anonymously authored document from 1938 titled "Intervention de l'aviation dans la bataille terrestre" (Aerial Intervention in the Land Battle) lays out some very cogent methods for the air force to intervene in the land battle.[65] Arguably, the most important single line of the document reads: "The synchronization of action between aerial and land forces needs to be as perfect as possible."[66]

This statement epitomizes the German methodology that led to France's defeat. The document goes on to explain exactly how aircraft can be employed to affect the land battle. Specifically, and tragically foreshadowing, the document emphasizes the extremely demoralizing effects that aerial attacks can have on ground troops specifically, "the extreme demoralizing effects of large bombs detonating."[67] Recall that many Luftwaffe aerial attacks in 1940 did little physical damage but were crushing to French morale.

Further, in describing action in Spain, the document details that ground troops without sufficient antiaircraft armament are particularly vulnerable.[68] The paper later mentions that fighters are the best defense against enemy aircraft.⁶⁹ Thus this document presented an argument that a unified approach to the land battle was required, and in addition to combined action, both the army and the air force needed to be prepared and properly armed against all threats. In short, the French military possessed documentation and analyses that basically described what would happen to the French army in May and June 1940.

Although the Stuka did not make a real impact on French psychology until after Poland, the Air Ministry and the FAF although late, were aware of the need of specialized aircraft for ground attack some time before the war began and they attempted (at least on paper) to get the project in motion: "The prototypes of these attacking planes had been studied by the technical services ... I [Pierre Cot] demanded ... the creation of such a force [in 1938–39]."⁷⁰

After Poland, panic began to set in. "The rapid collapse of Poland provided a sense of urgency to the creation of armored divisions that had not previously existed."⁷¹ Germany had been working with modernizing the concept of the armored division since 1933 and its experiences in the Spanish Civil War and during maneuvers led to the formula that quickly overran its opponents until the winter of 1941. The French army did not begin working with the concept of tank divisions per the World War II model until about January 1940, while France was already at war with Germany. Four months was not enough time to catch up to seven years of experimentation and experience.

In fact, the French Army expected the air force to fight its own air battle (and there is scant indication that the army ever tried to interfere with the air force in this matter) and provide support by attacking ground targets, but its main concern regarding the air force was that it would provide observation aircraft to spot artillery fires, and reconnaissance aircraft to provide information on the enemy. There was a major problem with this as well and it involved a particular inferiority, the radio. The army was simply unprepared to deal with coordinating the air battle over France in 1940; it was prepared to fight a 1914 style battle, as the French army in 1914 had been prepared to fight another 1870-style battle, especially when it came to technology.⁷²

The French army was arguably paralyzed in 1940 more by poor communications than any other factor. The simple reason was it was afraid of the radio. The perception was that the enemy would learn more from the army using the radio, than the army would gain from its use. Officers and men had to rely on runners or wired telephones and were only permitted to use the radio to transmit information after requesting permission usually from regimental officers or higher.[73] Without regular practice in the use of radio between units both ground to ground and ground to air and vice versa, there was little hope of making any air–ground cooperation meaningful on or over the battlefield. The fact the Gamelin did not have a radio in his headquarters at the Château de Vincennes outside of Paris, is indicative of how endemic this phobia was.

Did FAF Doctrine Make Sense?

Any fundamental criticism of FAF doctrine must first answer the question: did FAF doctrine make sense considering the overall French strategic outlook and doctrine overall, not just as it pertained to the air force? In short, the answer is yes, FAF doctrine did make sense as it pertains to overall national security posture and doctrine and the preponderance of evidence supports this conclusion.

Before 1928, overall French doctrine was offensive; the *offensive à outrance* (all-out offensive) had been a staple of French military thinking for more than a century. Until 1928 the French army carried the battle to the enemy from the very beginning with the goal of engaging in decisive actions to quickly overthrow the enemy. In 1928 France went in completely the opposite direction and switched to a defensive doctrine, but it maintained a significant offensive component as a symbiotic part of the overall plan. Thus, France was not relying on a solely defensive posture, and it did indeed have plans to carry the battle to the enemy after absorbing the initial shock of the enemy assault, presumably to the detriment of the same.

In theory, it was a beautiful plan. The exceptionally late problem of Belgium's switch to neutrality in 1936, and a hurried effort to cover the gap in the Maginot Line from the Belgian border to the sea did not fundamentally alter this plan. Nor did it change French operational concepts or national strategic thought processes and overall concept of operations.

The pattern of development of FAF doctrine makes sense under these circumstances because it embraced three key concepts that interlocked neatly with French national strategy. First, by 1938 FAF doctrine saw its air battle for the defense of French air space as the paramount mission, which is suggestive by the shift of the written priority list from 1933 to 1937.[74] This embraces the overall French defensive concept of using defensive firepower to wear down an enemy on the attack.

Second, FAF doctrine continued to embrace the established and vocalized needs of the army by providing ground attack missions, observation missions, and reconnaissance missions, all theoretically interfaced with the overall concept of methodical battle.[75] While this priority did shift, it never disappeared. The FAF never abandoned its cooperative missions with the army or for that matter with the navy.

Third, and this has been overlooked, the establishment of effective strategic bombing forces made sense in the French defensive paradigm even without considering the countries of the *Petite Entente*.[76] If everything worked as the French theorized it would (and before May 1940 most military people thought it would, including many Germans) then having a powerful bomber force available to strike targets inside Germany, whether they be military, industrial, governmental, or infrastructure made sense. If the Maginot Line had acted as a massively difficult barrier (much like an ocean or the English Channel) then development of a strategic bomber force in line with the British or American models and with a similar mindset made perfect sense. If the battle had held to the Maginot Line and the rough area of the Benelux, then it would have given France the ability to disrupt the German war effort by targeting deep interior assets. However, the story is more complicated than this.

Douhet and the FAF: A Driving Force in French Doctrine?

Douhet is mentioned in French military journals as early as 1934, the year the FAF physically began its independence from the army. The movement toward a strategically oriented air force also seems to suggest that Douhet had a direct influence on FAF doctrine, and perhaps overarching French political and military thinking on defense policy. Was this the case?

The answer is mixed. The evidence indicates that Douhet did not inspire French thought regarding air doctrine overall, rather he was an excellent outside spokesman who crafted a written work, which simply reinforced what many air force thinkers around the globe were already considering. The French, especially Pierre Cot, seem to have used his work to reinforce their pursuit of strategic air doctrine.[77] Three pieces of evidence indicate that much of what Douhet wrote in *Command of the Air* was under consideration in France well before Douhet could have had an effect through mass absorption by FAF personnel.

The French considered the possibility that weak morale could be broken through aerial bombardment quite early during World War I. The French were concerned that German bombing could sunder French unity. This trend continued up to 1940.

Well before aerial bombing was even practically possible, popular fiction (much like science fiction today) foresaw the terror potential of aerial bombing. Works such as H. G. Wells' *The War in the Air* in 1908 foretold death, fire, and destruction delivered by unstoppable aerial fleets upon virtually defenseless civilians with the newly invented airplane.[78] Progress made with dirigibles, and the persistent experimentation with what would become airplanes hinted at the breakthroughs just around the corner. In an era when nationalism was arguably beginning to peak, and social and political tensions seemed to be pushing Europe toward colossal conflict, this sort of fiction fueled fears of total war in ways unimaginable in previous conflicts.

By the Italo-Turkish War (1911–12), the fog cleared somewhat on the realities of the "next war."[79] People fully expected sooner rather than later that mass destruction would ensue from aerial attacks.

Nor was this generalized fear of aerial peril isolated to France. Considerable ink was spilled elsewhere concerning the imagined possibilities of aerial attack. In Britain for instance, Air Commodore L. E. O. Charlton wrote the following in *War from the Air: Past, Present, Future*: "This age will be the first to see a really revolutionary change in the art of war, in which the see-saw movements of attack and defence will eventually play no part. It will be more like a team competition in a shooting gallery. Neither of the opposing teams will interfere with one another, they will only be concerned with hitting their respective targets [from the air]."[80]

There was thus internationally a palpable fear of aerial bombardment, and French leadership was concerned about the potential effects of such on French morale well before *Command of the Air* was published. This concern continued in the 1930s, but it was a continuation of the original sentiment, not something seemingly forgotten and revivified merely because Douhet put it to paper. France was hoping at least in reference to the analogy above by Charlton, that two parties had to agree to compete at the shooting gallery.

France also had direct experience in attempting morale bombing, but admittedly against an adversary that could not return the favor, the Rif. During the Rif War the French used the bomber specifically to cripple enemy morale.[81] The results were marginal: the enemy combatants though "primitive" by European standards, quickly adapted: "All of the contemporary observers noted with awe the ability of the Rif populations to accept bombing attacks without a breakdown in morale."[82] The enemy in this case (the Rif) was reasonably unified and prepared to resist. In fact, the Rif were so effective they nearly drove the Spanish army out of Africa altogether. French intervention combined with use of firepower, airpower, brutal reprisals, creative thinking, and the Spanish use of chemical weapons specifically created with the aid of German scientists, finally brought the Rif War to an end.[83]

Regardless of how out of touch the independent bombing mission might have been with national policy, there was one scenario where it made sense. If France did get into a prolonged war with Germany, strategic airpower would have given France the ability to strike important targets beyond a static front. Again, this is counterfactual extrapolation, but there was no reason to assume Germany would not have conducted strategic bombing campaigns against France if Fall Gelb had bogged down into more of a World War I style set piece war. Indeed, it is likely France was spared strategic German strikes only because the Luftwaffe was too overbooked in the operational role trying to both dominate the air space over the battle area and provide flying artillery for the army. At no point during World War II did Germany ever demonstrate reluctance to strike civilian or infrastructure targets. French intelligence had excellent information on sensitive and vital locations that would have made excellent bombing targets.[84]

In this scenario, having a viable strategic air arm made perfectly good sense, but it still neglected what command and the army viewed as the air force's primary roles, reconnaissance, spotting, and direct support, which the above evidence shows moved further and further down the list of air force priorities as the 1930s moved along.[85] When battle came in May 1940, regardless of how gallantly the air force actually fought, the primary complaint against it in the immediate aftermath of the battle and indeed the war, was its so-called lack of support for the army. A reassessment of FAF performance is the primary focus of a later chapter, but this cannot be avoided in discussing doctrine. If the air force has any specific blame in creating ineffective doctrine considering French national requirements, doctrine, and needs, it certainly falls into this category.

Moving the bulk of the air force's efforts officially toward a strategic airpower mission meant that the air force had to de-emphasize its army support role. For the United States and Britain, this was not a potentially fatal decision; their likely enemies were beyond considerable bodies of water, and both had large and effective navies. However, France's primary security concern was its border with Germany. If the army did not survive in the field, there would be no France left to worry about much less German industrial targets. While the RAF and the U.S. Army Air Corps could afford to pull away from the army by asserting their independent strategic role, France in fact could not, neither could Germany or the Soviet Union, each of which had a strategic national security dilemma somewhat similar to France's in that both were really continental powers, not maritime powers. Both the Luftwaffe and the Raboche-krest'yanskaya Krasnaya armiya (RKKA, Red Army) were structured to have some strategic bombing capacity; in fact, the Luftwaffe seriously embraced, studied, and planned for it, but it did so alongside its operational airpower missions that it did coordinate as part of a cohesive whole of the Wehrmacht.[86]

Interestingly, Douhet had several proponents in Germany in the prewar period as well. Generals such as Milch and Wever seem to have been influenced by Douhet, and they certainly read him. However, Germany's conclusion was that overall the Luftwaffe needed to be flexible enough to conduct strategic bombing if it needed to, but that its primary role would be that of a partner in combined operations on a tactical/operational level.[87]

Further, in writing at least, it appears French command was correct about its theory of "Bomb not lest ye be bombed." While the evidence clearly demonstrates retrospectively that Nazi Germany had no qualms at all about bombing cities, towns, and villages in the 1930s, it was the Luftwaffe's policy that it would not initiate strategic bombing against enemy civil targets, out of the same fear that the favor would be returned.[88] The source of the fear was however different; Germany was afraid throughout the mid-1930s that the Luftwaffe would simply be overwhelmed by, of all opponents, the FAF. The newly minted Luftwaffe of 1935 was not the powerful and focused weapon of 1940. The critical years between 1937 and 1940 are where the FAF fell behind and the Luftwaffe lurched ahead.

The guilt in France cut both ways though. The army was by no means innocent although it tried to exculpate itself from June 1940, through Riom, which has to be taken as a smear on its honor to at least some extent, and into the postwar period. It is impossible to consider the defeat of the army or the air force in a vacuum—it was a mutual defeat caused by mutual failings, primary among which was a complete lack of understanding and communication.

Aloof and Apart: The Lack of Understanding

There was no effective combined operational/tactical doctrine between the air force and the army; in fact, there seems to have been little genuine attempt to understand each other on any level between 1933 and 1940. Three areas illustrate this failure. First, there was a great deal of talk about "integration" that clearly never took place; the air force and the army thought about their supposedly joint mission, but nothing ever came of the "thought" and this showed most clearly in May/June 1940.

But these were isolated observations, and what the Riom proceedings brought out was the two deadly mistakes of the command regarding the use of dive-bombing planes and the coordination of air and ground operations.[89]

There was a serious technological gap, enhanced by a communications security concern between the army and the air force regarding the use of the radio, and this fundamental rift caused extreme chaos in 1940. This was lightly described as "the imperfection of the liaison between land and air" by army officers desiring to preserve the honor of the army at Riom.[90]

Additionally, the army never seems to have had any idea what to do with a modern air force, or the reality of the effects of modern airpower upon untrained troops. Once the air force was returned to the army's operational control in 1938, the army proceeded status quo ante with their training cycles even though they had the air force effectively at their disposal and could have used it at their will as a valuable training tool.[91] While the army viewed the French squadron broken down from their prewar organization into penny packets as "co-operation aviation," it clearly had no idea how exactly to cooperate with it.[92]

However, the same criticism can be leveled specifically at the United States prior to 1940. The United States was heavily influenced by the French, and many regarded the French army as the finest in the world following World War I. It was only in the wake of the French defeat in 1940, that the U.S. Army finally gave the tank an independent role from infantry support and began meaningful work on combined operations.[93] France's failings were not hers alone. While criticism is certainly due, it is important to remember that the same mindset pervaded elsewhere.

Non-Integration

The air force seems to have seriously considered the importance of combined air defense well before hostilities in 1940. There are a series of documents in the SHAA that illustrate that some thought was put into how to best defend French air space in the event of war with Germany, the most likely and primary foe. The bulk of these documents concentrate on mutual (integrated between the army and air force) defense of the air space over Paris and covering northeastern France, the likely air and land invasion routes from Germany.

By 1918, France, especially in the area around Paris, had well-integrated air defense for the period. In addition to the forward deployed squadrons, the army had an impressive array of antiaircraft defenses deployed to deal with any potential German air threat.[94] The network was composed of listening posts, observations posts, central antiaircraft control centers, machine-gun posts, antiaircraft artillery posts, barrage balloon posts, and smoke screens.[95] These defenses were extremely thorough for the period.

Following World War I much of this system was dismantled, but the concept of integrating air defense did not fade, and from the 1920s-forward, extant documents suggest that France continued to think of air defense as an integrated duty, not solely the job of the air force. Writers such as Marcel Jauneaud commented as early as 1923 about the necessity of using a combination of fighters and ground-based air defenses to achieve the best results.[96] Colonel Hebrard commented on the efficacy of integrated antiaircraft defenses, especially regarding bombers, and the need to combine the efforts of both forces on offense and defense in the mid-1930s.[97] In theory, air defense even had its own organization dedicated to integrating combined air defense efforts, the DAT, or Défense Aérienne du Territoire.[98]

In theory, these integrated ground defenses were to overlap with air force areas of responsibility defined by the air force's new operational organization, which was designed along modern, coherent lines. The air force's organization, prior to its reversion to army control in 1938 stacked control and responsibility along hierarchical lines over well-defined geographic areas, with a clear command structure all of which was integrated by a modern radio communications system allowing for rapid response to any potential aerial or ground-based threat.[99] On paper, there was little to fault with this system. There were multiple flaws from a technological/doctrinal perspective that were never overcome and created massive problems for France in 1940. What the air force and the army drew up on paper, had little effect on reality.

There were major problems with this combined defense proposal before the air force surrendered its autonomy to an army that had little idea how to defend itself against aerial attacks, much less integrate an increasingly modern air force into its plans. First, France's antiaircraft guns were outdated and too few.[100] This problem was never resolved as war approached, although Gamelin tried to cover himself and the army by stating these problems had been examined.[101] Much like the rest of the French army, there was an unbelievable smattering of equipment, which constituted a logistical nightmare and made meaningful improvements in doctrine difficult. Just as the army brought Char B1 tanks, very modern designs for the most part, to bear against the Germans in 1940, it also brought FT-17 light tanks left over and unimproved from World War I into the fight as well, with predictable results. French army antiaircraft was improved only on a limited and tardy basis just before the war began: "Just as the French Army acted as if the equipment, training, and doctrine necessary for air-ground cooperation would materialize at need, it believed itself to already possess the constituents of an effective defence against German tactical aviation ... French leaders remained sanguine because they believed 'they could make a ... veritable forest of guns.' This confident assessment was not matched, however, by an effort to plant the required 'forest.'"[102]

This lack of modern antiaircraft weapons was exacerbated by an almost total lack air defense training in the army. Recall that one of the key takeaways from Spain was the effects of aerial attacks on untrained or poorly trained troops. Not only did the army apparently not pay attention to this, it proposed some ideas so incredibly ridiculous and curious that they defy all logic. One officer even suggested that planes were so loud, troops would have plenty of time to hear them and almost calmly take cover and hide, thus negating the effects of virtually any aerial attack.[103] This sounds utterly absurd, but ideas such as this made it into print. However, they were indicative of massive training shortfalls in the army as a whole. Even though some sort of training occurred in theory annually, French reservists were so poorly trained in 1940, many of them had no idea how to use core tools such as a hand grenade, and if fundamental training was neglected, it should come as no surprise that antiaircraft training was neglected.[104] France's investment in the Maginot Line was total; it was an all-in bet that technology and money poured into its construction would vindicate the neglect it forced upon the rest of the force due to its cost.

Thus, when war came in 1939, the army had little ability to defend itself in the field against aerial attacks (which proved fatal in 1940) much less aid the air force in a systematic air defense system designed to cover the most vulnerable parts of the country from Luftwaffe incursions. Finally, and perhaps most fatally, the army and the air force had a serious communication problem.

The army was somewhat technophobic. This applied especially in the case of the radio. To be objective, the army did have serious and legitimate concerns regarding communications security. Poor communications procedures led to many serious lapses during World War I. However, the French approach was fundamentally different from that of other militaries. Instead of trying to find more concrete ways to secure radio communications, the army shunned radios instead. This led to a dependency upon runners, field telephones, and the civil telephone network. It robbed the army of vital time in a fast-moving war that quickly grew beyond its means to manage. Crucially, as far as the air force was concerned it virtually severed rapid communications completely. Without the radio, effective strategic air defense was exceedingly difficult if not impossible.

There simply was no effective integration of the air force into the battle without the radio, and the army was fundamentally opposed to its use, demanding a series of time-wasting approvals, which normally only occurred after the critical moment had passed and initiative had been lost. The French army, which was supposed to coordinate and direct the efforts of the FAF from late 1938 forward, commanded the efforts of the air force with no effective means of communication. The slavish devotion to *bataille composée* (literally "compound battle") and the idea that modern battle could be choreographed like a play left no room and no consideration for integrating a modern air force into the equation. Foreign observers even noted what must have been viewed as very strange radio protocol within the army.[105] This is because although the army *had* radios, it apparently had very little concept how one might keep communications secure.[106] As explained to the author of the document in question, codes were apparently made up on the spot *if the army had to use the radio.*[107]

In view of the French Army's perceived fear of the radio, this is incredibly difficult to justify. From the outside it appeared that the army did not even try to create a useable, workable communications security policy other than what could be improvised on the fly if there was a *need* to use the radio. This was disastrous enough for the army in 1940 when it found that artillery and bombs quickly made a mess of any telephone lines strung between positions. Exactly how this theory was to reasonably be applied to communicating with the air force, which had to use radios is a complete mystery. Considering the most basic training shortcomings affecting the army in 1940, solving such a complex technical problem in an extremely short amount of time represented a titanic impossibility.

Thus, when Germany invaded in May 1940, the army and air force's lack of successful integration perhaps more than any other factor, led to France's rapid defeat on the battlefield. Ultimately, the majority of this guilt has to be laid at the army's feet. While a year may not have been enough time to completely retrain both forces for integration, little to nothing was done to attempt to do so as when war came the air force and the army effectively fought two separate battles rather than one combined battle. Differences regarding roles and employment of force that should have been settled clearly were not. The air force spent more time reacting to German raids after they hit their targets than beforehand, which undoubtedly took a severe toll on the Luftwaffe, as its own records reveal, but did little to keep the targets from being engaged.

Whither the Pilots?

When representatives of the French aeronautical industry met with Général Joseph Vuillemin in 1938, they were supremely proud to report that they could produce up to four hundred airplanes per month on the heels of their frantic and radical modernization and reorganization. Considering that the Allies were obsessed with production and potential production from at least 1935, and they were continually looking for ways to increase aircraft production, it seems logical that pilot training would have been an additional priority, but it was apparently overlooked by the air force. When war came, the air force was drastically short of key personnel, especially pilots, while it maintained bloated staffs that did nothing to ameliorate the crisis: "The HQs were overstaffed, the units had serious shortages—60 percent in NCOs and radio operators, 31 percent of air gunners... to meet the output of Plan V the Armée de l'Air between January 1940 and April 1941 would be short 1,800 pilots."[108]

Much like theoretical production was too little too late, so came the pilots, although there is clear evidence that the air force planned on training them. "On March 14, 1938, the Supreme Air Council recommended a new program calling for 1,600 additional officer pilots and a first-line STRENGTH OF *2,750 planes*. Fifteen billion Frances were said to be necessary to carry out this program."[109]

What is clear is that the pilots were not made available in the two years' time it took from this effort being approved, to the German invasion. Considering the above evidence, there were multiple critical personnel shortages in key areas that were simply never made good. The air force *talked* about training new pilots, like it *talked* about building a bomber fleet. The air force finally went into emergency mode, radically restructuring its thin and scattered air training facilities in 1939, but to no avail; when war came, it was still short of pilots.[110]

Additionally, from 1937 onward, the rest of the military attempted to expand at a time when manpower was the leanest *les années creuses* (the slow years), which were a product of low birth rates during World War I. The air force competed with the navy for technically proficient long service candidates capable of complex jobs such as flying, aircraft maintenance, and maritime engineering.

However, the air force did try to lure technically minded individuals for long-term service. It attempted to lure candidates in with interesting technical work and the lure of promotion, good pay, useful qualifications, and good benefits.[111]

The salient problem with the training structure for pilots and other key technicians seems to have been manning the training facilities in the first place. The fear of war and the seeming drudgery of the posting keep the training cadre small.¹¹² There was a generalized fear that a war might break out and experienced pilots would be stuck in training facilities.

Again, outside observers seemed acutely aware of French problems. The American attaché made specific note of the inadequacy of French training cycles.¹¹³ As Colonel Smith wrote, the FAF—especially the enlisted men—has a "short period of training."¹¹⁴ While Smith reserved more than limited criticism, the implications were clear: the FAF did not spend what in the American view was a sufficient enough amount of time in training to produce the sort of expertise and efficiency expected of modern air crew and maintenance crews in an increasingly complex and technical world.¹¹⁵

Summary: FAF

One can look at FAF doctrine in the light of the defeat of 1940 and call it a failure. Obviously, it did not protect France from being overrun, not that it could have done this alone; the failure of French arms was complete so far as the army and air force were concerned. However, this overlooks the fact that the FAF had to plan, like all other air forces, for a theoretical war at an unspecified time in the future; nobody could know all the details.

French doctrine failed for several reasons, but it reduces to a few key causes. First, FAF doctrine was out of touch with national strategic doctrine. France's leadership always showed reluctance to allow French aviators to bomb enemy infrastructure if there was any possibility of retaliation. The fact that FAF pursued a strategic doctrine instead of a tactical/operational doctrine in direct support of army operations directly contributed to France's defeat in 1940. However, the seeming lack of interest in the French army in anything pertaining to aerial warfare throughout the 1930s suggests that even if the air force had focused mainly on army support, problems such as poor communication and simple lack of knowledge on the army's part would have still yielded less than optimal results. While the argument can be made that strategic bombing made sense if France's battle unfolded into the long-term slugging match it envisioned, the complete and total reluctance of French national leadership calls this logic into serious question.

Second, the FAF and the French army spoke fundamentally different languages, and their cooperation was doomed from the very beginning.

On paper, both services spoke about the need to coordinate their battles and act as a unified tool to defend France and take the battle to the enemy. The ability of either service to cooperate jointly was almost nonexistent. The FAF was, to the best of its ability, technically advanced, and at least understood the importance of good wireless communication and fast reaction times in conducting a successful air battle. The French army, however, did not share the air force's vision, and its lack of training, combined with its primitive (for 1940) communications made successful coordination a nonstarter from the beginning. Further, the possibility of integrating an air defense with an army equipped with antiquated antiaircraft guns, and little to no training of most troops on how to deal with the threat of enemy aircraft grossly exacerbated the problem.

Last, France's inability to turn plans into reality meant that the pilots and planes that could have helped turn the tide against Germany with sheer weight of numbers alone never materialized. While nationalization went a long way to solving the airframe problem, doctrine and production never meaningfully crossed paths. Further, the FAF's inability to create a highly productive training system meant that when some of the matériel problems were finally alleviated, there were far too few key personnel to fly, fight, and service the aircraft. The FAF had key components missing from vital aircraft, and the key personnel missing to effectively utilize the aircraft it fielded. Creating doctrine around machines that only theoretically existed with pilots that only theoretically existed was simply an intellectual exercise, and not a viable means of national defense.

Unfortunately for the air force and for France as a whole, air force doctrine was full of holes and weaknesses. It was as much political as military, and it contributed greatly to the ultimate defeat. Perhaps most unfortunately, FAF doctrine built its hopes around a weak, disorganized, and outdated aircraft industry plagued with so many problems, it would have been comical had France's future not hinged at least partially on it. The massive strategically oriented air force envisioned never came to fruition largely because it partially hinged on an aircraft industry that could specifically support its technical and numerical needs.

6
LUFTWAFFE DOCTRINE AND TRAINING, 1934 TO 1940

CONSIDERING THAT the Luftstreitkräfte was dissolved in the wake of the Treaty of Versailles, and Germany had no real air force until 1934, it seems almost impossible that the Luftwaffe surpassed the FAF in the six years between its inception and 1940. One could be forgiven for assuming that the Luftwaffe would have to catch up on a decade and a half of airpower theory, but this was simply not the case. Although the Luftwaffe started virtually from scratch in 1934, a small but significant airpower brain trust operated throughout the 1920s and early 1930s as a part of the Reichswehr.[1]

This small group of aviators operated rather openly. They had no combat aircraft, but they did have eyes and ears, and curious and capable minds that understood airpower; Seeckt was well aware of airpower's potential, especially France's, and was cognizant of Germany's shortcomings under the Versailles strictures.[2] During a period of prolific writing on airpower, this small group digested much of the material that was printed. Combined with their previous experiences during World War I, and with a much-needed infusion of excellent officers transferred from the Heer to expand

and flesh out, the Luftwaffe rapidly developed workable doctrine almost from its inception, and developed it through experimentation, training, and direct involvement in the Spanish Civil War.

Further, Germany successfully circumvented many restrictions by operating inside the Soviet Union. While this arrangement certainly seems odd today, it made perfect sense for both Germany and the Soviet Union. The Soviet Union needed the know-how to produce modern aircraft, and Germany needed a place to continue working on modern designs well away from the eyes of Allied monitors. While much of the effort concentrated on technology and manufacturing, German officers were able to train on new aircraft and work with their Soviet partners to apply the new technology to existing ideas. These officers were a part of Seeckt's aerial brain trust that were cautiously sent to the Soviet Union so as not to create problems with the Allies.

Aircraft engineers and manufacturers also benefited from the cooperative program. Considering that aircraft technology advanced so rapidly in the 1920s and '30s, any lagging behind could have had serious consequences as the French discovered. Junkers was the most prominent of the German firms involved with the program, and although Junkers maintained a solid industry inside Germany producing transport aircraft, the work in the Soviet Union kept the firm abreast of the international competition.

One has to wonder how much and to what extent the Allies would have acted against Germany had the mission not been kept such a close secret. The flagrant and open discarding of the Versailles treaty resulted in no physical response. Occupying the Rhineland had no effect. In fact, gobbling up Austria and giving up Czechoslovakia along with the coming out of the Luftwaffe in 1935 seems to suggest little if anything would have been done if the program had been discovered. The cover-up was so well run that the Allies knew virtually nothing of it until after World War II.

While Luftwaffe doctrine evolved in the 1930s, the death of such important figures as General Walther Wever and the elevation of other officers had varying effects. Luftwaffe doctrine was coherent when the war began; it covered most possible missions and possibilities and was in many ways quite similar to that of the FAF or any other air force. The primary difference was that the Luftwaffe's doctrine and structure were primarily operational and well suited for army cooperation.[3] After all, the Luftwaffe had a usable intact doctrine left over from World War I. The best way to think of the Luftwaffe is as the Luftstreitkräfte in stasis or perhaps even long-term metamorphosis.

German Air Doctrine in 1918

Germany had a fully evolved air doctrine in 1918 that covered every known aspect of airpower at the time and worked so well that when Germany surrendered in 1918, its air force was the last truly effective and intact branch of service. In fact, one reason German airpower was specifically targeted at Versailles was because it was so effective; like submarines, tanks, and heavy artillery, German airpower had proved a genuine menace to the Allies during World War I, and along with the Royal Air Force (RAF), it was by far the most forward-thinking air service in the world.

Germany had some interest in airpower even before the invention of the airplane. It had invested considerable money, time, and thought into lighter-than-air aviation and its potential military applications. Most of Europe was in fact curious reading the possibilities as they existed before 1903, and writers such as H. G. Wells speculated in fiction as to the potential of aerial warfare once the technical problems (i.e., functional airplanes) were resolved in the same way writers such as Arthur C. Clarke speculated about man, technology, and the vastness of space.

Like Clarke, who envisioned the potential terrors of artificial intelligence gone awry, or Wells, who described vast fleets of airships of one kind or another delivering untold destruction to innocents and combatants alike. In fact, *The War in the Air* and *War of the Worlds* have a sort of symmetry.

While Germany was involved in several foreign adventures in Africa and Asia before World War I, it never had a chance to test its airships or later its airplanes in combat before World War I. It was in fact Italy that had the chance to explore the potential of airpower in minor conflicts immediately prior to World War I. Although Italian airpower had a limited impact, Italy's aviators, who to this day are not given enough credit for their thinking and contributions to airpower (other than Douhet), were the first to practice tactical bombing, something that remained only speculative even during the first weeks of World War I before armed aircraft became the norm.

When World War I began, all the major powers had some aircraft on establishment, but no completely clear idea how to use them outside of reconnaissance and artillery observation and spotting. In the opening weeks of the war, these aviators frequently passed each other on their daily duties with little to no hostility. Whether the story of bored or enraged aviators exchanging pistol shots like aerial cavalrymen is apocryphal or not, it took little time for the aviators of both sides to arm their aircraft and begin experimenting with the theories and ideas in place before August 1914. By January 1915, both sides raced to produce specialized aircraft and use them to help achieve the return to mobility that 1915 might promise.

As it turned out, 1915 yielded little on the ground on the western front other than blood and frustration. However, the air war evolved significantly, and Germany rapidly developed not only technology, but ideas that rapidly evolved into doctrine.

Experience Shapes a Coherent Doctrine

The doctrinal models concerning the three primary modes of aerial warfare (air superiority/combat, strategic bombing, and battlefield air attack) that the Luftstreitkräfte utilized in 1918, and that provided the foundation for Luftwaffe doctrine, were a direct result of combat. Three examples illustrate the rapid conceptualization, implementation, and analysis of German airpower doctrine during World War I, the air battle over Verdun, the strategic bombing campaign between Germany and Britain, and the coordinated battlefield air attacks during the German 1918 offensives.[4]

Describing the first aerial battles in 1914 and 1915 as chaotic aerial scrums is not entirely inaccurate. While the military aviators and their leaders were generally well versed in military theory for the time, aerial warfare was new. As a result, many aerial battles were random encounters. It is important to remember that there was no radar or any other functional and effective detection system, although later, auditory aircraft detectors yielded some results. As such, the air war was often a seesaw affair, and early aerial combat involved random and sometimes very lopsided encounters. On rare occasions, large numbers of aircraft collided and engaged in massive "dogfights" or "furballs" involving dozens if not hundreds of aircraft.

By 1916, the Luftstreitkräfte learned to control airspace and severely limit Allied access to specific areas. This was effectively demonstrated at Verdun. In France, Verdun is arguably the formative battle; the fight that epitomizes the French experience during the war. In a war often defined by waste and attrition, the German plan at Verdun, conceived by General Erich von Falkenhayn, was to maneuver German forces into a seemingly sensitive position to draw a continual stream of French forces that could then be decimated by the Germans. Verdun was to be a meat grinder. While the plan did not work the way Falkenhayn intended, the aerial portion of the battle, specifically operations before the ground offensive was launched, were particularly successful.

Prior to the battle, the Luftstreitkräfte isolated the airspace over the German concentration area by operating patrols that limited Allied reconnaissance in the area. This was vital in keeping the Allies from discovering German troop and logistic concentrations in the area that would have revealed the offensive before it was launched. This was achieved through systematic roving patrols that effectively controlled the length and depth of the area. In effect, the German created a "box" of their choosing in which they concentrated enough air forces that Allied aircraft found it particularly difficult to concentrate. Indeed, the Allies even noted the difficulty with aerial operations in the area but did not connect the activity to the pending offensive. As a result, the German offensive was a rather brutal surprise that initially achieved its objectives, although the ground plan unraveled and the battle, alongside the Somme, became synonymous with slaughter on the western front.

In spite of the problems on the ground, the Germans demonstrated that they could effectively control a limited amount of airspace for a specific amount of time with the appropriate number of aircraft. Today this is generally referred to as "air superiority" or "air dominance." Though the tactic became quickly obvious, the Germans continued to refine the model, combining it with ground-based antiaircraft defenses that increased in effectiveness and complexity throughout the war. Thus by 1918 Germany had an effective cooperative model that combined airpower with ground-based defenses that remained effective in limiting Allied airpower effectiveness almost to the very end of the war.[5]

While the Allies also designed ground-based antiaircraft defenses, the Germans excelled. Britain approached the problem in a different manner, combining ground- and air-based defenses to make Allied aerial forays into certain airspace extremely costly for the enemy. This makes sense, as both Germany and Britain bombed each other's countries with some regularity from 1915 to 1918 with mixed results. However, visions of doom simply did not materialize from strategic bombing, especially where enemy morale—both civilian and military—were concerned, and the Germans made good note of the fact. While "morale bombing" continued to be a favorite topic of theorists in the interwar period, many of whom assumed that "delicate" morale simply needed a few more bombs applied to it (or incendiaries or poison gas), the Germans determined that not only British civilian morale, but German civilian morale was hardly affected by bombing once the initial shock wore off. While bombing sensitive logistics, transport, or communications hubs generated very real and tangible results, troops prepared and armed to fight aircraft, and even civilians were greatly inured by the psychological effects of aerial attack.

Airpower could have appreciable effects of terrestrial battles, and by 1918 the Germans had a well-refined doctrinal model for ground attack. During the Kaiserschlacht (Kaiser's battle) offensive in 1918 that came very close to catastrophically rupturing Allied lines, German ground attack aircraft coordinated with ground units and suppressed Allied defenses, and damaged Allied transportation, logistics, command, control, and communications. Like Verdun, the Kaiserschlacht was a disappointment for the Germans, but nonetheless, German airpower performed its roles quite commendably. The new German purpose-made ground-attack aircraft worked well in the environment and demonstrated that in a very short span of time new aerial technology could be fused with new ideas to create effective results on and above the battlefield. In fact, this is where German airpower thrived in the operational arena during World War I and World

War II. While the Luftwaffe was eventually overwhelmed with missions, especially after 1943, for the first four years of the war, it was almost always able to control a specific piece of airspace for a coordinated effort with the army to achieve positive battlefield results.

When World War I ended, Germany had, in effect, an easily updatable, but more importantly effective doctrine that matched its strategic and operational needs quite well. In fact, after 1935 the core of the model was largely intact. Although improvements in communications and equipment enhanced German effectiveness, much of the air battle was eerily identical to the successful models and doctrine conceived during World War I. The integration of ground and airpower at almost all levels provided the strengths of the model in both World Wars.

By 1918 German flak and aircraft brutalized Allied bombers. German ground-attack aircraft cooperating with ground troops tore massive holes in Allied lines. German fighters were able to effectively dominate virtually any given area of air space for at least a limited amount of time. The Germans understood the limitations and the risks of strategic bombing, and their data proved accurate again during World War II. To use a sports analogy, Germany came back in the second half with new equipment and a refined playbook. The more interesting part, perhaps, is how poorly equipped the Allies were to deal with a model with which they were already essentially familiar.[6]

While it would not be accurate to state that German doctrine did not change at all between 1918 and 1939, it is certainly accurate to assert that the core experiences absorbed during World War I had a profound effect on the airpower doctrine of World War II. The Germans analyzed tactics in depth under Seeckt (while German military aviators and companies worked discreetly in the Soviet Union), and they were supported by civil aviation in Germany; these efforts were then openly developed under Hitler during the Spanish Civil War and brought up to speed for 1939 in terms of updating relative to technological developments that enhanced existing models. The 1939/1940 doctrine with which the Germans invaded France clearly demonstrated these updates.

The Importance of Heer Cooperation

The Luftwaffe was fundamentally an operational air force. It could do many jobs proficiently to a point, but its strength was operational airpower in conjunction and combined with land operations. The string of victories from 1939 up to the winter of 1941, then again through the summer of 1942, demonstrated a tremendous capacity for rapid victories over larger bodies of troops with more matériel, but less ability to maneuver and operate cohesively with ground forces to defeat enemies then pursue the penetrations to operational depths causing panic and collapse.

The winning combination for the Luftwaffe was the rapid establishment of air dominance combined with effective army cooperation. This was undoubtedly made more successful by the transfer of Heer officers to flesh out the Luftwaffe. Officers such as Albert Kesselring and Walther Wever came from an army background and then learned the business of flying. As a result, the Luftwaffe had a previously established army cadre that could "speak the army's language," and this greatly facilitated close cooperation with the army, which was a vital part of the Wehrmacht's success, especially before the tide turned in 1943, and the Luftwaffe's number of varied missions, shortage of aircraft and pilots, and ill-preparedness for strategic air warfare began to overwhelm it.[7]

The Luftwaffe and the army in the interwar years under Seeckt and his successors seriously evaluated the latter World War I campaigns. In 1918 close air support and army cooperation on both sides began to prove its decisive possibilities in conjunction with close army cooperation (for the period). Further, by 1918 both the Allies and the Central Powers had developed dedicated close air support aircraft such as the Salamander and the Halberstadt CL.II. More importantly, during the Spanish Civil War the Condor Legion gained firsthand experience with modern air warfare and began to solve the problems of air–ground cooperation well before they were needed in 1940.[8]

Although only certain Heer units had the ability to communicate directly with Luftwaffe units, modern radios and trained liaison personnel accompanied designated units enabling them to cooperate with a high degree of efficiency for the period. While the Condor Legion had to improvise a combination of landline and radio communication for coordination, by the 1940 campaign, dedicated radio sets eliminated the need for the complex and vulnerable combination of land and wireless communication. Unlike the French, the Wehrmacht developed extremely effective military radios and trained broad numbers of both men and women to use them efficiently. While Germany's trust in Enigma was ultimately misplaced, the belief in the utility of wireless in modern warfare was not. Without wireless as the French discovered, there was not meaningful air–ground communication and thus no meaningful battlefield cooperation.[9]

The close relationship developed between the Heer and the Luftwaffe was not only due to the number of former Heer officers who transferred to the Luftwaffe. Close cooperation in training exercises from 1937 to 1940, experience in Spain, then in combat in Poland in 1939 and in Denmark and Norway, gave the Wehrmacht ample time to "iron out" many problems. The result was that in 1940 the Wehrmacht was prepared to work closely as a team.

Much of this successful cooperation was directly due to Wolfram von Richthofen and his experiences in Spain. Difficulties and experiments during this conflict resulted in action between 1938 and 1940. By the time Germany invaded France on 10 May 1940, the Luftwaffe had refined its ideas twice—once after the Spanish Civil War, and once after Poland. The resulting improvements did good service in the West.[10]

A *Flivo* was the primary liaison officer responsible for coordinating direct cooperation with the Heer. *Flivo* units consisted of Luftwaffe personnel in vehicles that accompanied designated Heer units. The *Flivos* usually operated alongside their Heer headquarters and operations counterparts. Since they were effectively a part of the unit, cohesion grew through mutual experience and becoming familiar with men and officers; they came to understand the needs, methods, and thinking of the Heer, and demonstrated this in Poland.[11]

The *Flivos*' most important tool was the radio. The radios they carried were unique in Heer formations as they could communicate with aerial units. The usual method involved the request being passed to the *Flivos* from division staff, then the *Flivos* passing this up the chain via radio to the designated Luftwaffe support unit. Response times varied, but airpower on station within thirty to forty minutes was a typical norm. In addition, the *Flivos* could communicate with incoming units on preplanned strikes to help avoid the dreaded "blue-on-blue" casualties.

There was no organization like this in France. As previously illustrated, cooperation between the French air force (FAF) and the French army was, to be frank, extremely primitive to nonexistent. While the French army vacillated between giving no orders to the FAF units under its command and flailing madly about wondering where their air cover was, the Wehrmacht was innovating with air–ground cooperation models that are still in use today.

In addition, the Heer and the Luftwaffe placed great importance on the development and effective employment of ground-based antiaircraft defenses as part of integrated air–ground cooperation and tactical and strategic air defense. Germany had a well-integrated system of air defense by 1918 considering the technology available at the time, like the other doctrinal evolutions, flak was reassessed and restructured between 1935 and 1940. The essential model remained the same however: light, medium, and heavy. Light antiaircraft defenses were generally up to 20mm, medium up to 37mm, and heavy above 37mm, with the dreaded 88mm being the most famous, but exceeded in caliber by larger generally semipermanent emplacements usually inside Germany around sensitive installations and often of 105mm or above, and eventually radar directed. The guns inside the Reich played almost no part in the 1940 campaign, but the other guns that went to the field in 1940 were as vital a part of the German campaign as the Luftwaffe fighters.[12]

It is interesting that this aspect of the air war in Europe has hardly been covered considering the popularity of the topic as whole, and the impact that ground-based air defenses had in the air war in total. During the 1940 campaign, the impact of German flak was noticeable if not of prime importance, and most of this was due to emphasis on prewar doctrinal developments. As opposed to their French adversaries, the Germans had well-trained specialized ground-based antiaircraft units that provided at least some protection down to the platoon or company level in most cases. The standard MG34 machine gun was equipped with an antiaircraft tripod, and an antiaircraft sight that was usually carried in the gunner's accessory pouch along with spare parts, oil, tools, and an asbestos mitt to facilitate quick barrel changes. While the tripod was not usually carried in the assault, it was readily available as part of the standard equipment. This may seem petty or even truly minimal, but the evolutionary nature of the MG34, upon which arguably all general-purpose machine guns were modeled, and the flexibility of its mounting system combined with effective ammunition, made it a considerable threat to low-flying enemy aircraft of the era.

Further, Heer units were exposed to aggressive air attacks in training, and although the units of the higher numbered waves were not as well trained, they at least had some realistic exposure to dealing with enemy air attacks, whereas their French counterparts did not. This was of critical importance at places like Sedan in 1940, where light and poorly trained French antiaircraft defenses crumbled under vicious Luftwaffe attacks that did more morale damage than physical damage. The inability of French antiaircraft defenses to keep the Luftwaffe at least slightly at bay undoubtedly contributed to the crumbling morale of reservists with little to no effective training.

The "other side of the hill" at Sedan yielded very different results. Light through heavy flak decimated repeated Allied air assaults aimed at dropping the spans over the Meuse and stemming the flow of German troops. This was partly due to effective weapons, and partly due to effective training and doctrine. Heer units had a combination of inherent and independent ground-based air defenses. While most divisions had guns up to medium caliber, independent flak units belonging to both the Heer and the Luftwaffe were available to reinforce vital points of effort to ensure success.

While the internal politics of the division of identical duties between the Heer and the Luftwaffe is interesting, it had very little effect on effective employment of needed units, especially early in the war, and both branches cooperated with a remarkable degree of effectiveness because they were using the same playbook. Later in the war, most notably in North Africa and the Soviet Union, Luftwaffe flak units operated almost seamlessly with Heer units not only in the antiaircraft role, but anti-tank role as well. They provided critical support when Heer units were swarmed with aircraft and heavily armored tanks, such as the T-34, KV series, and even the Matilda, which the 88 called upon to counter for the first time during the 1940 campaign. The standard of training and the fusion of doctrine was simply so well developed that the separate branches of service meant little regarding effectiveness of communal effort, which was the opposite of what was witnessed in French service.

The Strategic Bombing Question and the Luftwaffe

Strategic bombing played a small role in the Battle of France compared to the rest of the war in the West through 1945. The Luftwaffe was primarily occupied with gaining and maintaining air superiority, air–ground cooperation, and interdiction (a strategic or operational role, depending upon purpose and perspective). In fact, the campaign developed so quickly there was arguably little ability to switch to the strategic bombing of infrastructure, national nerve centers, and so forth.

The Luftwaffe, like the FAF, studied the strategic bombing question in depth in the 1930s and incorporated it into its doctrine. The Luftwaffe had many adherents of strategic bombing, including General Wever, who was killed in an airplane crash before World War II, but had a lasting impact on development and operations.[13] The fundamental question for the Luftwaffe regarding strategic bombing was the same as the FAF's: how does it fit into national strategy? As far as the French Campaign is concerned, most strategic bombing was of little impact.

The Luftwaffe had doctrine in place to address strategic bombing, and for all intents and purposes it looked much like that of France, Britain, or the United States (on paper, at any rate). The German air force was geared toward being an operational branch that could do any job reasonably well and assert dominance over smaller operational areas on the continent; perhaps more importantly, it had a good relationship with the Heer. While the Luftwaffe neglected to produce an effective four-engine strategic bomber, aircraft such as the He 111, Ju 88, and Do 17 did yeoman's work in their absence. Unlike the French, if the German bombers were not perfect for the strategic bomber role, they were at least extant, complete, and modern. Although this deficiency had effects in the Battle of Britain and thereafter, it mattered little during the French Campaign. Germany developed systems such as the *Knickebein* bomb aiming device (which came into use just after the French Campaign) that unlike even the ultra-advanced Norden, was less subject to interference from weather. Until specific countermeasures were developed, it was remarkably effective.[14] In short, strategic bombing was another mission for which the Luftwaffe was much better prepared than the FAF.

Germany was also far more pragmatic than France when it came to the realities of strategic bombing. Unlike France, Germany understood that it was likely to be bombed when at war with a country that maintains a bomber force. As such, Germany developed extensive, modern air defenses integrating flak, radar, standard fighter aircraft, and night fighters (although the night fighters didn't come on line until shortly after the French Campaign). While there was debate over which arm (flak or fighters) was the most important, there seems to have been no illusion that Germany was going to be spared aerial bombardment.

Germany's defenses were far more like Britain's than France's. Every means available was integrated through land lines and radio communication, and these were guided by radar intercepts. Recall that France only had one radar set on 10 May 1940 (a gift from Britain). France's technophobia and ineffective organization meant that this sort of technologically viable and modern air defense integration was a nonstarter. Instead of deciding not to use a technology because of its potential vulnerabilities or the enemy's possible reaction, Germany chose to embrace and enhance its potential and strengths to mitigate enemy effectiveness. Although there was some infighting between the Luftwaffe and the Heer regarding flak defenses, most of these disputes were handled in such a manner as to not impact the effectiveness of the Wehrmacht's war effort as a whole.[15]

During the Battle of France, the Luftwaffe had little time to invest in strategic bombing outside of interdiction. One can argue whether interdiction should be classed as tactical, operational, or strategic. However, the Luftwaffe's deep strikes against clogged French road networks and immobile French army units produced a series of notable strategic effects. First, these strikes hampered a plodding French army that had not significantly increased its mobility since World War I. Slow moving units using clogged road networks slowed even further as airstrikes sowed chaos among men, horses, and machines; the added effects of civilian casualties due to the remarkable number of refugees, exacerbated the mobility problem. The distinct lack of effective modern antiaircraft weapons and training in the French army undoubtedly increased the effectiveness of these airstrikes. Thus, the Luftwaffe's interdiction of transportation hubs grossly impeded the French army's ability to maneuver. In a fast-moving war, the Luftwaffe quickly blunted key French defenses, producing a devastating strategic result.[16]

Second, these airstrikes made communications almost impossible for the French army. Aside from the damage inflicted on above-ground telephone networks, the French were dependent upon couriers. Even if the couriers survived the airstrikes unscathed, the road networks upon which they were dependent became so tangled, it severely delayed, if not denied entirely, a primary mode of communication. Since the radio was neglected or restricted to the point of ineffectiveness, this also produced a strategic result.[17]

Third, effective Luftwaffe interdiction created a logistical nightmare. The pace of the German advance following the fall of Sedan and the crossing of the Meuse left rail and road networks increasingly compromised. Luftwaffe strikes against rail facilities combined with those against road networks created a two-way logjam; supplies trying to get forward frequently butted heads with combat troops and refuges trying to retreat. Troops need fuel, food, and ammunition to fight. Luftwaffe interdiction dramatically decreased the effectiveness of French resupply efforts, again producing a strategic effect.

Fourth, the combined effects of all the above sowed confusion and severely hampered French morale. The Heer collected increasing numbers of French troops unable to shoot, move, or communicate during the first two to three weeks of the campaign. Although the French soldiers of 1940 were no less brave than those of 1914 to 1918, large numbers of troops simply left in lurch were bypassed and swept up, frequently having no real clue as to where they should have been going, or what they should have been doing.[18]

Last, Luftwaffe interdiction had effects on the FAF as well. While the dispersion of the FAF after it had reverted to army control arguably made it more difficult for the Luftwaffe to effectively target FAF airfields and facilities, the decentralization also meant that FAF support personnel, such as technicians and logisticians, had to resort to road networks for transportation. Many were lost in the swarm. Vital parts, ammunition, and fuel were lost as well, and many fully intact aircraft, unable to be evacuated, were left behind. It was bad enough that tens of thousands of French soldiers were unable to provide any effective resistance. It was even worse that the gutting of FAF organization, control, and centralization meant that it could not respond quickly enough to pressure to preserve its vital resources; the French army effectively forced the FAF to wear its lead shoes amid an aerial battle.

Objectively, part of the blame falls on the FAF and the French aircraft industry as well. Had the FAF standardized as the Luftwaffe largely had, the loss of technicians and parts would not have been as severe. However, the plethora of designs in service with the FAF meant that highly specific knowledge and parts were not to be found everywhere. One fighter airfield might have Curtiss Hawks, the next M.S.406s, the one after that D.520s; virtually all Luftwaffe fighter installations had Bf109s and the mechanics and parts to service them. Thus, the confluence of prewar dilemmas, decisions, social issues, industrial problems, and political entanglements by default increased the effectiveness of Luftwaffe interdiction. Even though the Germans most likely did not realize the impact of the variables, the French certainly felt them.

Only during the last two to three weeks of the French Campaign, while the Wehrmacht executed the Fall Rot offensive, did the French finally begin to rein in the chaos and fight in a truly effective manner. By that point, however, the Allies had already effectively lost.

From a speculative and counterfactual point of view, it is difficult to imagine that had the Luftwaffe engaged in strategic bombing of infrastructure and vital assets that the FAF or French ground-based defenses would have been able to do much to effectively counter the effort. As previously noted, although France had some effective antiaircraft weapons, they were poorly organized and trained. They had an inadequate early warning system, having invested virtually nothing in radar technology and French command having basically viewed the one British radar set they had been gifted as some sort of circus attraction or curiosity.

Although FAF fighter pilots and antiaircraft gunners engaged German aircraft when able, there was no centralized air defense command as later witnessed in Britain; again, the fear of radio communication virtually nullified this possibility, and the lack of centralized and effective air organization magnified the impossibility. During the very limited bombing of the Paris area toward the end of the campaign, Luftwaffe losses were minimal as it operated almost at will.

Whether or not French civil morale would have crumbled under Luftwaffe strategic bombing as the French leaders feared is also purely speculative. Retrospectively, the fears over French civil morale is likely best described as fear of a permanent and irreparable rift between the right and left resulting in defection to the Germans (à la Vichy and the French far right), mass refusal to fight, or a civil war on top of a German invasion had the war lasted longer (akin to Ukrainian partisans fighting both Russians and Germans) is also purely speculative. Considering the mass arrests before the war, the sabotage prior to and perhaps even during the campaign, and the true depth of the divisions, which frankly are still beyond the common understanding of most of the anglophone world, it is not beyond the pale of reason that long-term German strategic bombing would have exacerbated the divide. However, the corpus of the evidence concerning civilian morale from the Rif in North Africa to Britons in London suggests that French morale would have held together.

The other interesting possibility with German strategic bombing concerned Paris itself. Although France moved a good portion of its aircraft industry and ancillary components from the area, Paris still harbored the lion's share of French industry, government, infrastructure, and population with no other place in France well prepared to either absorb the population or the responsibilities, infrastructure, or production needs of the city. Another 1870-style scenario, from which many of the fears of French government and command stemmed, was certainly plausible.

Pilot Training

The Luftwaffe held a dramatic advantage over the FAF when it came to pilot training. This stems primarily from almost a decade of the Nazi regime encouraging and financially developing an active civilian and especially youth interest in aviation through organizations such as the Nationalsozialistisches Fliegerkorps (NSFK) and the Hitlerjugend. Both organizations began involving civilians in flight training from the early 1930s, although civilian clubs in fields as diverse as rocketry and gliding existed before the Nazis came to power. Although German military aviation was outlawed under the terms of the Versailles treaty, the exploits of World War I German pilots were still popular fodder during the interwar period, and when the Luftwaffe was reestablished it had no problem filling its ranks.

By the time of the French Campaign, the system in Germany produced a bumper crop of qualified pilots and thousands waiting in the wings to join. Juxtaposed to France, Germany produced more pilots than aircraft by May 1940. Unlike the French training system that languished, even in the late 1930s when the need was imminent, Germany produced a steady stream of pilots through expanding pilots training programs throughout the 1930s. As a result, Germany could afford to lose more aircrew than France, and it could put more pilots in the air in 1940.

While the German pilot training system eventually succumbed to attrition and an underprepared system resulting in a larger-scale collapse that resembled French problems in 1940, it was more than adequate considering the length of the 1940 campaign and the fact that the Luftwaffe was fighting the bulk of a poorly organized FAF, and only part of the RAF. Although the Battle of Britain obviously strained the Luftwaffe and pilot morale, it was never in a position where a shortage of pilots created a possibility of military collapse. To be fair, it was only after mid-1943, when the Luftwaffe had to fight the combined airpower of the U.S. Army Air Forces (USAAF), the Royal Air Force (RAF), and the Raboche-krest'yanskaya Krasnaya armiya (Red Army, RKKA), that the strain became so great as to tilt the balance.

The various civil clubs and ad hoc pilot training initiatives created a flow of Luftwaffe pilots that would have remained an overmatch for the FAF in virtually any conceivable scenario in which the war lasted even two to three years without a two front–plus war.

Luftwaffe Organization

One salient difference between the FAF and the Luftwaffe in 1940 was organization. Although the FAF made excellent strides toward creating a well-organized force prior to 1937, its reversion to army control meant that its units were dispersed into penny packets that always played a reactive role in the French Campaign.

The Luftwaffe was organized in a manner that suited the various doctrinal roles assigned to its personnel. These combined organizations, cooperating with, but independent of Heer command, enabled the Luftwaffe to operate as an organized whole and as a cohesive part of the Wehrmacht.

The *Geschwader* (squadron), which varied in size according to type (fighter, bomber, etc.) and the *Gruppe* (group) were the Luftwaffe's basic formations. These operated independently or in cooperation with other units of various type according to mission. They were fully capable of communicating with one another, and special aircraft could cooperate with ground units and their *Flivos*.

Like the Heer, the Luftwaffe was easily combined into various size groups that could be molded to fit almost any need over a short span of time. Although lack of resources and attrition as the war endured meant that the Luftwaffe was increasingly unable to effectively respond, during 1940 through at least mid-1943, it was able to transform and configure itself according to need. The standard operational-level organization, the *Luftflotte* (air fleet), had a mix of assets from top to bottom that enabled it to deal with most situations in its area of responsibility. At this level, it was fully capable of cooperating with Heer units at the division through corps to army level and respond to strategic air threats in cooperation with other air units.

The *Luftflotten* had a mix of units: fighters, bombers, and ground attack aircraft. They also usually included at least some transport capacity. In effect, the *Luftflotten* were ironically like the corps system developed under Napoleon: each could operate more or less like its own air force and was usually able to maintain superiority and operate independently over a designated amount of airspace for a specific amount of time. The extensive training and common doctrine meant that any units could effectively be mixed and matched at any time because they were trained to do so and "spoke the same language." Compare this to the organization of the FAF, which by the time of the 1940 campaign was fragmented, dispersed, and unable to operate in a unified manner, and the advantages for the Luftwaffe were obvious.

The Luftwaffe entered the 1940 campaign with an extremely flexible organization compared to its FAF counterpart. Due to the nature of the organization, and the command structure, the Luftwaffe was able to morph according to size and need and address any given threat effectively. Although at points, such as the Dunkirk evacuation, the Luftwaffe was pressed to maintain dominance, during the 1940 campaign it could and did achieve air superiority at any given point when it chose to do so and was shuffled to create the correct organization to achieve the desired result.

Compare this to individual FAF squadrons being assigned to infantry divisions with which they usually had no communication when airborne, and the advantages are obvious—and the results were devastating.

Conclusions

It is difficult to overstate how great a difference the approaches to war through doctrine, organization, and training made during the air campaign in 1940. Consider this within the context of operational air warfare from an air–land cooperative perspective. While there are multiple reasons why the Luftwaffe succeeded as well as it did against fierce, but scattered, French resistance, it was the integrated battle that produced such impressive results for the Wehrmacht, not just the Luftwaffe. It was the lack of fundamental meaningful modern integration between the army and the FAF in France that contributed in a direct military sense to France's defeat. Although the sources of the lack of French unity of battle go well outside the military spectrum, the direct defeat does not.

The Luftwaffe fought an operational war with three goals: eliminate enemy airpower (a strategic airpower goal), overwhelm the French army (an operational goal), and defend airspace as a combined effort between ground- and air-based defenses in cooperation with the Heer (arguably tactical, though strategic in design). While the Luftwaffe had its strategic goal as often defined and delineated as a key factor in interwar arguments for independent air branches in defeating the enemy air force, it never lost sight of its operational mission of cooperating with the Heer to achieve Germany's strategic goals.

One can argue as to which aspect was most important, but it is difficult to argue against the primacy of cooperation between the Luftwaffe and the Heer in France in 1940. While each branch had units fulfilling independent jobs, the "magic," so to speak, happened where they fundamentally cooperated to achieve goals. Whether it was the density and effectiveness of a combined air defense, or the violence of ground assaults supported by overwhelming airpower at key points, the joint effort had the most dramatic effects.

The virtual opposite was witnessed on the French side, with an almost diametrically opposed training and organizational concept. While FAF doctrine always mentioned the importance of army cooperation, in practice the idea was moot; they were not trained to operate together, they were technologically incapable of doing so, and the organization of the FAF in 1940, largely decided by political infighting, left the FAF in a flailing and reactive posture. Last, but also of critical importance, the absolute state of neglect in training, equipment, and organization of antiaircraft defenses in the French army left French troops extremely vulnerable if not at many points completely at the mercy of the Luftwaffe.

While the implications of airpower to strategy and grand strategy often overshadow those of air war at the operational level (outside of discussions of the Normandy campaigns in 1944), it was the operational level of air–ground cooperation that led to Germany's success on the continent between September 1939 and December 1941 and in the East until the strains of a two-front war began to cause the Luftwaffe's collapse beginning in mid-1943. Whereas the FAF was by 1940 largely composed of insiders and restructured to support Pierre Cot and his beliefs (viewed at best as alien by the army), the Luftwaffe's leadership in large part came from the Heer in the beginning. Though there was interservice competition, this largely political element is also important in understanding this story.

7

POLITICS AND AIRPOWER IN FRANCE
A Nation and Its Services Divided

ANY MILITARY ORGANIZATION accused of failure must seriously examine its leadership. The French air force's (FAF's) leadership was condemned in the immediate aftermath of the defeat informally by French and Allied soldiers and officers, and formally, if extremely subjectively at Riom.[1] "Vichy could not accuse me [Cot] without accusing La Chambre, for its thesis was that the inadequacy of French aerial armament was the result of bad policy."[2] The FAF's leadership—more than any other factor, due to its influence on every facet of the equipment, personnel, doctrine, and operations—is most to blame for the failure. It was, after all, their collective decisions that led to the aforementioned failures, disorganized doctrine, poor equipment, and a poor overall fit in the established French national strategic outlook. The FAF had no strong, consistent, long-term leader like Billy Mitchell, Erhard Milch, or Hugh Trenchard after it gained its independence. It needed somebody to represent the educated opinions of a professional long-term soldier who was also an aviator to forcefully represent it at the highest levels of military and government. Due to the rapidly changing nature of French politics and the frequent changes at top positions that came along with this, combined with an almost incomprehensible degree of paranoia and distrust between the French Left and Right, it never happened. Further, it is not clear that such a leader existed in the hierarchy of the air force who could have filled the role.

The failure was both military and civil. On the military side, Général Vuillemin had more influence over the FAF than any other officer in the prewar years, as his tenure at the top lasted longest. He was an impressive character, but he was judged rather harshly by most. Major-General Sir Edward L. Spears posited, "There were few officers in the FAF of really first-class mental caliber.... On the other hand, there were many General Officers who had been very brave pilots in the last war but were not sufficiently educated to command important formations now. Among these ... must be included General Vuillemin."[3]

However, assessing the quality of FAF officers was a complex task, and one finds that contemporary assessments of officer quality tend to be complex (as they rightfully should be). While Spears had excellent firsthand experience dealing with French higher leadership, his communication with more junior level officers seems to have been limited due to his elevated position. Further, Spears leaned heavily upon Colyer's opinions published ten years after the war in writing his memoirs.[4]

Other foreign contemporaries presented a more balanced view of the officers inside the FAF. The American attaché, Lieutenant Colonel Ralph C. Smith, commented on the quality of FAF leadership at various levels, but in general, he seems to have been impressed with the more junior level officers with whom he was in contact.[5] He did not stop there in his leadership assessment. He reserved particular criticism for the effects that French politics were having on the effectiveness and morale of the FAF. While he does not name names, there is little doubt where exactly this criticism was aimed: "The division of France into two political groups has impacted the morale of the air army. Communist propaganda is more acute, and a certain discontent has been noted among the most patriotic officers. Promotions are going to the adherents of the Popular Front."[6]

Although Smith does not mention Cot by name, there can be no doubt exactly who this comment was aimed at. Further, even though Cot left the Air Ministry in 1938, this revised amendment appeared in 1940.[7] Although Cot was gone, *his* air force endured through his careful selection of officers, formidably reshaped by his bloodless purge. Careful analysis of Smith's verbiage might lead one to conclude he either sided with or was influenced by what remained of the conservative cadre in the air force, or perhaps a source inside the army whom he never mentions.

This is further revealed by his assessment of French airborne troops that he described as unimpressive, but impossible to ignore.[8] This is at odds with most other accounts, which paint prewar French airborne troops as rather impressive, even discounting Cot's probably too glowing praise. Thus, it seems that even foreign officers were drawn into the French political game before the war began. By the time the war began the FAF had been under Vuillemin's leadership for over a year. Smith's reservation of criticism for a general that by most accounts was legitimately one of Colyer's "brave pilots, but poor generals" is further evidence that Smith at least tacitly sided with French conservatives in his estimation of the FAF.[9]

Even much later, Cot questioned Vuillemin's intelligence in an interview about the FAF during World War II.[10] Vuillemin saw some of the imminent flaws and shortcomings, and although he was vocal in his pessimism, he did little overall to rectify the problems and did not act as a forceful advocate for the air force, especially after it reverted to army control.[11]

On the civil side, Pierre Cot and Guy La Chambre were the most influential air ministers. Cot was a radical leftist. He was undoubtedly an outspoken advocate for the air force and airpower, but his ulterior motives were always in question in a highly charged French society and government. La Chambre was neither terribly outspoken nor influential, and in a tragic way a good match for Vuillemin as a pair of rather compliant milquetoasts; neither effectively represented the air force in the lead-up to World War II.

The army was partially responsible for the air force's failure as well, and Général Maurice Gamelin must bear a considerable burden of the guilt as he controlled French defense in the 1930s: "Neither the French army nor the FAF was organized for total warfare."¹²

While the political divisions in France understandably distanced the army from a rather leftist air force, the army's almost complete and quite willful ignorance of modern air–ground interface left it poorly equipped to fight the Wehrmacht, and almost completely unable to cooperate with the air force even though it controlled the air force from 1938 to 1940.¹³ The stifling of anything other than the official opinion, especially in the last eighteen months or so before the war, did nothing to ameliorate the crisis.

While air forces in Britain and the United States certainly had their share of ineffective leaders, seemingly good ideas on paper that played out poorly in reality, and some internal enemies, the FAF's civilian and military leadership problems were unique. The failures of the FAF in battle in 1940 resulted more from leadership failures than anything else.

A Poor Helmsman with Rudder Afoul

When one examines prewar air forces in Britain, the United States, Germany, and even the Soviet Union, one notices strong, vocal leaders who forcefully represent the thoughts and desires of the air force effectively over the long term. The United States and Britain were gifted with many such as Billy Mitchell, Carl Spaatz, Arthur "Bomber" Harris, and Hugh Trenchard. Germany had among others Erhard Milch, who helped mold the Luftwaffe. The Soviet Union had some excellent prewar air generals who were every bit as competent as their Western counterparts, but they were purged alongside the Soviet Union's other great thinkers like Mikhail Tukhachevsky, the "Red Napoleon."¹⁴ All of these leaders enabled their respective air forces to grow and develop profitably, even if they did not have all the answers that were ultimately revealed through war.

What the FAF lacked was the sort of long-term semipermanent leadership and representation that the other air forces found. Why is this important? Much like the bicameral U.S. Congress, power in military organizations is often the result of seniority and time in service. The higher ranks of the different services get to know each other over time as does the national political leadership. The result is usually profitable to all, even if there are arguments over the what, how, and when.

However, this sort of relationship is also dependent on stable long-term governments and a reasonable sense of national unity. In the United States and Britain, military leaders could depend on working with most civilian leadership over a period of years; the dictatorships in Germany and the Soviet Union were even more stable from this perspective. The French government dramatically fluctuated from left to right over the course of the 1930s, as did the leadership of the FAF. Beginning with Cot and his bloodless purge of senior air officers in 1934 and 1935, the FAF never found a strong military voice with staying power that represented it effectively at the highest levels to the best interest of not only the air force, but France as a whole. The problem with this model is that the frequent changes of control meant that not only staffs, but entire services had to constantly readjust to the new chief every few months. For small organizations, this is not such a big issue. If a small staff of twenty has a new chief every year, they can probably adjust quickly, but it will still hurt their efficiency. However, a complex organization with hundreds of thousands of members all divided into complex departments with highly specialized jobs does not adjust quickly to such frequent changes.

TABLE 4. HEADS OF THE FAF, 1933–1940

Head of FAF	Term
Général Joseph Barès	January 1933 to April 1933
Général Victor Denain	April 1933 to February 1934
Général Joseph Barès	February 1934 to September 1934
Général Bertrand Pujo	December 1935 to October 1936
Général Phillipe Féquant	October 1936 to February 1938
Général Joseph Vuillemin	February 1938 to September 1939
Six chief of staff changes	Just over five years

Source: Robin Higham, *Two Roads to War: The French and British Air Arms from Versailles to Dunkirk*. Annapolis: Naval Institute Press, 2012, 97.

TABLE 5. FRENCH AIR MINISTERS, 1933–1940

Air Minister	Term
Paul Painlevé	June 1932 to January 1933
Pierre Cot	January 1933 to February 1934
Général Victor Denain	February 1934 to January 1936
Marcel Déat	January 1936 to June 1936
Pierre Cot	June 1936 to January 1938
Guy La Chambre	January 1938 to March 1940
André Laurent-Eynac	March 1940 to June 1940
Général Bertrand Pujo	June 1940 to July 1940
Eight different ministers	Just over seven years

Source: Robin Higham,. *Two Roads to War. The French and British Air Arms from Versailles to Dunkirk*. Annapolis: Naval Institute Press, 2012, 97.

The argument could reasonably be made that this sort of shift can and has worked in the past. A country may lose a prominent general or politician yet witness itself and its military stay the course; for instance, FDR's death did not significantly disrupt the U.S. war effort as some in Germany hoped it would.[15] However, in these instances there was a common purpose, even if there was disagreement in how to see it through. Further, changes in government in countries such as the United States did not always equate to changes in top military posts. This was, however, the case in France. The result was unstable leadership. There was no clear, strong long-term advocate for a modern air force of any type (operational, strategic, tactical, or otherwise) who was able to steer the FAF through the 1930s with a firm, resonant voice. France's internal instability was more to blame for this than any other factor.

While internally the air force pressed toward a strategic outlook as the 1930s progressed, the national outlook did not change on a military or political level; recall that the air force was restrained from bombing valuable German targets in the opening phases of the French Campaign when they could have made a difference. Unfortunately, nothing effective had been done at a command level to change this attitude.

There were two arenas in which the air force could have made a difference swaying people to their point of view in the 1930s, the national command structure, and the professional education system in France. Unfortunately, the air force failed to make significant inroads in either area. This is where the lack of a solid, long-term leader was most missed.

This problem was sociopolitical. The level of distrust among the French Left and Right was so severe it ended up dramatically and fatally affecting the efficacy of the FAF in 1940.[16] While Cot's views and writings must be viewed through the filter of his extreme left wing politics, many of his statements were quite accurate: "Communist senators and deputies were dismissed from Parliament. . . . Moreover, under the simple pretext of Communism, and sometimes mere denunciation, militant anti-Fascists, who have never been Communists, were molested and subjected to irritating police investigations."[17] The fact that Cot purged "Fascists" from the air force, did not make it into his text without some sterilization.[18] Both sides were culpable, both sides purged effective officers, men, and ideas, and this internal fighting, the result of a conflict in leadership, was more to blame than any other factor.

Pierre Cot

Pierre Cot was a divisive voice in prewar French politics, and although he had a very direct effect on the development of the FAF and its internal culture, he seems to have been treated like Akhenaten by many of his contemporaries who, even when they wrote of the defeat after World War II, seemed reluctant to even mention his name. Weygand does not mention Cot in *Recalled to Service*.[19] Even Gamelin, for whom Cot reserves profuse vitriol, avoids discussing Cot in his memoirs.[20] Perhaps it was because Cot had (seemingly) clean hands in the 1940s and 1950s. Perhaps it was because Cot and the French Left had a plethora of ammunition at their disposal in the wake of Vichy and World War II, and anything that smacked of fascism, including too overt criticism of the French Left by the men who "lost" the war for France, would seem to shout *collaborateur*! Perhaps it is because the French Left was powerful and popular following the war, whereas the right was permanently tainted with the guilt of Vichy. While

Cot was far from the most powerful, his ambitions were virtually limitless as he worked with the French Left, mostly through the Front Populaire, to gain greater control over French national policy throughout the 1930s. Even in exile, Cot was too dangerous for many; de Gaulle refused any help from Cot in assembling a Free French response under Allied leadership as he was felt to be "too conspicuous."[21] In reality, de Gaulle consistently, but indirectly, questioned Cot's overall loyalty always connecting him with communists in thinly veiled negative overtones.[22]

Pierre Cot moved further to the left as his political career progressed, but he was apparently more conservative in his youth.[23] Cot also served as an officer in the army for four years during World War I, and he knew the dangers of war.[24] His interest in airpower developed later, but by the 1920s, Cot was a devotee, even if he was an amateur. By 1933 Cot was fully at work to achieve independence for a French air arm. At the time, he was air minister under Édouard Daladier. Cot had been involved in the establishment of Air France a few years earlier, and regardless of later justifiable criticism on various levels, he was a competent air minister. He knew his business and was familiar with the issues of the day, as he began to lay the groundwork for an independent air force that looked much like those of other major powers at the time; he kept current with issues related to airpower as they developed from the late 1920s through the 1930s.[25] He was quite familiar with Douhet, as were many in France by the early 1930s.[26] By 1934 Douhet was being discussed not only in French journals, but in books that were written either to support Douhet or decry him.[27]

However, the French—like everybody else—wrote independently on airpower issues prior to Douhet's work, and Douhet's concepts were well understood long before 1928.[28] While Cot agreed with Douhet, as did many in the United States and Britain, they all did so even before *Command of the Air* was released; that was the true power of the book. Douhet simply wrote what became the canon of airpower and presented it to a willing body of preexisting disciples.[29]

What is particularly interesting about Cot, is that from a very early point, he viewed airpower as a diplomatic tool.[30] Cot saw the prospect of strategic airpower as a leg on the stool of the *Petite Entente*.[31] From

1933 to 1934, with the specter of German power rising under Hitler, the multiple ties France had with smaller European states such as Poland and Czechoslovakia still seemed to have enough muscle to act as a potential counterbalance. By 1935 and 1936 after the Luftwaffe was revealed and the first grossly overinflated estimates of German airpower began to pour in, the countries of the *Petite Entente* and even the supposed security of the Maginot Line were questioned in France. French leaders began to look for more powerful allies as the threat loomed.

There were three serious possibilities for France: ally with Britain, ally with Italy, or ally with the Soviet Union to counterbalance an increasingly powerful Germany. There were problems with all three options. Britain was reluctant but viewed by many as necessary. Italy was a possibility. Italy was not allied concretely with Germany in the 1930s. However, Italian relations with Britain were tense, and a French alliance with Italy could have alienated Britain. France was extremely reluctant to do anything to deter the one ally they viewed as absolutely vital as its position vis-à-vis Germany from a population point of view alone was critical.[32] France had good relations with the Russians in the past fifty or so years, but the Soviet Union presented problems. First, it might have alienated Britain, which was none too cozy with the Soviets; second, the Soviets were a bit of an unknown quantity militarily in the early to mid-1930s; and third, communism made many in France, especially conservatives, quite nervous.[33]

France and Britain did not immediately discard the possibility of allying with the Soviets, however. Both France and Britain sent military delegations to the Soviet Union in the mid-1930s. This period was the height of Soviet development of combined arms theory under the yet unpurged intellectual leadership of Tukhachevsky. Both delegations were thoroughly impressed with what they witnessed; it was clearly not what they expected.

Regardless of how impressive the Soviet army was, especially before the purges, it was still a part of the Soviet Union, and that was a problem for many politicians, French, British, and otherwise. This was not in any way reflective of a positive outlook toward Germany; the Soviet Union, and the Soviet Communism that came with it were considered as dangerous if not more so than Nazism.[34] Communism was not a peaceful political movement.

The fact that the Comintern had a clear, vocal, international mission to convert as it were, the rest of the world to the communist system made the Soviet Union an especially odious ally. Although Weygand for instance stated, "I had always thought that we should only be able to succeed against Germany by compelling her to fight on two fronts."[35]

There was little overall enthusiasm for bringing France in any way closer to the Soviet Union from the French Right and Center. Any effort to do so was viewed suspiciously due to France's deep internal divisions.[36] French leadership was pulling the French military, doctrine, and policy in two decidedly different directions, one more pro-Soviet with strategic airpower as a tenant of foreign policy under Cot, and one more pro-British (although Cot was not anti-British) with a conventional French doctrine that did not embrace strategic bombing of enemy infrastructure à la Douhet.

The late 1930s did nothing to improve the West's outlook toward the Soviet Union. The Soviet nonaggression treaty with Germany combined with the invasions of Finland and Poland convinced the West that their caution regarding the Soviet Union was well justified. In fact, France and Britain arguably came quite close to intervening directly against the Soviet Union after it invaded Finland.[37] Although Weygand for instance was notable in retroactive support for an alliance with the Soviet Union, he also freely admitted to the crises of conscience developed by the Allies in trying to deal with the Soviet menace to the Baltic states and Finland: like many other generals after World War II, he subtly admitted his own faults, but was careful to give them as positive a veneer with as minimal discussion as possible before moving along to the next topic.[38]

France was particularly nervous about such an alliance. France, unlike Britain, had a strong communist movement. Although French communists as such were relatively small in number, the party's power and influence, especially inside the Front Populaire frightened many in the center and right including, perhaps most importantly, Gamelin.[39] Although Gamelin and the French Right largely avoid detailed discussions or any mention of their own culpability in neglecting the Soviet Union as an ally, Cot certainly did not shy away from criticism.[40] However, Cot also provided the Soviets with an out, explaining that they had no choice but to treat with the Germans for their own security in 1939.[41] The deeper one probes into leadership and the failure of the French battle in 1940, the picture the review of the primary source material paints is one in which both sides of the argument gently deflect any admission of failure while heaping scorn upon their political opposites. Even after the war, the argument continued.

If Gamelin, the overall commander of the French military establishment, was specifically nervous regarding communism internally, the possibility of allying with an external communist ally—especially one as large and ominous as the Soviet Union—was not likely if he had any influence in the matter. Even when France finally was at war with Germany, communists were singled out for arrest and persecution even though the very real threat of the Wehrmacht was poised on the border, preparing to cross at any time.[42]

In this atmosphere then, Pierre Cot's persistence throughout the 1930s in trying to get France to ally with the Soviet Union created tension between Cot and the more conservative elements in France, especially the army. Cot was inseparable from the air force, and with good reason—he had left indelible marks on that branch early on, and he was in and out of the Air Ministry during the 1930s, holding the office from 1933 to 1935 and again from 1936 to 1938, with multiple air ministers in between.

Cot was not always a staunch leftist. He was a captain in the army during World War I, and he was conservative during this period by French standards. Following the war, Cot began to move left politically, a course upon which he held steady throughout the remainder of his life. Cot was first interested in matters relating to airpower in the mid- to late 1920s, just as France was completely revamping its military outlook, and preparing to wager its national security on defensive firepower embodied in the Maginot Line. Cot was involved in the establishment of Air France, and he, like others in France, began to look at the independent air forces with strategic capabilities as models for an independent FAF, which would then enable France, to better provide for her own defense, while striking vital targets inside German territory.[43]

The 1920s witnessed a great deal of military soul searching for most of the combatants of World War I. In the United States, the air corps and the navy, sometimes at great odds with each other, developed concepts of land-based and sea-based strategic airpower. In Britain, the RAF grew, once even thankfully, due to a laughable and mythical French boogeyman, while the army conducted a series of remarkable experiments in mobility demonstrating the theoretical power of not only fast armored vehicles, but of the radio as well. While the Soviet Union was still sorting its internal affairs, and operating unsuccessfully against some of its weaker neighbors, it grew its industrial base, and set some its best thinkers to work on the war of the future. Germany, very quietly, kept abreast at least in its professional reading and thought, while surreptitiously developing armor and aircraft well inside the Soviet Union. Ten years after World War I, the world prepared for a second global conflagration.

The FAF was born in this atmosphere, and it is Pierre Cot's legacy. Cot's ideals were so well ingrained in the air force, even after the defeat in 1940, that as late as the 1990s, popular sentiment suggested that the air force was still the branch belonging to the Front Populaire. As an unnamed source told historian Elizabeth Kier, "Between you and me, the air force is the Popular Front's air force. That says it all."[44] What exactly did Cot do to create this internal leftist culture in the air force, and how deep and how strong were the roots?

Cot took two actions early on that could only be regarded as both controversial and political. First, he purged the newborn air force of many officers and promoted new officers from the ranks, and second, he used government funds to force open elite aero clubs so middle- and lower-class students with talent could learn to fly independent of air force training. The bloodless officer purge was controversial to say the least. However, it did two things for Cot: it eliminated many officers in the air force who were not of the same thinking or whose politics might create some problems, and second, it created a bond of loyalty between Cot and the newly promoted officers; he clearly viewed the subversive presence of "fascists" as severely as he judged the right of doing the same to communists.[45] From a strictly military point of view, it also purged a great deal of experience, regardless of which way the senior officers leaned. It forced a group of untrained NCOs into roles they most likely were intelligent enough to fill (the air force and navy NCOs were generally technically and mentally adept long-term service members), but with which they had no experience.

In 1934, with war still a distant and uncertain possibility (at least outside of Hitler's mind), the purge was not nearly as damaging as the later Soviet purge that lobotomized the Red Army and air force. However, it did cause a significant period of readjustment that would have been smoother had Cot gradually, if even at a slightly accelerated pace, weeded out officers that might have caused him problems.

Combined with the movement to make the aero clubs in France more egalitarian, there could be little doubt as to Cot's purpose. Deliberately invading a leisure domain of the rich and conservative, even under the guise of the national preparedness (which ironically, it did pitifully little to promote, as France never created the pilot base it needed) could have been viewed again as a hostile move against the right.

If these events occurred in a microcosm of military reorganization and preparedness, they likely could have stood and been accepted and forgotten to an extent. However, Cot was simultaneously active in the international and domestic political arenas in ways that left little doubt in a divided France as to where he would like to lead the country as a whole.[46]

Although Pierre Cot was a devotee of airpower, he had higher aspirations; he hoped to be appointed foreign minister. His best shot before World War II was under Blum, who offered him the Air Ministry again. He accepted this, but it was not what he wanted. It did put him back into a powerful position, but it was too far removed from the inner core that made major decisions and movements possible.[47]

Regardless of his lack of direct access to the power of the inner circles of French government, Cot worked throughout his career to bring France closer to the Soviet Union.[48] Further, his actions were overt. Cot visited the Soviet Union multiple times throughout his career, both before and after World War II; he was not hiding his preferences and ideals.[49]

He continually pushed for closer relations with the Soviet Union in the prewar period. On the surface, the Soviet alliance made sense as a counterbalance to rising German power. The Soviets obviously had a large military and massive resources. However, there was a problem with Soviet power; it had to move through or over client states of the *Petite Entente* to be effective. Even before the Cold War, the Soviet Union made countries as nervous as did an increasingly powerful Germany. Poland fought (and won) a brief war against the Soviet Union in the 1920s. As the 1930s wore on, Soviet expansionism justified the nervousness. It would be difficult, if not impossible, to convince already nervous countries such as Poland and Czechoslovakia to allow "friendly" Soviet troops to pass through or over their territory.[50]

Further, an alliance with the Soviets would have pushed the vital ally, Britain, further away. The British were not keen on allying with the Soviet Union, and the eventual alliance between the Soviet Union, the United States, and Britain was one of necessity, and only made possible by Operation Barbarossa and the German declaration of war against the United States a week after Pearl Harbor. The relationship was never one of great trust between the anglophones and the Soviet Union, and the immediate decline in relations following the defeat of Nazi Germany is obvious proof.

None of this deterred Cot; neither did the Cold War after World War II. Following World War II, Cot continued his close relationship with the Soviet Union, and his efforts to bring the two countries closer together. How deep were Cot's convictions and how close was his relationship with the Soviets?

The Venona decrypts finally enabled the United States to read Soviet diplomatic traffic, but only after World War II. Whatever happened during the war years was already done, but the information was still immediately valuable. Not all of the traffic was deciphered. Many of the transcripts are marked "unrecoverable," meaning that a word, phrase, page, and so forth was not visible for some reason or another.

There were a great many surprises in the decrypts. The greatest of which, perhaps, was information regarding Cot's acting as a spy for the Soviet Union. To be sure, the information is fragmentary. Some have previously suggested Cot *might* have been a spy.[51] However, transcripts from the Comintern archives confirm one thing: Pierre Cot was a Soviet spy.[52]

The evidence indicates that Cot was a spy for the Soviet Union during World War II. The date of his service begins about mid-war after Cot had fled France (wisely, one must argue). In the Venona decrypts Cot is given the code name "Daedalus," a remarkably appropriate name indeed. It was also perhaps far too obvious.[53]

While the evidence clearly indicates that Cot began spying for the Soviet Union after France fell, one is left to wonder exactly how much Allied intelligence might have suspected regarding Cot. There is circumstantial evidence that Cot may have been suspected by the Allies after France fell. For instance, de Gaulle would not give Cot any sort of post in the government in exile even though in de Gaulle's words Cot begged him for any sort of position.[54] There is distinct evidence that the U.S. Army viewed the revived FAF as suspect as early as 1946, perhaps not ironically, as Cot was then again for a short time air minister.

The fact that the Soviets formally recruited him after 1940 strongly suggests that he was not on their payroll in any manner before that point. However, Cot's closeness to the Soviets in general, and his continual efforts to move France and the Soviet Union closer together are in the least, quite suggestive. That there were Soviet spies in France, Britain, and the United States is beyond doubt. Additionally, the Parti communiste français communicated regularly with the Comintern.[55] Although the French communists wanted to maintain uniquely French communism, the flow of information back and forth was quite fluid, and no doubt Moscow had good information, often inside and probably at very high levels, on the doings of the French.

Pierre Cot was a divisive figure in a divided country. His actions, though designed to strengthen the air force, cannot be considered apart from French politics and culture. While his efforts to create a functional, modern air force and a modern aircraft industry were serious, his ultimate goals must be questioned, undoubtedly as his political enemies did. His overt efforts to tie France closer to the Soviet Union and his desire to eventually attain the Foreign Ministry, could not be taken as anything other than an effort to shift France decisively to the left.

Cot's version of anti-fascism seems to have been a jaded and as poorly judged as the right's version of anti-communism. Cot did not acknowledge much in the way of a center in his discussion of prewar and wartime events.

His verbiage indicates he saw the struggle both inside and outside of France as one essentially between fascism and communism. While Cot was not a card-carrying communist before the war, preferring to connect himself more generally with the Front Populaire specifically, and with communism more tangentially, his verbiage, especially in *Triumph of Treason*, left little doubt that he essentially viewed the world as a struggle between communism and fascism, and eventually one would be forced to take one side or the other: "It is not France, nor Germany, but the whole of Europe that must be organized and purged of fascism," he declared.[56]

While this seems like a legitimate statement, especially in the middle of World War II, it is important to remember that Cot's verbiage tends to color all those opposed to him on the right as fascists. By the time Cot wrote *Triumph of Treason* his language is distinctly pro-communist, and although he veiled this feeling well enough before the war, it seems likely his opponents had little doubt regarding his communistic inclination. That taint could not be taken lightly by the French army, nor its leadership that also leaned progressively further right with Gamelin, to an extent Weygand, and ultimately Pétain. Thus, while the army might well have drowned out any other practical requirements, ideas, and concepts beyond its relatively narrow and focused doctrine centered on the Maginot Line and the "methodical battle" concept (seeing the primary role of the air force as reconnaissance and spotters practically up to the very last minute before the invasion), it always eyed the motives of the air force suspiciously, which might explain why leadership was so eager to break the air force down into ineffective elements.[57] Whether Cot became increasingly leftist because of the actions of the right is debatable; his actions indicate he seemed to steer that course ably on his own without any particular aid.

From a strictly military point of view, Cot's devotion to French strategic bombing was foolish. First, there was no indication that the French fear of reprisal bombing had diminished enough to give this serious consideration. Second, although the aircraft industry was partially modernized, it was never—not even in June 1940—capable of producing modern, viable bombers in sufficient quantity to create a viable strategic bomber arm, especially compared to Germany.[58] There is no indication that six months or even a year might have solved the bomber production problem, although it might have begun to fix the fighter problem by 1941. Cot's bloodless purge also robbed the air force of a great deal of experience and potentially useful relationships that might have greatly assisted the air force in operating more productively with the army and as part of the national defense structure.

Cot arguably did more damage to the air force by alienating it from the army on political grounds. The purge certainly raised concerns. The nationalization of the aircraft industry (which could not be separated from the communist ideology of nationalization) in peacetime made the wedge broader. However, what might have had the greatest impact was Cot's continual endorsement of labor, since that was where the communists were the strongest, and where ultimately, they did the most damage to a vital industry. These views were not only internal, but external as well. While the external critics might have missed the undertones, these certainly would not have been lost on the French Right, and Cot clearly viewed Riom as their attempt to castigate and eliminate any and every policy of the left.[59]

Ultimately, Pierre Cot, the scion of the FAF and French airpower in the 1930s contributed to the failure of 1940 by putting the air force on a track it could not manage militarily. This put the air force on a collision course with the army and its leadership, by far the most powerful armed institution in France. Counterfactually, given more time the air force might have been able to create a viable model. However, considering the rapidity with which the military reverted the air force to army control after Cot left the ministry in 1938, this is highly doubtful. The army through training and general knowledge truly had no idea what to do with the air force, and the events of May and June 1940 verify this. The army did not retake control of the air force because it thought it could fight it better than its own officers, it retook control because it feared Cot's motives, the Left's motives, and ultimately what might happen under the right conditions. Cot specifically illustrates this point by suggesting the airborne troops were eliminated because of the specific fears of communists in the ranks.[60] In light of Cot's muddled loyalties it might be tempting to ignore this, there was a very real purge of French communists in France well before the capitulation. If Gamelin lost sleep worrying about arming army reservists—many of whom were communists under the control of conservative leadership—it does not take much extrapolation to comprehend the potential fears he entertained regarding the air force.

Guy La Chambre

Guy La Chambre was effectively the last air minister before the invasion. Taking over from Cot in March of 1938, La Chambre inherited possibilities and problems simultaneously. On the positive end, La Chambre inherited an improved, if not completely renovated aircraft industry. There were still significant problems in major areas such as engines, gauges, and armament, problems that could have been solved by foreign sourcing relatively easily. The air force was also in good shape organizationally, if still lacking in equipment and pilots.

La Chambre had an opportunity to continue to develop the air force. In many ways, he had a better opportunity than Cot. La Chambre was not divisive like Cot. In fact, he was arguably made air minister because he was more pliable. However, La Chambre had virtually no experience with aviation; he was largely involved in local politics before his promotion.[61] Unfortunately for the air force, one of the first things that happened under La Chambre's guidance was the reversion to army control, breaking up the potentially effective organization the air force had constructed. Now, instead of an air force–controlled air defense network that was reasonably well organized and under air force control, the air force en masse migrated to army control where squadrons were often broken down into tiny units, sometimes as small as one squadron per infantry division.[62] This might not have been as much of a problem if the army was well trained in air matters, but the army was pathetically prepared to deal with control of the air units that were once again its responsibility.[63] Professional training relating to air issues, especially since air force independence, was almost completely absent in the army. Gamelin was right; the French had "concentrated on their army," but he failed to mention that in the process, the army had almost completely ignored professional training regarding airpower.[64] The army's interest in the air force never changed; the army expected the air force to provide reconnaissance and artillery spotting, and that was the extent of its interest and, frankly, its abilities. The air force was expected to maintain air superiority, and conduct what other independent mission it was allowed, on its own accord, but do it under an ignorant army command.

The problem with this was that with the air force broken down into small elements (not unlike tanks) and relegated to what was arguably a sort of support role under the command of officers who did not know how to use it, it was rendered uniquely unable to act effectively against aerial threats.[65] The air force indeed had the right idea as was proven throughout the war: unified command of air force assets was necessary to organize an effective aerial defense.[66] The air force, and France, had just been stripped of this ability, and Air Minister La Chambre was as responsible as anybody else for this occurrence.

The nationalization and reorganization begun under Cot did finally yield results under La Chambre, but the results came quite late with impressive monthly production numbers being realized by 1939. While the process was controversial from the beginning, by May 1940 the French aircraft industry was cranking out aircraft at an impressive rate, even if the Byzantine procurement process often meant that what was on hand in squadrons never matched what was officially produced.[67] Wastage, or flawed aircraft unacceptable for delivery and use also remained high. However, between the deliveries by French industry and American industry (according to more than one source), the air force made up its combat losses so well, that it ended the air battle in 1940 with almost as many aircraft as it began with.[68]

While Cot was divisive, his ability to keep one foot on each side of the aisle, juggling the now nationalized industry with labor issues, was unique. La Chambre was unable to do this. There are indications that excessive protectionism was rampant in France.[69] France could ill afford protectionism in this area. While the aircraft situation was improving, it clearly was not solved. There were multiple models available for sale, especially in the United States. While France did procure many aircraft in this way, there is evidence that reports and evaluations of foreign aircraft were intentionally falsified to make French models appear inferior, when they in fact were not.[70]

It appears that France may have ordered less potent models from the United States to make them appear less capable or at least only on par with French models. For instance, the Curtiss Hawk could have been procured with more guns than those with which they were equipped for France.[71] Further, problems that France had not yet coped with, such as effective aircraft machine guns, could easily have been solved by ordering or manufacturing U.S. models under license.[72] These weapons were not protected under U.S. arms export laws, and nothing in theory would have stopped France from ordering them.

These decisions in the final months before the war could have and should have been influenced by the Air Ministry under La Chambre. Cot later testified that one of his primary concerns was to acquire aircraft in volume by any means necessary.[73] In light of this information, and considering the growing nature of the threat, La Chambre should be tagged with much of the blame for leaving the air force less well equipped than it could have been in May 1940. Cot let La Chambre off rather lightly, probably in an attempt to deflect some of the guilt away from himself and simultaneously strengthening his charge against his real target, Riom and the French Righ.t[74]

Général Vuillemin

Général Joseph Vuillemin led the air force under La Chambre, and shares the blame with La Chambre for these fateful decisions in the final months before World War II. Like La Chambre, Vuillemin's greatest sin was likely also the reason he was appointed in the first place, his compliance. There is no known evidence to suggest that Vuillemin protested air force transfer to army control, nor does the evidence suggest that Vuillemin acted to solve the worst of the air force's other problems, even though, like La Chambre, he had some time to do so. Although he was consistently worried about the number of German aircraft in service, he seems to have been far less concerned with how to fight them cohesively when they did come; Vuillemin played perfectly into the army mindset of the notion of a controllable process of war with a predictable timetable that was manageable so long as the flow of matériel was maintained.

Vuillemin was frankly a bit of a pathetic figure. His inaction generally indicates he was probably operating far above his skill level. Even unbiased observers felt Vuillemin to be outside of his comfort zone: "Vuillemin certainly made a poor impression. He looked what in fact he was, a pilot of the last war who had gone to seed. NCO was written all over him. Rather fat, rather pasty, bursting out of a uniform several sizes too small, which is a common filing of both French airmen and sailors, his bovine blue eyes had the same expression of rather hostile bewilderment to be observed in oxen as they watch the trains go by."[75]

Vuillemin had a front-row seat to the possibilities of the Luftwaffe's power. He visited Germany before the war, and although there was a bit of deception upon the part of the Germans, Vuillemin returned to France predicting France's airpower would last less than a fortnight: "I am quite convinced that if a conflict erupts this year the FAF would be wiped out in a few days."[76]

What is remarkable about Vuillemin is that he did little to demand more for the air force even though he led it. In fact, Vuillemin is best described as apathetic from 1938 to 1940. When the aircraft industry approached him indicating they could likely start producing aircraft in the hundreds per month, he simply responded that he only needed forty or so since he could not produce more pilots than that, rather than give the orders to redouble the efforts of the air force to produce pilots to fill the seats of the aircraft that would begin to become available.

During the Riom Trial, sham though it was, the bulk of the blame for the defeat was laid at the feet of the air force. Although Cot was not present, wisely fleeing for his personal safety, La Chambre and Vuillemin did not. If Vuillemin was incompetent, he was defiant. He was not called to testify at Riom, even though one of the main goals seems to have been to eviscerate the air force and subsequently the Left. He may have been "very inadequate," but he was no coward.[77] Vuillemin was a patriot through and through, and although he was a bit of a yes-man, he resisted the urge to capitulate, and his outward courage and defiance made the prosecutors cautious and unwilling to let him testify on record; even Cot described him as a "true patriot."[78]

More than any other factor, leadership was the ultimate cause of the FAF's failure in 1940. No single leader bears most of the responsibility; there was plenty of blame to go around.

Cot was without a doubt, supremely divisive. His politics, beliefs, and actions—such as purging the officer corps and nationalizing the aircraft industry—could easily be regarded as a move toward communism, which it probably was if one digests it with the corpus of Cot's written material in the immediate postwar era. However, Cot and his disciples were correct on many counts. The air force did need a unified centralized command; its inability to strike cohesively and concertedly against the Luftwaffe was the most decisive factor in its defeat. The aircraft industry was primitive, vulnerable, and not up to the challenges of modern combat aircraft manufacturing demands. The process was slow, and it caught up very belatedly, in fact too late, falling behind in technology and never resolving its quality and technology issues. Cot's insistence upon building a massive strategic bomber force was always unrealistic, considering the state of the aircraft industry, and overall French national strategy and perceptions regarding bombing.

Conversely, Gamelin, army leadership, and the Right share a sizable portion of the blame. They killed promising programs such as the Infanterie de l'air and inhibited the air force not only by lobotomizing a reasonable command structure just when it was beginning to show promise, but recall they went so far as to inhibit the air force from attacking vulnerable German columns, an act that might well have seriously stalled not only German progress, but rattled German nerves as well in the early stages of the campaign and bought France the time it desperately needed. Gamelin's attempts to keep his control over the establishment were not unusual, but his paranoia and his desire to somehow avoid conflict altogether were so irrational that even Paul Reynaud wanted rid of him.[79] Gamelin was the personification of what the Germans called *Straußmanöver* (ostrich maneuver), basically ignoring reality as a defense. However deep the sociopolitical rifts in French society were, it was unforgivably shortsighted for command, especially Gamelin, to do as Cot suggested and fear the Left in France more than the fascists in Germany.[80] While Cot's lacquering of the French

Right with the same brush as the Nazis was also deeply unfair on many levels, the occupation and the Vichy government add some weight to his arguments even now, although most of this also delaminates under close scrutiny. The French Left and Right may well have detested each other only marginally less than the Nazis in Germany, but they both genuinely loved France even though extreme examples on both poles are frequently used to counter this argument.

La Chambre and Vuillemin basically played the roles assigned to them and rocked neither the command nor political boats in France, even though they should have. La Chambre did an admirable job of realizing the modernization of the air industry so that by 1940, even with all the political intrigue, labor issues, and technological problems, the air force had a steady supply of at least decently modern aircraft. The primary problem was that the air force was chained in penny packets to army officers who had literally no idea how to use the aerial forces at their disposal. Further, the lack of unified air force command meant that the FAF always fought at a disadvantage. Although it took a serious toll on the Luftwaffe even in its disorganized and depleted state, one is left to wonder what it could have done had it been properly organized and led by men willing to fight for its interest, but still palatable to the powers that be.

The very nature of leadership demands that those in power must make the most difficult decisions based upon often limited and uncertain information. This is one of the reasons societies tend to idolize exceptional leaders and demonize those that fall well short. In the end, it is the failings of leadership that most often translate into ultimate defeat.

8
REASSESSING THE AIR BATTLE OVER FRANCE IN 1940

THE FRENCH AIR FORCE (FAF) has been continually maligned in the anglophone world since the summer of 1940. In relatively short order, the francophone world followed suit. There were many complaints when suggested the FAF was almost a nonentity: "The extent to which our air force was outclassed was truly appalling."[1]

Anglophone discussions of the FAF have been pervasively hostile and critical from the very beginning. In fact, it may have been a British officer, Air Commodore Colyer, who set the tone for the history of the French air battle as early as June 1940. Colyer was the British air attaché stationed in Paris. His first report dated 30 May 1940 was particularly condemnatory of the FAF, and this report arrived in London in medias res.[2]

In his report, Colyer describes the combined efforts of the French Air Ministry and the aircraft industry as "inefficient well-meaningness [sic]."[3] Although he gave credit to FAF generals for being brave pilots, he assessed their generalship as being of quite poor quality.[4] Further, he suggested that there was a lack of a will to fight on the part of the FAF in general.[5] However, the last paragraph of his report was something of a hammer blow to the reputation of the FAF as a whole. "The French Air Staff, in my opinion, is not fitted to deal with the broad aspects of coordinated offensive air action against Germany and will only act as a brake on the Allied effort so long as they are allowed independence in this matter."[6]

This is the earliest wartime "official" opinion yet discovered offering an assessment of the FAF in combat from the point of view of an experienced air force officer. Coyler was the man on the ground in Paris offering an assessment, which cannot help but have had a tremendous impact on British points of view during and after the war regarding the FAF. If there is any doubt of this, one need go no further than examining the postwar memoirs of General Sir Edward Spears.[7] These copies of Colyer's reports were located in Spears' papers in the B. H. Liddell Hart Archive at King's College, London.[8]

In the eighty years since France fell, few have questioned these pervasive opinions. Even though the evidence has been available for years, few have examined the Luftwaffe's losses to determine exactly how hard-fought the air battle over France was in 1940, and what the long-term results were.

Due to the lack of research in general regarding the FAF, many of the criticisms have been a bit oblique and indirect. Alistair Horne suggested it was simply overwhelmed.[9] Early on, B. H. Liddell Hart seemed to forget that the FAF was even a factor, and such conspicuous absences of its discussion might well be a source of the "no-show" verbiage.[10] Later works dealing with doctrinal or military failure, such as Meir Finkel's, often discuss the French defeat with little or no mention of the FAF.[11] Airpower generalists often used very brutal and sometimes quite overstated and inappropriate verbiage such as Stephen Budiansky: "Every link—command, doctrine, organization, tactics, equipment, training, intelligence, morale—was weak and each broke as the strain fell upon it."[12] Only recently have authors begun to scratch the surface of the real effectiveness of the FAF in such works as *Unflinching Zeal*.[13]

In fact, the evidence and basic conclusions have been available in print since the 1980s. In *Strategy for Defeat: The Luftwaffe 1935–45*, Williamson Murray detailed the Luftwaffe's losses during the Battle of France.[14] Murray's data was taken not from the Allied kill claims, but German reports on losses incurred during the campaign. Further, his incisive and detailed loss returns can be compared to those from the Battle of Britain, and the Blitz to compare and contrast exactly how severe the fighting was. Murray clearly states,

> Tables III through VI underscore the extent of German aircraft losses in the Battle of France. They suggest the tendency [in the Luftwaffe as well as among the Allies] to view the Battle of Britain a separate episode from the defeat of France does not do justice to the resistance of Allied air forces in the Spring of 1940 and distort the fact that for five months, from May through September, the Luftwaffe, with only a short pause, was continuously in action. The break in morale of the bomber pilots, reported over London in mid-September 1940, thus was the result not only of the strain of fighting over Britain, but of operations that had been continuous from the previous May.[15]

It is difficult to argue with his conclusion based on the data. The losses the Luftwaffe incurred during the air battle over France were such that it could not replace its losses in either pilots or machines before the Battle of Britain. The Luftwaffe's losses during the Battle of Britain, then the Blitz exacerbated the shortage of pilots and airframes, which perpetuated itself again and again in Russia, in Africa, and in the air battles over Germany from 1943 to 1945. The critical point is that the Battle of France put the Luftwaffe on course for a flat spin from which it would never recover.

As for anglophone authors, very few and really only one—Robin Higham—truly even attempts to at least restore the good name of the individual French pilots in the Battle of France. "The story of the Armee de L'Air in the Battle of France has been tinted and tainted by disaster to the Armee de Terre, and by the shameful neglect by French historians of this part of their own history . . . their materiel was very poor, yet on the other, the experienced [French] pilots acquitted themselves quite well."[16] However, Higham also reflects some generalities about the FAF that simply were not accurate. "The roots of the defeat of the FAF went deep. They included a lack of focus, lack of doctrine, and a lack of communications."[17]

What Higham truly missed here was that the FAF had excellent concepts of all three components above, and that these were systematically repressed or dismantled by the French army and general staff between 1938 and 1940.

This was systematically dismantled by the French army after the FAF was returned to its control in 1938 due primarily to a distinct failure on the part of army dominated French command to understand the importance and efficacy of airpower: "The French General Staff admitted the *indirect* use of airpower in warfare, particularly in attacking supply columns and harassing lines of communication, but not its *direct* participation on the battlefield."[18]

This, of course, leaves conventional historiography with a significant problem. If the FAF simply failed to show up, and did a poor job defending the metropole against the Luftwaffe, then how and why did the Luftwaffe suffer so grievously? If one accepts that the FAF did little damage to the Luftwaffe that leaves only three possibilities as to how and why Luftwaffe losses were so high. First, many losses could be purely maintenance or accident related. Second, the Royal Air Force (RAF) could have caused the bulk of the damage with its limited commitment of fighters. Third, the French army could have caused most of the damage with its inherent antiaircraft defenses.

The Air Battle in 1940—Broad Strokes

The air battle over France technically began on 3 September 1939 with the French and British declaration of war on Germany following the invasion of Poland. During the Phony War, there were somewhat regular air skirmishes, often glorified in the French press, and that probably painted an overly rosy picture.[19] Not to be outdone, the somewhat similar German press would later make the efforts of German aviation over France, especially that of the Stukas, equally rosy and less (German) bloody than honest on the part of the Luftwaffe.[20] When the invasion came on 10 May 1940, the serious problems began within the first week. The failure of the Dyle Plan, combined with the unexpected move through the Ardennes, quickly upset the well-laid plans of Allied command. Although there were significant indications that strong German forces were maneuvering in the area, the FAF was restrained from attacking due to ingrained fears of German retaliation.

The air battle concentrated early in the north and quickly around the Sedan area, where the FAF made almost suicidal attacks against the German breakthrough that threatened the entire Allied line. Although the

FAF and the RAF were significantly damaging the Luftwaffe, the lack of ground-based antiaircraft defenses, and loss of territory leading to overrun airfields and losses in parts, planes, and personnel, meant that the air battle, at least from the French point of view, seemed to grow more difficult every day, even though somewhat heroic efforts were made on the part of industry through improvisation and scavenging; far too slowly, France began calling in squadrons from less-threatened areas, such as North Africa.[21]

As the Wehrmacht pried the Allied armies apart and overran more and more territory and (subsequently) airfields, the position of the FAF deteriorated. By the end of May, although it continued to fight on, the loss of pilots, machines, and personnel made the effort less effective. It was only toward the end of the French Campaign that the Luftwaffe did any real strategic bombing against French infrastructure. It was minimal, had no noticeable effects, and is almost unmentioned in histories. One thing it does indicate, though, is that the Germans had their hands far too full supporting the air–land battle to consider moving on to more strategic efforts; this "never quite enough" problem followed the Luftwaffe throughout World War II.[22] The FAF and the RAF in France in 1940 were the only Allied air forces *not* destroyed mostly on the ground, but in the air, even when the situation became dire. Although the infrastructure delaminated along with Allied command's plans, the FAF bled as much to stave off defeat as the Luftwaffe did to achieve victory; it was not a pushover.

Luftwaffe Losses in 1940

What exactly were the Luftwaffe's losses in 1940? The best records to consult are the Luftwaffe's own. Considering that enemy air forces grossly inflate kills against enemy air forces, often to the point that an enemy at some point loses more aircraft that it owns, admitted losses are typically more accurate.

What remains a bit shocking about the Luftwaffe's losses in the French Campaign is that although they were tremendous, and resulted in the loss of airframes and pilots that could never be fully replaced, this has largely been ignored. Speculatively, there are two reasons for this. First, the Battle of Britain and the Blitz have become the salient air battles of early World War II. While both battles were crushing to the Luftwaffe, they were an exacerbation of losses it could not afford that had occurred in France. However, these losses fit into the anglophone paradigm that France was inherently unreliable and incompetent.

Operation Barbarossa in 1941 is often considered the tipping point for the Wehrmacht as a whole. The massive losses incurred from June 1941 to January 1942 are often considered decisive. Indeed, the Wehrmacht did lose a considerable number of irreplaceable men and precious equipment, and arguably lost what was left of the superbly trained junior to mid-level officers and NCOs who were the professional core of the prewar Wehrmacht that provided Germany with the stunning victories of 1939 to 1941.

While both above assumptions are to a point quite correct, they need to be reevaluated, a task—specifically in reference to the Luftwaffe—which has largely been accomplished by Williamson Murray. However, this needs to be refined. What Murray did not fully illustrate and what has largely been ignored since June 1940, is that much of the damage inflicted on the Luftwaffe was the result of FAF action. Much of the problem in assessing this damage has been perception. It was not that FAF was not present. It was not that the FAF was not having an effect (truly rather significant) on the Luftwaffe; the data will prove this. The ultimate problem was that the FAF was fighting from a reactive stance during virtually the entire campaign due to poor communications and a lack of a good early warning system, under army command that did not understand airpower, and with qualitatively inferior equipment.

As a result, the FAF unfortunately did more damage to the Luftwaffe after it had already launched its attacks than before. When eyewitnesses, even French eyewitnesses like Marc Bloc made comments such as, "Where was the air force?" it set the tone for the postwar assessment. Explaining how the FAF was as effective as it actually was challenging, and it actually goes against what has come to be accepted as fact.

Combat and Noncombat Losses

Williamson Murray's excellent research and writing clearly distinguish between the Luftwaffe's combat losses and its maintenance/accident losses based upon the original records from 1940.

TABLE 6. LUFTWAFFE AIRCRAFT LOSSES

Type	Strength 4.5.40	Due to Enemy	Not Due to Enemy	Total	Destroyed Not on Operations	Total All Causes	% as Total of Initial Strength
Close Recce	345	67	5	72	6	78	23%
Long-Range Recce	321	68	18	86	2	88	27%
Single-Engine Fighter	1,369	169	66	235	22	257	19%
Twin-Engine Fighter	367	90	16	106	4	110	30%
Bombers	1,758	438	53	491	30	521	30%
Dive Bombers	417	89	24	113	9	122	30%
Transport	531	188	18	206	7	213	40%
Coastal	241	20	16	36	3	39	16%
TOTAL	5,349	1,129	216	1,345	83	1,428	28%

Source: Williamson Murray, *Strategy for Defeat: The Luftwaffe 1933–1945*. Maxwell Air Force Base, Montgomery, AL: Air University Press, 1983, 40.

The Luftwaffe's combat losses for the French Campaign total 1,428 aircraft.[23] Combined with the noncombat losses, this total equates to 28 percent of its overall strength.[24] By any estimation, this represents a significant depletion of overall airpower, especially considering that the Battle of Britain and the Blitz followed hard on the heels of the Battle of France. Thereafter, the Luftwaffe was continually engaged in Europe, the Mediterranean, Africa, and eventually the Soviet Union with virtually no pause or break.

As Murray illustrates, this first massive loss of strength is never fully recovered, and the Luftwaffe fought at a disadvantage throughout the remainder of World War II. The important fact is that noncombat losses alone certainly cannot account for the overall percentage of losses from which the Luftwaffe never recovered. Thus, the idea that simple maintenance or accidents overwhelmed the Luftwaffe and accounted for its dramatic losses over France in 1940 can be dispelled. This leaves two remaining possibilities.

The French Army

Perhaps, then, the French army caused significant damage to the Luftwaffe during the campaign, and this explains the losses incurred in 1940. The problem with this argument is that the French army was poorly prepared to defend itself against aerial attack. First, it was poorly equipped to deal with modern aerial threats. The bulk of its antiaircraft guns were antiquated compared to those of the Wehrmacht. Second, its troops were by the army's admission poorly prepared to mentally cope with the stress of aerial attack. Third, the after-action accounts of the French army's defeat all point to the fact that the French army viewed aerial defense as the job of the FAF. This final notion was that with which the army decidedly and shamefully sacrificed the air force to the puppet fascist state at Riom.

French soldiers were almost helpless when it came to inherent antiaircraft defense: "The division's major deficiency was in anti-aircraft weapons. Unfortunately, this deficiency existed throughout the French army. In its 1938 program, the army sought to create 923 antiaircraft batteries with a total of 6,739 weapons, 90 percent of which were 25-mm guns. But this huge number exceeded the production capacity of French industry, annual production being about 300 weapons per year, and the army decided to give priority to other weapons."[25]

The shortage of antiaircraft weapons as a critical fault was obvious in the immediate wake of the defeat, and was due to what Pierre Cot at the time referred to as "the decadence of the Army."[26] The significant lack of antiaircraft defenses at FAF installations (by May 1940 scattered in penny packets and assigned on as low a level as a squadron to an army division) also aided the Luftwaffe in suppressing the FAF. "French air power also lacked adequate anti-aircraft protection for its bases and fields. Here the air force paid for the errors of the General Staff of the Army."[27]

Further, the antiaircraft weapons France did possess were mostly assigned to defend the interior of France with very few deployed forward to cover the army or air force ground installations. "According to the statement made by General Marescaux, director of aerial defence, before the court of Riom, 600 cannon were assigned to the army zone and 1,500 to the interior. It was considered more important to protect property than fighting men; yet it was the fighting men who were attacked by the German aerial forces, not the interior of the country."[28]

While the French army revisited antiaircraft weapons in 1940 and French industry responded by stepping up production, it was too little, too late, and there are also some suggestions that indicate that French antiaircraft weapons that were available in 1940 were deliberately sabotaged by the workers who made them.[29] If this was indeed the case, and French antiaircraft weapons had been systematically sabotaged for some time, it detracts even further from the notion that the French army could have been primarily responsible for the Luftwaffe's losses in May and June 1940.

It is, however, irresponsible to suggest that the army or general staff had no concept of antiaircraft defenses, nor any notion of their importance. Their attempt to produce more antiaircraft armament is at least suggestive of that. However, the tremendous amount of material printed in France between World War I and World War II indicates that the French were actually quite aware of the problems associated with air defense and the intricacies thereof. This makes the condemnation of French command even more powerful.

The final version of the *Manuel du gradé de D.C.A.* printed in 1940, just before the war began, indicates that at least academically, the French army understood the modern theory of antiaircraft defense.[30] The manual opens by defining the general role of ground-based antiaircraft defenses as "one of the principal elements of aerial defence."[31]

The 25-mm through 105-mm guns intended to be employed by the French army covered the theoretical spectrum of low-, mid-, and high-altitude engagement ranges for antiaircraft purposes. Recall that both German and later British and American antiaircraft defensive fires organized into these categories proved remarkably effective when dealing with both German and Japanese aircraft.

The manual also reveals an underlying problem with French antiaircraft defenses—their antiquity. For instance, the 75-mm antiaircraft gun was in production before World War II, and the *Manuel du gradé* included ballistic charts and tables for slightly modernized fuses and explosive shells dating to 1916 and 1917, respectively, with little to no improved ballistic performance, and paling in comparison to the German 88-mm gun or American 90-mm gun.[32] Regardless, it is clear the bulk of these guns were positioned to have no effect on the air battle on the front where they were most needed.

While this mistake was basically inexcusable on the part of the general staff, there was a peculiar French mindset that helps to explain it: the French fear of German strategic bombing. France embraced strategic bombing early in World War I, then walked away from it out of fear of German reprisals French command and government felt would be far worse than anything they could inflict in return, even when it was clear the German army was on the run and the war would soon be over in 1918. During the interwar period, the FAF embraced the strategic airpower concept as did many other air forces. Douhet was extremely well read in French air circles, and books such as *La doctrine de guerre du Général Douhet* were popular and available.[33] Books such as *Défense aérienne du territoire* also illustrate that these lessons were quickly readily absorbed, analyzed, transmitted, and discussed.[34] Among the more general air defense topics included in this treatise, the authors spend some time discussing the most peculiar and particular aspects of Douhet's formula: aerial poison gas attacks upon the population.[35] However, French aviators and their leaders were well aware—or should have been—of the potential morale effects of aerial bombardment. Works released well before Douhet's magnum opus, such as *L'aviation militaire et la guerre aérienne*, discuss bombing and morale effects in 1923 and earlier.[36]

Indeed, this may well explain exactly why the general staff deployed its antiaircraft defenses so heavily in rear areas, the fear of the morale effects specifically upon the French population that German bombing might have caused. "Might" is the operative word, because extremely little of what could be considered German strategic bombing was conducted in 1940. The Luftwaffe instead devoted the bulk of its aircraft to the battle space immediately over the front, exactly where the French antiaircraft defenses were the thinnest.

Ergo, with poor equipment poorly positioned, the possibility that the French army could have been responsible for the bulk of the Luftwaffe's losses is untenable. In the wake of the defeat, French generals even admitted to their troops' relative helplessness in the face of aerial attack.

The RAF

The final possibility is that the RAF did the bulk of the damage to the Luftwaffe during the Battle of France. The RAF sent units to France soon after Britain and France declared war on Germany. There was little doubt, and rightly so, that France would soon become a battlefield. Both France and Britain had reason to question the efficacy of French airpower. Spears noted, "Morale was as patchy as the [French] Air Force was uncoordinated. Colyer had concluded that not only the FAF was hopelessly inadequate, but that the Command was quite uncapable [sic] of making a plan or indeed of using such resources as were available."[37] He was correct; while overall French higher command was ineffective, it was French army command that was incapable and culpable in this instance.

The RAF deployment was a great relief to France. From 1938 forward, even the most staunchly pro-army elements in France began to dread the anticipated potential of German airpower. Arguably, the concessions in Munich were at least partially due to the specter of massive waves of Luftwaffe aircraft pounding the unprepared Allies. Allied estimates of German airpower were grossly inaccurate. However, by the time the air war over France was analyzed by Cot in 1944, the total of German aircraft available at the time was remarkably accurate when compared to German records: Cot submits a total of 5,200 German aircraft engaged, which was within 149 of the official German records quoted above.[38]

The invasion of Poland most certainly was not subject to much misinterpretation. Although the Allies declared war seemingly without fear, the conclusions drawn from the Polish campaign caused even more concern in France. While faith in the Maginot Line and planning remained strong, at least overtly in France, the rapid German victory induced a sort of quiet panic in some circles in France. From October 1939 to May 1939, the French tried to improve and adapt, trying in effect to hedge their bets, maintaining public confidence in the established plan, but quickly trying to remedy deficiencies by creating, for instance, armored divisions. At the same time, French command made the critical and fatal decision among the reform to dismantle air force centralized organization and command.

The RAF was needed in France; it was not a passing concern or whim. The FAF had many inherent problems, but the most immediate was a lack of modern, first-rate, frontline aircraft. While the French aircraft industry was beginning to produce better quality aircraft, and the promise of delivering these in quantity was real given time, the FAF was largely equipped with planes that were simply outclassed by their German adversaries.

The RAF has been celebrated since May 1940. Few, if any, have criticized its performance. In fact, the RAF's poor performances—such as the extremely costly early strike missions against German targets—mostly due to German antiaircraft defenses, have been somewhat glorified. The RAF also covered the evacuation at Dunkirk, with British fighters loitering over the evacuation beaches during the entire cycle of Operation Dynamo. In a strange way, even though France fell and the British Expeditionary Force was evacuated leaving almost all of its equipment behind, the RAF came away from the Battle of France seemingly a victor of sorts both in the press at the time, but in the historiography as well. Therefore, the RAF must have inflicted the bulk of the crushing damage against the Luftwaffe, except the data does not reflect that.

This perception, this victory out of defeat, was not in any way transferred to the French. However, the original tally of victories for both air forces is remarkably close, with Britain claiming 821 German aircraft destroyed and France claiming 853, though the French total includes kills supposedly logged by antiaircraft as well.[39] Combined, these numbers far exceed German records of losses above, especially with other Allied claims included.[40]

Without speculating and somewhat randomly designing formulas to apply to the actual number of Luftwaffe aircraft lost and their presumed source during the Battle of France, if one evenly splits the total tally of Luftwaffe combat losses of 1,129 and removes 10 percent for Dutch and Belgian claims (probably an overestimate) that leaves approximately 1,000 Luftwaffe aircraft to be split between the FAF and the RAF.

Considering the disadvantages of the FAF, this must be assessed as a greater victory overall for the FAF than the RAF, although this has been contested. Higham admitted his initial perception was perhaps that the loss was a sort of moral victory, his perceptions in writing seem to change.[41]

As for the Armée de l'Air, its fate in 1940 was sealed by inappropriate prewar decisions. It lacked doctrine, command, control, and communications, aircrew able to withstand the attrition of war, as well as competitive thoroughly tested machines with suitable, reliable engines and an accountable production and delivery system.[42]

Higham nudges up to many important points, but ultimately falls short in his analysis. Why is this so? What Higham failed to mention was that the FAF did have doctrine, it did have command, and it did have an excellent concept of centralized control along with a functional grasp of wireless battlefield communication. The FAF had modern, centralized organization, clear doctrine on paper that was very similar to most other air forces, and modern communication. However, when it reverted to army control, all of this vanished. These criticisms are not particularly valid when aimed at the air force; they should have been directed at the army instead.

In fact, the disadvantages under which the FAF fought fully justify the contention that the air battle over France in 1940 was indeed at least a moral victory. The FAF's technological disadvantages, organizational disadvantages, and a simple analysis of the available data regarding the sorties, replacements, and ratios, without any creative formulas applied completely change the visage of the battle of the FAF in 1940.

A Little More Data

It has long been accepted that the FAF was simply a no-show. Even though Luftwaffe losses during the air battle of May and June 1940 have been known for decades, they have been ignored, speculatively, because it detracts from the narrative of the Battle of Britain. A significantly weakened Luftwaffe having lost irreplaceable pilots and airframes, battling of all people the French, detracts from the anglophone narrative between the invasion of France and the entry of the United States in December 1941. Considering all of the above, before illuminating all the disadvantages under which the FAF fought, there may be those who still doubt the efforts made by the brave French pilots who fought with almost every disadvantage possible arrayed against them. Therefore, a little more data from the German side is in order.

The following information was derived from German loss reports on a daily basis from May 1940. These numbers reflect only loss or damage reported on an official basis by the Luftwaffe from 10 to 16 May 1940, the first week of action. The losses are divided between damage or loss as a result of engaging British aircraft and French aircraft.[43]

TABLE 7. LUFTWAFFE AIRCRAFT LOSS AND DAMAGE, 10–16 MAY 1940

Date	Lost/Damaged by British Aircraft	Lost/Damaged by French Aircraft
10 May	36	46
11 May	26	23
12 May	28	21
13 May	18	16
14 May	31	24
15 May	17	18
16 May	11	13
Totals	167	161

The following table represents German claims against British and French aircraft over the same period.[44]

TABLE 8. GERMAN CLAIMS AGAINST BRITISH AND FRENCH AIRCRAFT, 10–16 MAY 1940

Date	British Aircraft Claimed	French Aircraft Claimed
10 May	6	6
11 May	12	25
12 May	37	18
13 May	14	29
14 May	50	37
15 May	20	37
16 May	11	13
Totals	150	165

A quick look at the data from the Luftwaffe perspective reveals something shocking: during the first week of the war, when the FAF was nowhere to be seen, the Luftwaffe claims that out of the aircraft lost and damaged in aerial combat, 167 were due to British action, and 161 were due to French action. In that same period, the Luftwaffe claimed 150 British kills and 165 French kills. This equates to the FAF by Luftwaffe admission damaging or destroying 96 percent as many German aircraft as the British. It also means the Luftwaffe claimed 90 percent as many French kills as British.

Why is this significant? Because the Luftwaffe did not lose planes and claim planes from the FAF at an almost identical rate as the RAF if the FAF did not show up to fight. The FAF very much *did* show up to fight, and it did so effectively, arguably more so than the RAF considering the sizable number of disadvantages arrayed against it. Many of the FAF's woes were due to decisions based upon bad judgment or even paranoia on the part of French command, dominated by conservative French army leadership.

One salient conclusion that Higham reached that is even more revealing about the above data is that since the aviators of the FAF were flying fewer sorties on average than their RAF comrades, their sortie-to-kill ratio was much higher.[45] Thus, the above losses to the FAF, confirmed by the Luftwaffe, represent a higher efficiency rating for the average FAF pilot than that of an RAF pilot.

Technology

The FAF was ill equipped to fight the Luftwaffe in 1940. While the French aircraft industry had been nationalized, reorganized, and many of its production facilities modernized and moved to less vulnerable areas (away from Paris and the northeast), it was technically behind the Germans. Although most French aircraft factories were modernized, there were still grievous deficiencies, and outside views were very critical and like those of de Seversky.[46] Many subindustries, such as engines had not been reorganized or modernized. As a result, France began to produce more airframes, but many of these airframes lacked vital components such as engines, gauges, or even armament, in fact an almost myriad number of deficiencies, which Higham points out.[47]

The French models were technologically inferior. The most numerous of the French fighters, the M.S.406, was notoriously problematic.[48] It was slow compared to its primary adversary, the Bf 109, it was under-gunned, and those weapons it did have were often unreliable. To make matters worse, even the newer M.S.406s (those produced after modernization) had severe structural problems and failures that often made the aircraft more dangerous to the French pilot than the German. The newest French fighter—the D.520—was a significant improvement over the M.S.406, but it was still at a disadvantage to the Bf 109 in power and armament. It was also only available in small numbers, with approximately forty being in service on 10 May 1940.

Additionally, the number of types of fighters in French service was a problem. France fielded American types, such as the Curtiss Hawk, in addition to numerous French-made models, some of which were either completely obsolete or rapidly approaching it. Thus, France had to cope with equipping and repairing a large number of types of fighters. Although the Luftwaffe had more than one mark of Bf 109 in service most of the essential parts were interchangeable or easily modifiable. One Bf 109 mechanic could repair another Bf 109 as the knowledge was essentially transferrable. However, on the French side, a Curtiss Hawk mechanic was not necessarily familiar with the M.S.406, the D.501 or D.520, and so on. Obviously, the parts were not interchangeable. When the French Campaign began on 10 May 1940, the Luftwaffe primarily utilized one type of fighter to supply and repair, and it was superior to every French model in service. The Luftwaffe had similar advantages in strike and bomber aircraft.

The Luftwaffe's bomber and attack aircraft also presented an interesting problem for the FAF: they were almost as fast, if not faster, than many French fighters. Whereas the RAF's Hurricanes and Spitfires had little problem catching the German bombers launched against Britain, French aviators operated at a disadvantage versus the German bombers, which were numerous, well-made, and high-performance aircraft for their day in 1940. Of course, the RAF also had the advantages of radar, centralized control, and excellent communications during the Battle of Britain and the Blitz later in the year, something the FAF definitely did not enjoy.

Organization: Command, Control, and Communications

Many air forces gained complete (or at least significant) independence from their respective armies before World War II. Even the U.S. Army Air Corps (which was redesignated the U.S. Army Air Forces in 1941, and the U.S. Air Force in 1947), enjoyed de facto independence well before the war, although it technically remained a part of the army. The FAF gained its independence in 1933. Although it continued to acknowledge its responsibility to the army throughout the 1930s, the FAF—like the RAF and the USAAC—focused upon strategic airpower, a goal for various reasons it never achieved. In 1938, the FAF reverted to army control. Up until that time, its efforts to create a modern air force resulted in a fairly well-organized and considered network designed to defend French airspace.

Unfortunately, the French army possessed neither the knowledge nor the communications network to effectively operate the FAF that it absorbed just prior to May 1940. When the air force was divided up piecemeal, its units went from direct air force control by air force officers, divided roughly into a group/wing/squadron structure, to being commanded by as low as the divisional level by army officers having little idea what to do with them.[49]

The French army was fatally technophobic when it came to the radio.[50] While telephonic communication was viable, it is impossible to communicate with airborne units without using a radio. Although France possessed good radios, the army was reluctant to use them.[51] No single example illustrates this fear or reluctance more than the fact that Gamelin did not have a radio in his headquarters at Vincennes, where he typically ensconced himself in a sort of self-induced reclusiveness. Additionally, even when the army was in dire straits, its radio procedure was so clumsy and weighty that it made their possession almost pointless. When Germany attacked, the FAF was deployed piecemeal and under the command of army officers untrained to command them, handicapped by poor communications.

Contrast this with the Luftwaffe, which although committed thoroughly to operational airpower during the French Campaign, cooperated with the Heer rather than being controlled by it. The Luftwaffe was controlled by air force officers who understood airpower, as well as being organized by the same. The Luftwaffe not only communicated with its units via radio, but it also employed this technology when communicating with the Heer in both planning and while on active operations. "Co-operation with the Luftwaffe was arranged. I was to be in touch with the leader of the close support planes, that exceptionally brave man, General von Sutterheim, and simultaneously with the Fliegerkorps [roughly: air group] commanded by General Lörzer. In order to establish a sound basis for co-operation, as quickly as possible, I had invited the airmen to my planning exercises, and I also took part in an air exercise that General Lörzer organized."[52]

The Luftwaffe was not strictly an operational army-focused air force. It was multifaceted, and if one looks at the doctrinal structure of the FAF before it fell under army control, the two foes resemble each other in thought, if not in action.

When the true air battle over France began on 10 May 1940, the Luftwaffe's command, control, and communications positioned it well against the FAF. Poor communications, bad control, and frankly ignorant command in the guise of the army, conspired to relegating the FAF to a reactive posture. Even when opportunities arose to take the initiative, the army (or national command) denied the air force excellent opportunities that could have fundamentally altered the course of the French Campaign. "General Réquin, who nevertheless upheld the excellence of the French doctrines of war, was obliged to admit (March 19) the imperfection of the liaison between the land and air."[53]

While the FAF's problems ran much deeper than the merely technological or organizational, the pilots, service personnel, aircraft, and command met head to head with their German adversaries. Ultimately, France lost this battle. The recriminations against the FAF began immediately and have never been satisfactorily explained. It has been accepted "fact" until now that the FAF was a virtual nonentity in 1940, and few have had any idea of the outrageous disadvantages under which French aviators fought against the Wehrmacht as a whole, and the Luftwaffe in particular.

In spite of these disadvantages, the data demonstrates that not only did the FAF fight exceptionally hard against the Luftwaffe with one hand proverbially tied behind its back, but it also managed to cause an exceptional amount of damage in the process. The Luftwaffe did not walk over Britain or Russia although both suffered under its attacks. The record must now indicate, perhaps now a bit more clearly, that not only did the Luftwaffe not walk over France or the FAF, it actually never fully recovered from the battle to regain its dominance as demonstrated against Poland, Denmark, Norway, and Holland.

The Insidious Political Wrinkle

If it can be accepted that the FAF fighting in retrograde motion with its supplies, airfields, and pilots constantly dwindling in a manner unlike any other major opponent of the Wehrmacht (excepting the Red Air Force), there are a few questions that still need to be answered. Primary among these is why the FAF, remarkably effective as it was, suffered from what Higham referred to as a lack of "doctrine . . . command, control and communications"?[54] Further, why was the FAF chained to the French army's limitations, and why—if Higham and other authors are correct—did the FAF have no coherent doctrine?

The answer is grounded in the French army, French command, and conservative French politics. In fact, the FAF *did* have a coherent doctrine. It had a well-organized prewar system to defend the likely areas of incursion by the Wehrmacht. Although its bombing-focused doctrine was out of line with French national strategic outlook and planning, it developed along very similar lines as RAF and USAAC doctrine.

The FAF was stripped of its doctrine when it reverted to army control in 1938 after five years of independent development. The ultimate reason for the devolution of French air theory was political rather than military, and it was illuminated during the war by the man who was arguably both father and undertaker of the FAF, Pierre Cot.

Cot was a highly influential figure on the French Left, and the driving force behind both the establishment of an independent air force and nationalizing the French aircraft industry. Cot also viewed airpower as a diplomatic tool.[55] Cot desired a close alliance with the Soviet Union; he intended to use French strategic airpower as an effective tool to isolate Germany with the Soviet Union's cooperation.[56] In a starkly divided France, whose sociopolitical rivalries, often violent, go back to 1870 if not 1789, this leftward, communist alignment was anathema to the French Right and French command that it dominated.

Whether or not the French Right had any concrete evidence against Cot or his circle before World War II is difficult to say. One thing is certain: Cot did eventually become a spy for the Soviets during the war, verifying the worst of the French Right's fears.[57] In Cot's own words: "It is not France, nor Germany, but the whole of Europe which must be organized and purged of fascism."[58] Clearly, Cot viewed the struggle as that essentially between communism and fascism, and his verbiage and attitude toward the French Conservative Right left little room for interpreting exactly how he viewed them.

This internal struggle for the soul of the FAF did not escape outside observers. The American air attaché in Paris, Lieutenant Colonel Ralph C. Smith, made a crystal clear and unambiguous statement regarding his observations in an amended report dated April 1939: "The division of France into two political groups has impacted the morale of the air army. Communist propaganda is more acute, and a certain discontent has been noted among the most patriotic officers. Promotions are going to the adherents of the Popular Front."[59]

French command reverting the air force to army control made no military sense; the army had no idea how to use the air force, and the campaign in 1940 proved that. What the army feared and what the French Right feared was the French Left. This is why French command dismantled the Infanterie de l'air.[60] This is why communists were dismissed wholesale (if not imprisoned) in 1939 and 1940; the Right was more afraid of communists inside France than Nazis in Germany.[61] This is why French command turned a well-organized air force with a modern, if somewhat inappropriate, doctrine over to the army that had no idea how to use it. This is why the FAF did not perform even better than its undeniably excellent results achieved under desperate circumstances.

It would not be fair to state that the FAF did not have good doctrine, organization, or communication—it did have them. Unfortunately for France, it was stripped of them before they could be put to good use. The brave and effective French airmen made an excellent accounting of themselves anyway. Their "lost cause" was factual, not a postwar fantasy designed to exculpate themselves.

Conclusions

It is difficult to try to develop formulas with scant, incomplete, and often inaccurate information, and expect the results to be conclusive. One of the major problems in assessing the overall effects of the air battle over France, and how history should judge the performance of the French airmen in that epic fight, is that disjointed information from sources with an obvious bias (even if some of their observations are perfectly accurate) tends to lead to conclusions that are not as finite as historians would like. As such, there are times where the information has to be digested and condensed, and conclusions drawn that reflect the knowable from the unknowable information.

The simple fact is that the FAF and its allies fought the Luftwaffe at a distinct disadvantage. It would be more accurate to say that they fought the Wehrmacht—which acted as a more cohesive whole—at a distinct disadvantage. The FAF and the RAF fought largely separate battles, both with tragic results, but not without taking a tremendous toll on the Luftwaffe in the process.

The FAF flew fewer sorties—that fact is undeniable. Although no accurate tally has been arrived at, the obvious reactionary stance of the FAF, its problem acquiring missions from an army that had no idea what to do with it, and the rapid rate at which it had to retreat to new bases due to loss of territory leaves little room for speculation on this point. Poor organization due to army negligence exacerbated this problem. As Higham concluded, "It has been said that the air Battle of France was more intense than the Battle of Britain . . . but that was because the command and logistics structure collapsed and *escadrilles* were constantly on the move, ill-housed and ill-fed, overworked, and under the constant strain of uncertainty. Life was chaotic."[62]

The FAF seems to have made good on most of its losses, at least during May, which enabled it to keep fighting.[63] Further, many French pilots were recoverable when lost over their own territory. In addition, most of the French pilots were far more experienced than their British or German adversaries.⁶⁴

German bombers were perceived as a greater threat, and the response to the bombers and dive bombers was greater than the response to German fighters. Losses in both categories were noticeably high, based on Luftwaffe records.⁶⁵ Bombers had more aircrew per plane, meaning personnel losses were unavoidably higher. In addition, the Luftwaffe put its best pilots in bombers, not fighters, a by-product of its early commitment to strategic bombing.⁶⁶ The result was that the Luftwaffe lost a higher percentage of its best pilots. Records indicate there was a distinct lack of experience among many Luftwaffe pilots, but especially fighter pilots, even at this early stage of the war.

In essence, better French pilots in inferior aircraft, who were poorly coordinated due to a virtual total lack of knowledge from their army commanders, operating with dreadfully poor communication, fighting in a reactive posture against a well-coordinated Wehrmacht caused irreplaceable losses, a problem that was never satisfactorily remedied. If this does not constitute a moral victory, and in some ways a victory for the Allies in the long game that went on until 1945, it is difficult to imagine what a true moral victory might actually look like.

While a number of authors from Paul Martin to Robin Higham have done an excellent job of rehabilitating the reputation of individual French airmen, their revelatory work has fallen on deaf ears. This aerial campaign has been slighted from the German side as well, perhaps understandably due to its short duration in comparison with the Wehrmacht's other campaigns. The examination of the air war in 1940, involving the minor allied powers, such as Denmark and Holland, have been even more neglected. The deep causes of the French aerial defeat have been almost ignored by military historians from the sociopolitical/military point of view. It is time not only to finally, loudly, and permanently set the record straight that the FAF performed well—especially considering its circumstances—but to examine the deep causes of the FAF's defeat as a social, political, and military defeat caused by fundamental divisions in French politics and society, and a sense of paranoia that ultimately resulted in France's defeat and occupation.

Several questions remain. One of which is, Did France and the FAF misread the contemporary lessons of modern aerial warfare? Were they simply drawing perennially from 1918? Did the French, and specifically the FAF, spend any time staying abreast of current developments? The answer to this question lies in examining the French analysis of the Spanish Civil War, an event close to home not only militarily, but politically for the French.

CONCLUSION

HISTORIANS, generals, coaches, and sports fans all want simple answers for defeat. Surely, there must be one reason that explains any loss. It is certainly convenient, and perhaps even desirable to do so. However, these answers are almost universally disingenuous if not outright dishonest. Complex systems interact and compete across a broad matrix of categories and levels. The FAF lost in 1940 because it was simply outmatched in most categories and at almost every level. However, it was not nonexistent as it often seems to be described or at least alluded to being, and the Luftwaffe's significant losses prove that even fighting at a severe disadvantage the FAF's pilots were brave, resolute, skilled, and often more than a match for their Luftwaffe opponents who fought with almost every advantage.

On a technical level, the FAF's aircraft were behind those of the Luftwaffe by at least three to six years, realistically more when it comes to bombers. Although planes like the D.520 were in service, they were not available in great enough numbers, and they were still inferior to the Bf 109, which although of the same general vintage as the D.520 and even the M.S.406, had been consistently improved and upgraded since its inception. Many of the improvements to the Bf 109 were the result of the Luftwaffe's experiences in the Spanish Civil War. The early Bf 109s were more lightly armed and had less powerful engines and somewhat less stout airframes. Although the M.S.406 and other French fighters could have been improved, and to some extent they were, when manufacturing processes were modernized during the partial nationalization of the French aircraft industry, there is evidence that some felt that too much improvement would lead to an arms race with Germany. The irony is that the arms race was underway, and Germany was already ahead, and there was no point at which Germany de-escalated. The French were on the verge of releasing a significant number of newer aircraft that they could have produced in solid numbers when the war began. Unfortunately, too few made it off the production lines. French airmen fought at a distinct disadvantage when it came to aircraft quality vis-à-vis their German opponents.

Somewhat inferior aircraft was clearly not the decisive factor, regardless of how popular technology and performance are topically. Technical specifications are easy to read, digest, and compare, and they are perennially debated in popular histories, periodicals, and documentaries. Luftwaffe loss reports indicate many technically superior German aircraft were lost to inferior French-flown aircraft. Although machine performance weighed against French pilots, they still took a serious toll. This was not the only time this theme played out during World War II, or even during the French Campaign: on the ground, inferior German and Czech tanks often overwhelmed better French tanks for the same reason, crew quality and training. While it made the FAF pilots' jobs even more difficult, it certainly did not stop them from literally decimating the Luftwaffe. Excepting multigenerational or quantum technology gaps this factor rarely plays the most significant role in defeat. It is however useful if one wishes to appeal to "gear junkies" who need that next book on any given tank or plane. It is also useful inside the Beltway to sell the next newest and best thing in planes, ships, and tanks. *Wunderwaffen* (wonder weapons) are extremely popular, even though the Panzer VI and the Me 262 did not win the war for Germany, nor did superior Western technology outlast the iron will of various guerrilla groups over the decades.

Technology is important, however, and one piece of technology was significant in explaining French defeat in the air and on the ground: the radio. The lack of effective radio communication was one of the pillars of French defeat. While the FAF used the radio as much as any other air force, the army had an almost irrational technophobia that would have hampered cooperation with the FAF had that branch had remained independent, and it virtually stymied the FAF's efforts once the air force reverted to army control. Although telephone lines and couriers might work on the land (*might*: they were quite easy to disrupt or destroy), they certainly did not work with air-to-ground communications. The record clearly illustrates French army–air force cooperation was incredibly poor, and although the dubious Riom Trials shamed and dishonored the French army on more than one level, perhaps none was more gross than laying its salient failures at the feet of the FAF. Army commanders could not or would not use the radio.[1] Further, the almost complete lack of training and modern doctrine in the French army regarding airpower, air defense, and air–ground cooperation meant that the army was largely incapable of defending itself against the Luftwaffe and totally incapable of meaningfully utilizing the FAF assets distributed piecemeal often at the divisional level to officers who through no fault of their own had any clue how to effectively utilize airpower, and for the most part were incapacitated in communicating with air assets.

Ground-based air defense discussions are largely neglected in the historiography of World War II, but the impact of the same coordinated with effective airpower should not be underrated and was also key to explaining the failure of the FAF. This is a multifaceted discussion worthy of a volume of its own. Ground-based air defenses contribute directly to the outcome of battles for air superiority by degrading the capacity of enemy airpower through increased diversion of resources and through attrition. The Wehrmacht effectively demonstrated this concept during the French Campaign. German flak proved extremely effective against concentrated, but often ill-considered and planned aerial attacks.

French troops had few modern antiaircraft weapons, and very little training against aerial attack. Even though the physical results of German aerial attack were frequently overrated, the intent of the attacks, to dislodge

French defenders, was successful.[2] The army was as much, if not fully, to blame for its troops' poor performance against German aerial attack as decades of neglected training and equipment updates took a serious toll on unprepared troops who felt themselves at the mercy of the Luftwaffe. Further, with the FAF effectively under army control, the army was doubly to blame for the punishment its troops endured from the air. The army did try to play catch-up with equipment and training in the last weeks before the war began, but it was too little too late, just like the tank formations that only began to take shape and discover problems Germany had wrestled with (and solved, to some extent) in the years before the war.

The Spanish Civil War provided lessons that were largely ignored by France, and utilized by Germany, and the potential efficacy of battlefield air attack was among them. However, there were multiple others, and perhaps the most interesting part is that France had much indirect access to almost the same lessons as Germany. While France was intent on distancing itself from the war out of fear of the war spreading to a very divided France, the literature available in France provided accurate assessments from both French and foreign observers in substantial quantities. This is also true of the German experience, but the direct experience and lessons from the Condor Legion were crucially important to the early successes of the *Bewegungskrieg*. Not only were the *Flivos* added as a permanent part of force structure, making air–ground cooperation timely and possible, but everything from effective fighter versus fighter to fighter versus bomber tactics were evaluated by Germany and integrated into training and doctrine before World War II, and continually enhanced because of combat performance.[3] The Bf 109 received significant upgrades as a result of combat in Spain, even though it was already superior to virtually everything in the air in the late 1930s. This pattern of updates, although creating a morass of variants at times later in the war, made the Bf 109 in particular viable until 1945.

The experience in Spain not only developed tactics and improved machine performance, it developed leaders for Germany. Many of the famous aces and generals from Luftwaffe cut their eye teeth in modern aerial warfare in Spain and were then able to put these lessons to good use in World War II. Contrast this with the FAF, that effectively lost its independence in 1938, less than five years after its separation, while the Luftwaffe was still learning and evolving in Spain. The information was available in France until the military press was effectively shut down by Gamelin in a fit of stupidity and hubris, but how was the FAF to even consider implementing the lessons from Spain when it was broken into penny packets and returned to army control? While the FAF was far from perfect, it was generally a progressive force, but not all its ideas were sound or indeed well-suited for French defense requirements.

Doctrine was one of the two most significant factors in the FAF's defeat, and in France's defeat in 1940. The tragedy is that the FAF had basically sound air doctrine on some levels but was not allowed to employ it. Prior to the dissolution of the FAF, it had a sound squadron to group organization that mirrored most other air forces' and was designed and employed to cover the main threat from Germany in eastern and northeastern France. It was designed to be controlled by a series of air force commanders and centralized. Although it was not put into practice, it would have put the Luftwaffe up against a much more centralized command and control system. Considering the impressive losses the FAF inflicted upon the Luftwaffe when operating with little meaningful doctrine and direction, one is left to wonder what the results may have been had the FAF been able to fight the battle it had planned throughout the 1930s.

However, FAF doctrine was not perfect and some of the ideas pursued in the 1930s made sense for France, and others did not. Strategic airpower, more specifically strategic bombing as envisioned in the interwar period, did not make sense, and the FAF spent too much time pursuing it. While strategic bombing was in vogue and "Douhetian" ideas were used as a cornerstone to establish the need for independent air forces internationally, based on consistent reluctance to bomb Germany from World War I forward, the FAF should have known that creating a strategic bomber force whose target was strategic, German assets in Germany's interior was a waste of time. There was simply no way the government or higher command was going to allow strategic bombing on the scale envisioned against Germany. Whether French morale was ever as fragile as imagined, French political divisions were exceptionally deep, and the FAF's independence, its pursuit of perceived dangerous ideas, and its erstwhile mentor, Pierre Cot, were all inextricably commingled. It is not difficult to imagine ultraconservative army officers questioning whether the FAF wanted to provoke Germany into bombing France to create a morale crisis whereby a civil war could be ignited that the Left thought it could win.

While Germany was deeply divided in the 1920s and early 1930s, Hitler's rapid rise to power and his draconian policies quickly quashed any dissent. The military, including the Luftwaffe (which is sometimes considered the most pro-Nazi of the German services outside the Waffen SS), had no such sociopolitical restraints or quibbles to restrain it, and it pursued doctrine that would provide victory at an operation level in conjunction with the Heer as part of a more unified strategic outlook that paid solid dividends at least through June 1940.

While the Luftwaffe became increasingly strained as it was stretched beyond its limits, its doctrine was sound and effective in 1940. Luftwaffe doctrine focusing on an operational level air war that was closely coordinated with offensive operations on the ground, but did not neglect the necessity of air supremacy, especially over vital limited spaces of critical need, worked well until at least mid-1943. The French Campaign is probably the best example of this. Although the Luftwaffe was not designed to be a primarily strategic air force, it had no internal restraints inhibiting its ability to conduct such operations as later campaigns would demonstrate.

The depth of division between the Right and the Left in France is difficult to fathom, even for societies such as the United States and Britain that imagine their political situations at any one point cannot possibly get any worse. Cot was without a doubt incredibly controversial, and the Right's fear of him was well founded (though it is unclear when Cot actually began spying for the Soviet Union). The internal divisions, dating at least as far back as the Dreyfus affair (a debilitating event for the army) if not the Paris Commune—or perhaps even the French Revolution—permeated the military establishment as well. Whether it was the dismembering of the paratroops (a promising unit), or the mole hunt for agents in the intelligence corps at the lowest level, these debilitating actions had a clear effect on the morale and cohesiveness of the FAF and the military.

While this distrust applied to the FAF as a whole, the intelligence corps, perhaps the most promising organization in the military, was a perfect example of not only political but organizational dysfunction. The Deuxième Bureau was, as primary source evidence proves, remarkably accurate in its assessments and information regarding the Luftwaffe and the Wehrmacht. Not only did the French understand Luftwaffe and Wehrmacht equipment and doctrine, but it also had a most clear picture of Luftwaffe bases and organization. They also had actionable intelligence about critical infrastructure targets, many of which were within range of their limited bomber force (had it been allowed to bomb anything when it might have been effective in the opening two to three days of the campaign). If any branch or service of the French military establishment was reasonably guilt-free in June 1940, it was intelligence. Unfortunately, all the clarity in the world on German preparations and intentions was not enough to avoid defeat.

Intelligence was not only ignored, but the information it provided, especially after Poland, was feared. It provided excellent assessments of events of the Spanish Civil War as did the open press. Many articles were published in French professional journals that were also prophetic and accurate such as the limited effectiveness of bombing on morale, and the vulnerability of the bomber. The stark warnings regarding the effectiveness of battlefield air attack on unprepared troops were also ignored, and this bad bet cost France dearly, especially at Sedan. Any idea that ran afoul of accepted doctrine was eventually completely shut down because leadership was afraid it would sow too much discord; professional journals were silenced because the contents frequently disagreed with accepted policy. Fear made decision-making progressively worse as 1940 approached.

The irony is that Germany's military intelligence was not taken that seriously either. Intelligence postings were mostly temporary assignments, and there were very few committed professionals. Although Germany's intelligence regarding France was generally accurate, many of its officers felt that intelligence was poor and lacking depth when it came to the overall picture of France and its capabilities and defenses in 1940. The Wehrmacht found few surprises in France pertaining directly to the military.[4] Although intelligence was neglected in Germany, it was still effective enough under the circumstances.

The Wehrmacht was well aware of French methods and also knew of the FAF's problems; the reorganization of the French aircraft industry was no secret, neither was French procurement of American aircraft. However, German leadership still had a healthy respect for the army that defeated them in 1918 and understood that any action in France could have ended in disaster. In the end, the experiences during World War I also led to the French army abhorring the radio and relying on telephone lines and couriers. The fact that Gamelin did not have a radio at Vincennes is one of the most starkly baffling facets of the campaign. One of the more currently unanswerable questions remains: after the events of World War I, why did French leaders imagine that the Germans would show any restraint regardless of French actions?

Leadership, both military and political, was the salient factor in the failure of the FAF in 1940. While one could arguably blame or credit leadership in most instances for critical failures or successes, military organizations often find a way to muddle through. In France's case, there was no time to do so; the pace of war surpassed the time France had to exchange. French leadership was plagued with fears, both imaginary and real, and a sense of impending doom seemingly combined with blind confidence and paranoia pervaded.

Part of the problem was simple pigheadedness and ignorance. In a real sense, doctrine was dogma in France, and this made deviation from doctrine heresy. This was combined with a unique and seemingly perpetual political instability that never allowed new courses to be set with any firmness; France was the epitome of the "weak democracy." Fear combined with mental rigidity created a leadership situation that resembled more ancient ideas of absolutism (perhaps appropriate for the army's political leanings); if things were going well or tolerably, the monarch (Gamelin) loosened the leash and allowed some liberties, but as soon as genuine pressure for reform presented itself, the velvet glove came off the iron fist. By the time the need for reform was apparent, it was simply too late—the guillotine's blade was falling.

Pierre Cot and the Left in its various guises such as the Front Populaire deserve an equal share of the blame. While independent air forces were generally logical, Cot's name was tied to the entire enterprise from beginning to end whether or not he was air minister, and his bloodless purges and overt sympathies (not to mention the covert spying) for the Soviet Union made the Right even more paranoid, and perhaps justifiably so. The fact that the Right could not separate good ideas from their "bad" sources was an intellectual failing on their part, however. That there was never any meaningful liaison between the army and the air force, and the military education system neglected to train its army officers in the role of airpower in modern warfare, in light of the events such as the Spanish Civil War, further emphasize the rigidity in the leadership structure.

Thus, the FAF was hamstrung with monolithic and toxic leadership. In spite of the excellent intelligence, the turnaround in the aircraft industry, the competent pilots, modern organizational ideas that were doctrinally sound, and accurate, prescient analysis of current affairs in airpower, it could not succeed. Ultimately, it was dismantled, restrained, and misguided.

In a strange way, France fought 1940 from 1918 backward, and Germany picked up in 1918 and went forward. There was no revolution at all in military affairs between 1918 and 1940, and if one is to be completely objective, there was little real evolution. That is the first part of explaining what the Luftwaffe did right that helped it triumph over the FAF. However, many of the Luftwaffe's failings later in the war ironically mirrored or paralleled those of the FAF in 1940.

On a final note, the reputation of the French airmen who flew against Germany in 1940 deserve a complete reevaluation and frankly an apology. These men flew at almost every disadvantage and still pummeled the Luftwaffe. Whether it is the anglophone historiography—obsessed with its own eventual victories in the Battle of Britain and from late 1942 onward—postwar NATO politics, or the often-concealed realization that a British or American military in the same situation as France's in 1940 would have suffered the same defeat, the reputation of the French airmen deserves serious review. Perhaps more than any other French troops during World War II, they are deserving of *la gloire*.

Notes

INTRODUCTION
1. Geoffrey P. Megargee. *War of Annihilation: Combat and Genocide on the Eastern Front, 1941.* New York: Rowman & Littlefield, 2006.
2. David M. Glantz. *The Gates of Stalingrad: Soviet-German Combat Operations April to August 1942.* Lawrence: University Press of Kansas, 2009.

CHAPTER 1. COMBAT AIRCRAFT
1. Barry R. Posen. *The Sources of Military Doctrine: France, Britain, and Germany between the World Wars.* Ithaca: Cornell University Press, 1984: 109.
2. Posen, *Sources of Military Doctrine*, 122.
3. Richard P. Hallion. *Strike from the Sky: The History of Battlefield Air Attack, 1910–1945.* Washington, DC: Smithsonian, 1989: 16.
4. Hallion, *Strike from the Sky*, 16.
5. Général Charles Christienne and Général Pierre Lissarrague, *Histoire de l'aviation militaire: L'Armée de l'Air 1928–1981.* Paris: Charles-Lavauzelle, 1981: 125.
6. Christienne and Lissarrague, *Histoire de l'aviation*, 125.
7. James S. Corum. *The Luftwaffe: Creating the Operational Air War, 1918–1940.* Lawrence: University Press of Kansas, 1997: 275.
8. Williamson Murray. *The Luftwaffe: Strategy for Defeat 1933–1945.* Maxwell Air Force Base, Montgomery, AL: Air University Press, 1983: 32.
9. Dominique Breffort and Andre Jouineau. *French Aircraft from 1939 to 1942: Fighters, Bombers, Reconnaissance and Observation Types.* Vol. 2, *From Dewoitine to Potez.* Paris: Histoire & Collections, 2005: 49–50.
10. Breffort and Jouineau, *French Aircraft*, Vol. 2, 48.
11. Breffort and Jouineau, *French Aircraft*, Vol. 2, 48.
12. Breffort and Jouineau, *French Aircraft*, Vol. 2, 49.
13. Gaston Botquin. "The Morane Saulnier 406." *Profile Publications Number 147*: 7.
14. Botquin, "Morane Saulnier," 8.
15. Breffort and Jouineau, *French Aircraft*, Vol. 2, 48.
16. Breffort and Jouineau, *French Aircraft*, Vol. 2, 48.

17. Ministère de l'Air. "Équipement et armement de l'avion Morane type 406, moteur Hispano-Suiza 12 y-31 1860 cv." 3 October 1938: 12.
18. Camille Rougeron. "Chasse française et chasse allemande." *L'Illustration* no. 5053, 6 January 1940: 11–14.
19. Breffort and Jouineau, *French Aircraft*, Vol. 2, 67.
20. Breffort and Jouineau, *French Aircraft*, Vol. 2, 67.
21. Breffort and Jouineau, *French Aircraft*, Vol. 2, 67.
22. Breffort and Jouineau, *French Aircraft*, Vol. 2, 67.
23. John F. Brindley. *French Fighters of World War II*. Vol. 1. Windsor: Hylton Lacy, 1971: 14.
24. Brindley, *French Fighters*, 14.
25. Brindley, *French Fighters*, 16.
26. Brindley, *French Fighters*, 17.
27. Ministère de l'Air. *Extrait du tableau de composition du l'avion Bloch 151*, 1939: 1–169.
28. Ministère de l'Air. *Extrait du tableau*, 1–169.
29. Ministère de l'Air. *Extrait du tableau*, 1–169.
30. Dominique Breffort and Andre Jouineau. *French Aircraft From 1939 to 1942: Fighters, Bombers, Reconaissance and Observation Types*. Vol. 1, *From Amiot to Curtiss*. Paris: Histoire & Collections, 2004: 36.
31. Breffort and Jouineau, *French Aircraft*, Vol. 1, 36.
32. Breffort and Jouineau, *French Aircraft*, Vol. 1, 36.
33. Ministère de l'Air. *Notice technique de la mitrailleuse M.A.C. modèle 1934, type aile; type touselle*, 1936: 11.
34. Ministère de l'Air. *M.A.C. modèle 1934*, 12.
35. Ministère de l'Air. *M.A.C. modèle 1934*, 25.
36. Ministère de l'Air. *M.A.C. modèle 1934*, 18.
37. Ministère de l'Air. *M.A.C. modèle 1934*, 40–44.
38. Major Alexander de Seversky. *Victory Through Air Power*. New York: Simon & Schuster, 1942: 190–91.
39. de Seversky, *Victory Through Air Power*, 68–69.
40. de Seversky, *Victory Through Air Power*, 69.
41. Pierre Cot. "Technical Mobilization: Hearings before a Subcommittee of the Committee of Military Affairs of the United States Senate." 77th Congress, 1st sess. on S. 2721: A Bill to Establish an Office of Technical Mobilization, and for Other Purposes. December 12, 14, 17, 18, and 19, 1942. Vol. 3. Washington, DC, 1943: 605–606.
42. Maxwell Air Force Base. Air Force Historical Research Agency. Microfilm Reel A2873. Lieutenant Colonel Ralph C. Smith, "French Combat Estimate 1937–1940": 57.
43. Smith, "French Combat Estimate," 57.
44. Smith, "French Combat Estimate," 57.

45. Bill Gunston, ed. *Jane's Fighting Aircraft of World War II*. New York: Crescent Books, 1994: 176.
46. Anis El Bied and Andre Jouineau. *The Messerschmitt Me 109*. Vol. 1, *From 1936 to 1942*. Paris: Histoire & Collections, 2001: 36
47. El Bied and Jouineau, *Messerschmitt Me 109*, 36.
48. El Bied and Jouineau, *Messerschmitt Me 109*, 36.
49. Anthony Pritchard. *Messerschmitt*. New York: G. P. Putnam's Sons, 1975: 50.
50. Pritchard, *Messerschmitt*, 50.
51. El Bied and Jouineau, *Messerschmitt Me 109*, 45.
52. El Bied and Jouineau, *Messerschmitt Me 109*, 45.
53. Pritchard, *Messerschmitt*, 181.
54. Pritchard, *Messerschmitt*, 181.
55. Gunston, ed., *Jane's Fighting Aircraft*, 128.
56. Gunston, ed., *Jane's Fighting Aircraft*, 129.
57. Gunston, ed., *Jane's Fighting Aircraft*, 128.
58. Robert Jackson. *Spitfire: Life of the Legend*. New York: Metro Books, 2010: 42.
59. Jackson, *Spitfire*, 21. Author's emphasis.
60. Gunston, ed., *Jane's Fighting Aircraft*, 139.
61. Gunston, ed., *Jane's Fighting Aircraft*, 141.
62. G2 Report. 14 February 1936. "France: Bombardment in the Organization of the Air Army." Air Force Historical Research Association, 248.501–56: 1.
63. E. Severac. *Dans le ciel de France*. Paris: Cieux Collection, 1947: 3, 8–11.
64. Christienne and Lissarrague, *Histoire de l'aviation*, 125.
65. Christienne and Lissarrague, *Histoire de l'aviation*, 125.
66. Williamson Murray, *Strategy for Defeat*, 32.
67. Breffort and Jouineau, *French Aircraft*, Vol. 1, 58.
68. Breffort and Jouineau, *French Aircraft*, Vol. 1, 59.
69. Breffort and Jouineau, *French Aircraft*, Vol. 1, 59.
70. Breffort and Jouineau, *French Aircraft*, Vol. 1, 60.
71. Breffort and Jouineau, *French Aircraft*, Vol. 2, 39.
72. Breffort and Jouineau, *French Aircraft*, Vol. 2, 40.
73. Breffort and Jouineau, *French Aircraft*, Vol. 2, 41.
74. Breffort and Jouineau, *French Aircraft*, Vol. 2, 41.
75. Breffort and Jouineau, *French Aircraft*, Vol. 2, 41.
76. Breffort and Jouineau, *French Aircraft*, Vol. 2, 20.
77. Breffort and Jouineau, *French Aircraft*, Vol. 2, 21.
78. Breffort and Jouineau, *French Aircraft*, Vol. 2, 21.
79. Breffort and Jouineau, *French Aircraft*, Vol. 1, 46.
80. Breffort and Jouineau, *French Aircraft*, Vol. 1, 46–47.
81. Breffort and Jouineau, *French Aircraft*, Vol. 1, 47.
82. Breffort and Jouineau, *French Aircraft*, Vol. 1, 175.
83. Breffort and Jouineau, *French Aircraft*, Vol. 1, 18.

84. Breffort and Jouineau, *French Aircraft*, Vol. 1, 18.
85. Breffort and Jouineau, *French Aircraft*, Vol. 1, 19.
86. Breffort and Jouineau, *French Aircraft*, Vol. 2, 32.
87. Ministère de l'Air, *Notice technique des bombes d'aviation*, 1936: 44.
88. Ministère de l'Air, *Bombes d'aviation*, 45–47.
89. Ministère de l'Air, *Notice technique sur les fusées d'aviation*. 1936: 12.
90. Murray, *Strategy for Defeat*, 15.
91. James S. Corum. *The Luftwaffe: Creating the Operational Air War, 1918–1940*. Lawrence: University Press of Kansas, 1997: 166.
92. Corum, *Luftwaffe*, 166.
93. Corum, *Luftwaffe*, 187.
94. Eddie J. Creek. *Junkers Ju 87: From Dive Bomber to Tank-Buster, 1935–1945*. Surrey: Ian Allen, 2012: 11.
95. Creek, *Junkers Ju 87*, 332.
96. Richard P. Hallion. *Strike from the Sky: A History of Battlefield Air Attack, 1911–1945*. Washington, DC: Smithsonian, 1989: 142–43.
97. Anthony G. Williams and Emmanuel Gustin. *Flying Guns of World War II: Development of Aircraft Guns, Ammunition and Installations 1933–45*. Shrewsbury: Airlife Publishing, 2003: 65.
98. Williams and Gustin, *Flying Guns*, 312.
99. Williams and Gustin, *Flying Guns*, 313.
100. Botquin, "Morane Saulnier 406," 7.
101. Williams and Gustin, *Flying Guns*, 88.
102. Williams and Gustin, *Flying Guns*, 91.
103. Patrick Facon. *Histoire de l'Armée de l'Air*. Paris: La Documentation Française, 2009: 161.
104. Anthony Christopher Cain. *The Forgotten Air Force: French Air Doctrine in the 1930s*. Washington, DC: Smithsonian Press, 1992: xiii.
105. Partick Facon. *Le bombardement stratégique*. Monaco: Editions du Rocher, 1995: 52.
106. G2 Report, February 14, 1936. "France: Bombardment in the Organization of the Air Army." Air Force Historical Research Association, 248.501–56: 3.
107. Military Attaché Report France (Aviation). "General Disposition of French Air Army in May, 1940; Summary of Activity Prior to Armistice; Conclusions." Maxwell Air Force Base, Montgomery, AL: Air Force Historical Research Association, 170.2278–28.

CHAPTER 2. THE FRENCH AND GERMAN AIRCRAFT INDUSTRIES

1. Robin Higham. *Unflinching Zeal: The Air Battles Over France and Britain, May–October 1940*. Annapolis: Naval Institute Press, 2012: 198.
2. Patrick Facon. *Histoire de l'Armée de l'Air*. Paris: La Documentation Française, 2009: 161–69.

3. Herrick Chapman. *State Capitalism and Working Class Radicalism in the French Aircraft Industry*. Berkeley: University of California Press, 1991: 108–10.
4. Anthony Christopher Cain. "L'Armée de l'Air, 1933–1940: Drifting toward Defeat." In *Why Air Forces Fail: The Anatomy of Defeat*. Robin Higham and Stephen J. Harris, eds. Lexington: University Press of Kentucky, 2006: 57.
5. Chapman, *State Capitalism*, 226.
6. Alistair Horne. *The Fall of Paris: The Siege and the Commune 1870–71*. London: Penguin, 1990: 426.
7. Andre Van Haute. *Pictorial History of the FAF: Volume I 1909–1940*. London: Ian Allan, 1974: 26.
8. Dr. James J. Davilla and Arthur M. Soltan. *French Aircraft of the First World War*. Stratford: Flying Machines Press, 1997: 1–20.
9. Davilla and Soltan, *French Aircraft*, 1–20.
10. Davilla and Soltan, *French Aircraft*, 1–20.
11. James S. Corum and Richard R. Muller. *The Luftwaffe's Way of War: German Air Force Doctrine 1911–1945*. Baltimore: Nautical and Aviation Publishing, 1998: 6–7.
12. Chapman, *State Capitalism*, 143.
13. Eugenia C. Kiesling. *Arming Against Hitler: France and the Limits of Military Planning*. Lawrence: University Press of Kansas, 1996: 130–35.
14. Thierry Vivier. *La politique aéronautique militaire de la France: Janvier 1933–septembre 1939*. Paris: L'Harmattan, 1997: 88–90.
15. Cain, "L'Armée de l'Air 1933–1940," 57.
16. Gaston Botquin. "The Moraine Saulnier 406." *Profile Publications No. 147, 1966*: No. 7.
17. Botquin, "Moraine Saulnier 406," 7.
18. Chapman, *State Capitalism*, 37.
19. H. G. Well's *The War in the Air* was among the first to address this after the advent of the airplane. There were numerous others, but imagining the effects of aerial bombardment had been a topic of popular fiction since well before the first airplane flew.
20. Williamson Murray. *Strategy for Defeat: The Luftwaffe 1933–1945*. Maxwell Air Force Base, Montgomery, AL: Air University Press, 1983: 8–9.
21. Murray, *Strategy for Defeat*, 8–9.
22. Karl-Heinz Frieser. *The Blitzkrieg Legend: The 1940 Campaign in the West*. Annapolis: Naval Institute Press, 2012: 20.
23. Alistair Horne, *Fall of Paris*, 428.
24. Elizabeth Kier. *Imagining War: French and British Military Doctrine Between the Wars*. Princeton: Princeton University Press, 1997: 25.
25. Chapman, *State Capitalism*, 57.
26. Susan B. Whitney. *Mobilizing Youth: Communists and Catholics in Interwar France*. Durham: Duke University Press, 2009: 16–17.
27. Whitney, *Mobilizing Youth*, 171.

28. Janusz Piekalkiewicz. *Ziel Paris: Der Westfeldzug 1940.* Berlin: F. A. Herbig, 1986: 321.
29. Chapman, *State Capitalism*, 83.
30. Emmanuel Chadeau. *L'industrie aéronautique en France: 1900–1950.* Paris: Fayard, 1987: 234–35.
31. Chapman, *State Capitalism*, 221.
32. Patrick Facon. *Histoire de l'Armée de l'Air.* Paris: La Documentation Française, 2009: 145.
33. Facon, *Histoire de l'Armée de l'Air*, 139.
34. Robin Higham. *Two Roads to War: The British and French Air Arms from Versailles to Dunkirk.* Annapolis: Naval Institute Press, 2012: 169.
35. Kier, *Imagining War*, 25.
36. Generalleutnant a.D. Andreas L. Nielsen. *The Collection and Evaluation of Intelligence for the German Air Force High Command.* Maxwell Air Force Base, Montgomery, AL: Air Force Historical Foundation, 1955. K113.107–71 8-1115–20: 118.
37. Nielsen, *Collection and Evaluation*, 119.
38. The discussions of these issues are many and varied. Of the U.S. Air Attaché reports from Paris, especially from 1936 to 1940, those from Lieutenant Colonel Fuller tend to be the most detailed. Lieutenant Colonel H. H. Fuller. Report No. 24,257-W. May 9, 1938: 1. 4711–136 France. Maxwell Air Force Base: Air Force Historical Foundation.
39. Captain Townsend Griffiss. "Difficulties with Gnome-Rhone Engines." Report No. 22,904-W, November 3, 1936. 4711–136 France. Maxwell Air Force Base, Montgomery, AL: Air Force Historical Foundation.
40. Lieutenant Colonel H. H. Fuller. Report No. 24,257-W. May 9, 1938: 1. 4711–136 France. Maxwell Air Force Base, Montgomery, AL: Air Force Historical Foundation.
41. Fuller, "Report No. 24,257-W," 2.
42. Fuller, "Report No. 24,257-W," 2.
43. Fuller, "Report No. 24,257-W," 3.
44. Fuller, "Report No. 24,257-W," 3.
45. Lieutenant Colonel H. H. Fuller. "Government Contracts with Aeronautic Interests." Report No. 24,326-W. May 28, 1938. 4711–136 France. Maxwell Air Force Base, Montgomery, AL: Air Force Historical Foundation.
46. Lieutenant Colonel H. H. Fuller. "Aircraft Program & Orders." Report No. 24,113-W. 4711–136 France. Maxwell Air Force Base, Montgomery, AL, Montgomery, AL: Air Force Historical Foundation.
47. France No. 268. "The Morane 406 Fighter." 4711–136 France. Maxwell Air Force Base, Montgomery, AL: The Air Force Historical Foundation. Author's emphasis.
48. France No. 268, "Morane 406 Fighter," 1. Author's emphasis.
49. Edward L. Homze. *Arming the Luftwaffe: The Reich Air Ministry and the German Aircraft Industry 1919–39.* Lincoln: University of Nebraska Press, 1976: 1.

50. E. R. Hooten. *The Luftwaffe: A Study in Air Power 1933–1945*. Hersham: Classic Books, 2010: 17–19.
51. Hooten, *Luftwaffe*, 17–19.
52. Murray, *Strategy for Defeat*, 13–15.
53. Homze, *Arming the Luftwaffe*, 35.
54. Homze, *Arming the Luftwaffe*, 35.
55. Homze, *Arming the Luftwaffe*, 63–64.
56. Murray, *Strategy for Defeat*, 1–5.
57. Adam Tooze. *The Wages of Destruction: The Making and Breaking of the Nazi Economy*. New York: Viking, 2006: 328–29.
58. Tooze, *Wages*, 328–29.
59. James S. Corum. *The Luftwaffe: Creating the Operational Air War, 1918–1940*. Lawrence: University Press of Kansas, 1997: 61–66.
60. Homze, *Arming the Luftwaffe*, 161–68.

CHAPTER 3. FRENCH AND GERMAN INTELLIGENCE, 1934 TO 1940

1. Pierre Cot. *L'Armée de l'Air, 1936–1938*. Paris: Grasset, 1939: 37.
2. Robert J. Young. "French Military Intelligence and Nazi Germany, 1938–1939." In *Knowing One's Enemies: Intelligence Assessment Before the Two World Wars*. Ernest R. May, ed. Princeton: Princeton University Press, 1986.
3. "L'aviation de chasse en Espagne." SHAA MO 064, 64.
4. "L'aviation de chasse," SHAA MO 064, 64.
5. "L'aviation de chasse," SHAA MO 064, 65.
6. "L'aviation de chasse," SHAA MO 064, 75.
7. "L'aviation de chasse," SHAA MO 064, 77.
8. "L'aviation de chasse," SHAA MO 064, 77.
9. "L'aviation de chasse," SHAA MO 064, 77.
10. "Renseignements fournis par les aviateurs gouvernementaux sûr la guerre d'Espagne." SHAA MO 064: 41.
11. "L'aviation de chasse," SHAA MO 064, 82.
12. "Renseignements," SHAA MO 064, 41.
13. "Renseignements," SHAA MO 064, 38.
14. "Renseignements," SHAA MO 064, 38.
15. Pierre Cot. Technical Mobilization: Hearings before a Subcommittee of the Committee of Military Affairs, United States Senate, 77th Congress, 2nd sess. S.2721: A Bill to Establish an Office of Technical Mobilization, and for Other Purposes, v. 3, December 12, 14, 17, 18–19, 1942, Washington, DC: Government Printing Office, 1943: 605.
16. Cot, Technical Mobilization, 605.
17. "Renseignements," SHAA MO 064, 28.
18. A. Odier. "Will the Pursuit Type Be Eliminated by New High Speeds?" *Revue de L'Armée de l'Air*. September 1936: 965–76. Trans. R. Garnier. AFHA 4624–47.
19. "Renseignements," SHAA MO 064, 31.

20. "Exemplaire No. 41: Attaque et defense des terrains en Espagne," SHAA MO 064, 47–49.
21. Robert A. Doughty. *The Breaking Point: Sedan and the Fall of France, 1940*. Hamden: Archon, 1990: 68.
22. Commandant Marcel Jauneaud. *L'aviation militaire et la guerre aérienne*. Paris: Ernest Flammarion, 1923: 169.
23. P. E. "La guerre d'Espagne." *Revue de L'Armée de L'Air*. May–June 1939: 313–19.
24. Eddie J. Creek. *Junkers Ju 87: From Dive Bomber to Tank-Buster 1935–45*. Hersham: Ian Allen, 2012: 49–50.
25. "Renseignements," SHAA MO 064, 34.
26. "Attaque et defense," SHAA MO 064, 8–9.
27. "Attaque et defense," SHAA MO 064, 9.
28. "Les troupes de transmissions de l'Armée de l'Air Allemande." 16 November 1936: 72–82. SHAA MO 055.
29. "Les troupes de transmissions," SHAA MO 055, 73.
30. "Les troupes de transmissions," SHAA MO 055, 72–76.
31. "Les troupes de transmissions," SHAA MO 055, 78–79.
32. Robert J. Young. "French Military Intelligence and Nazi Germany 1938–39": 276.
33. Cot, Technical Mobilization, 606.
34. Murray. *The Luftwaffe: Strategy for Defeat*, 104–106.
35. Murray, *Luftwaffe*, 104–106.
36. Murray, *Luftwaffe*, 18.
37. Major General Sir Kenneth Strong. *Intelligence at the Top: The Recollections of an Intelligence Officer*. London: Cassels, 1968: 58.
38. Pierre Cot. *Triumph of Treason*. New York: Ziff Davis, 1944: 277–79.
39. Karl-Heinz Friesser. *The Blitzkrieg Legend: The 1940 Campaign in the West*. Annapolis: Naval Institute Press, 2005: 35.
40. Général [Maurice] Gamelin. *Servir: Les armées françaises de 1940*. Paris: Plon, 1947: 221–34.
41. Gamelin, *Servir*, 224–26.
42. Gamelin, *Servir*, 275.
43. Young, "French Military Intelligence," 276.
44. Young, "French Military Intelligence," 297.
45. Young, "French Military Intelligence," 300.
46. "Exemplaire No. 41," SHAA MO 064.
47. Young, "French Military Intelligence," 299.
48. Air Commodore Douglas Colyer. Report: "Paris, June 1940." 30 May 1940. B. H. Liddell Hart Archive. King's College London. Spears 11/1.
49. "Géographie aérienne de l'Allemagne." SHAA MO 61/2.
50. Centre des hautes études aériennes. Map: Dépôts d'essence et de munitions en Allemagne. 1939. SHAA MO 43/1.

51. *Exercice sur la carte 1938–1939*: 5. SHAA MO 43/1.
52. Cot, *Triumph of Treason*, 277–79.
53. Cot, *Triumph of Treason*, 195.
54. James S. Corum. *The Luftwaffe: Creating the Operational Air War, 1918–1940*. Lawrence: University Press of Kansas, 1997: 275–77.
55. Pierre Cot. *L'Armée de L'Air*. Paris: Grasset, 1939.
56. E. R. Hooton. *The Luftwaffe: A Study in Air Power, 1933–1945*. Hersham, Surrey, UK: Classic Books, 2010: 68–69.
57. There were an amazing number of books on doctrine, air forces in general, and aircraft published in both French and German that discussed the same basic precepts of modern aerial warfare. Many of these emphasized strategic air war such as Colonel Vauthier's *La doctrine de guerre du Général Douhet* that appeared in German as *Die Kriegslehre des Generals Douhet*; both editions were published in the same year, 1935.
58. Horst Boog. "German Air Intelligence in World War II." In *Aerospace Historian* 33, no. 2 (June 1996): 122.
59. Corum, *The Luftwaffe*, 275–77.
60. Corum, *The Luftwaffe*, 275–77.
61. Boog, "German Air Intelligence," 124.
62. Robert Hutchinson. *German Foreign Intelligence from Hitler's War to the Cold War: Flawed Assumptions and Faulty Analysis*. Lawrence: University of Kansas Press, 2019: 33–35.
63. Hutchinson, *German Foreign Intelligence*, 122.
64. Hutchinson, *German Foreign Intelligence*, 122.
65. John Erickson. "Threat Identification and Strategic Appraisal by the Soviet Union, 1930–1941." In *Knowing One's Enemies: Intelligence Assessment Before the Two World Wars*. Ernest R. May, ed. Princeton: Princeton University Press, 1986: 285.

CHAPTER 4. THE FRENCH AIR FORCE, THE LUFTWAFFE, AND THE SPANISH CIVIL WAR

1. Général Maurice Duval. *Les leçons de la guerre d'Espagne*. Paris: Librairie Plon, 1938.
2. The main file in the SHAA archive concerning the events in Spain is MO 064 Espagne, which contains a number of different reports from open sources to classified attaché reports.
3. "La guerre en Espagne," SHAA, MO 064.
4. "La guerre en Espagne," SHAA, MO 064.
5. Duval. *Les leçons*.
6. "L'aviation de chasse en Espagne." SHAA, MO 064, 61.
7. "L'aviation de chasse," SHAA, MO 064, 61.
8. "L'aviation de chasse," SHAA, MO 064, 62.

9. "L'aviation de chasse," SHAA, MO 064, 62.
10. "L'aviation de chasse," SHAA, MO 064, 62.
11. "L'aviation de chasse," SHAA, MO 064, 64.
12. "L'aviation de chasse," SHAA, MO 064, 75.
13. "L'aviation de chasse," SHAA, MO 064, 77.
14. Anthony Pritchard. *Messerschmitt.* New York: G. P. Putnam's Sons, 1975: 35–38.
15. Pritchard, *Messerschmitt*, 37–38.
16. "L'aviation de chasse," SHAA, MO 064, 82.
17. "L'aviation de chasse," SHAA, MO 064, 82.
18. Generalleutnant a.D. Andreas L. Nielsen. *The Collection and Evaluation of Intelligence for the German Air Force High Command.* USAFHA Maxwell AFB. 8-1115-20.
19. Stephen L. McFarland. *America's Pursuit of Precision Bombing, 1910–1945.* Washington, DC: Smithsonian, 1995: 75–87.
20. McFarland, *America's Pursuit*, 41
21. McFarland, *America's Pursuit*, 41.
22. M. Duncan Sandys. "Les bombardements aériens de Barcelone." *Revue de l'Armée de l'Air,* June 1938: 691.
23. Sandys, "Les bombardements," 692.
24. Sandys, "Les bombardements," 694.
25. Sandys, "Les bombardements," 694–96.
26. AFHA 4624-47. A. Odier. "Will the Pursuit Type Be Eliminated by New High Speeds?" *Revue de l'Armée de l'Air.* September 1936: 675–76. Trans. R. Garnier.
27. Anonymous. "La guerre aérienne en Espagne." *Revue de L'Armée de L'Air.* February 1937: 195–96. Emphasis added.
28. P. E. "La guerre d'Espagne." *Revue de L'Armée de L'Air.* June 1938: 690.
29. P. E. "Une controverse italienne sur la chasse en Espagne." *Revue de L'Armée de L'Air.* May–June, 1939: 313–19.
30. P. E., "Une controverse italienne," 316.
31. P. E., "Une controverse italienne," 316.
32. P. E., "Une controverse italienne," 318.
33. P. E., "Une controverse italienne," 316.
34. P. E., "Une controverse italienne," 316–18.
35. P. E., "Une controverse italienne," 318.
36. James S. Corum and Richard R. Muller. *The Luftwaffe's Way of War: German Air Force Doctrine 1911–1945.* Baltimore: Nautical and Aviation Publishing, 1998: 5.
37. H. B. "La guerre aérienne en Espagne." *Revue de l'Armée de l'Air,* February 1937: 812.
38. Richard P. Hallion. *Strike from the Sky: The History of Battlefield Air Attack, 1911–1945.* Washington, DC: Smithsonian, 1989: 19–20.
39. Hallion, *Strike from the Sky*, 196.
40. Hallion, *Strike from the Sky*, 196.

41. H. B., "La guerre aérienne en Espagne," 812.
42. H. B., "La guerre aérienne en Espagne," 812.
43. H. B., "La guerre aérienne en Espagne," 814–15.
44. Williamson Murray. *Strategy for Defeat: The Luftwaffe 1933–1945.* Maxwell Air Force Base, Montgomery, AL: Air University Press, 1983: 15.
45. Pierre Cot. *L'Armée de l'Air.* Paris: Grasset, 1939: 21–22, 43.
46. Cot, *L'Armée de l'Air,* 37–38.
47. Pierre Cot. *Triumph of Treason.* New York: Ziff Davis, 1944: 297.
48. Cot, *Triumph of Treason,* 227.
49. Major George Fielding Eliot. "France's Weygand." *Life,* 20 May 1940: 102.
50. Cot, *Triumph of Treason,* 196.
51. Cot, *Triumph of Treason,* 336–37.
52. P. Mikhailow. "Tactical Employment of Pursuit Aviation: Experience of the Spanish Civil War." *Krasnaya Zvezda,* 16 May 1938. Charles Berman, trans. U.S. Army War College, March 1938.
53. Mikhailow, "Tactical Employment," 2.
54. Mikhailow, "Tactical Employment," 2.
55. Mikhailow, "Tactical Employment," 4.
56. Mikhailow, "Tactical Employment," 6.
57. Mikhailow, "Tactical Employment," 11–12.
58. G. Gagarin. "Aviation in Defensive Actions: Experience of the Spanish Civil War." *Krasnaya Zvezda,* 16 May 1938. Charles Berman, trans. U.S. Army War College. June 1938.
59. Gagarin, "Aviation in Defensive Actions," 2.
60. Gagarin, "Aviation in Defensive Actions," 3.
61. Gagarin, "Aviation in Defensive Actions," 7.
62. Martin Alexander. *The Republic in Danger: General Maurice Gamelin and the Politics of French Defence 1933–1940.* Cambridge: Cambridge University Press, 1992: 160.
63. Cot, *Triumph of Treason,* 227.
64. John Terraine. *A Time for Courage.* New York: Macmillan, 1985: 53.
65. Raymond L. Proctor. *Hitler's Luftwaffe in the Spanish Civil War.* London: Greenwood Press, 1983: 21–22.
66. Proctor, *Hitler's Luftwaffe,* 25–29.
67. Robert M. Citino. *Quest for Decisive Victory: From Stalemate to Blitzkrieg in Europe, 1899–1940.* Lawrence: University Press of Kansas, 2002: 224.
68. Citino, *Quest,* 225–35.
69. Proctor, *Hitler's Luftwaffe,* 48–49.
70. Proctor, *Hitler's Luftwaffe,* 21–22.
71. David Johnston. *German Eagles in Spanish Skies: The Messerschmitt Bf 109 in Service with the Legion Condor during the Spanish Civil War.* Atglen, PA: Schiffer, 2018: 141.

72. Proctor, *Hitler's Luftwaffe*, 182.
73. James S. Corum. "From Biplanes to Blitzkrieg: The Development of German Air Doctrine Between the Wars." *War History* 3, no. 1 (1996): 98.
74. Corum, "From Biplanes to Blitzkrieg," 97–100.
75. E. R. Hooton. *The Luftwaffe: A Study in Air Power 1933–1945*. Hersham, UK: Classic Books, 2010: 44–45.
76. James S. Corum. *The Luftwaffe: Creating the Operation Air War*: 209–12.
77. Corum, *The Luftwaffe*, 211.

CHAPTER 5. FRENCH DOCTRINE AND TRAINING, 1934 TO 1940

1. Alistair Horne. *To Lose a Battle: France 1940*. New York: Penguin, 2007: 125–28, 164–65.
2. Barry R. Posen. *The Sources of Military Doctrine: France, Britain, and Germany between the World Wars*. Ithaca: Cornell University Press, 1984: 133.
3. Anthony Cain. *The Forgotten Air Force: French Air Doctrine in the 1930s*. Washington, DC: Smithsonian Press, 2002.
4. Robert Forczyk. *Case Red: The Collapse of France*. New York: Bloomsbury, 2017: 409–10.
5. Max Schiavon. "La doctrine des forces aériennes françaises 1912–1976." *Revue historique des armées* 265 (2011): 125.
6. Richard Overy. "Airpower, Armies, and the War in the West, 1940." *Harmon Memorial Lectures*. No. 32. Colorado: United States Air Force Academy, 1989: 6–7.
7. Robert Allan Doughty. *The Breaking Point: Sedan and the Fall of France, 1940*. Hamden: Archon, 1990: 267.
8. Herrick Chapman. *State Capitalism and Working Class Radicalism in the French Aircraft Industry*. Berkeley: University of California Press, 1991: 221–29.
9. Pierre Cot. *Triumph of Treason*. New York: Ziff Davis, 1944: 284–89.
10. Colonel P[aul]. Vauthier. *La doctrine de guerre du Général Douhet*. Paris: Berger-Lavrault, 1935.
11. Camille Rougeron. *Das Bombenflugwesen*. Berlin: Rowolht, 1938.
12. James Sterrett. *Soviet Air Force Theory 1918–1945*. London: Routledge, 2007: xii–xiii.
13. James S. Corum. *The Roots of Blitzkrieg*. Lawrence: University Press of Kansas, 1992: 168.
14. René Martel. *French Strategic and Tactical Bombardment Forces of World War I*. Allan Suddaby and Steven Suddaby, trans. Lanham: Scarecrow, 2007: 98–99.
15. Martel, *Strategic and Tactical Bombardment Forces*, 98–99.
16. Partick Friedenson and Jean Lecuir. *La France et la Grand-Bretagne face aux problems aériens 1935–mai 1940*. Vincennes: Service Historique de l'Armée de l'Air, 1976: 191–93.
17. George K. Williams. *Biplanes and Bombsights: British Bombing in World War I*. Maxwell Air Force Base, Montgomery, AL: Air University Press, 1999: 59.

18. Williams, *Biplanes and Bombsights*, 59.
19. Richard M. Watt. *Dare Call It Treason: The True Story of the French Army Mutinies of 1917.* New York: Dorset, 1969: 231–45.
20. Colonel Hébrard. "Sur le bombardement aérien dans son interdiction diurne." SHAA MO 38/8.
21. Hebrard, "Sur le bombardement," 15.
22. Cot, *Triumph of Treason*, 322–23.
23. Martin S. Alexander. *The Republic in Danger: General Maurice Gamelin and the Politics of French Defence, 1933–1940.* Cambridge: Cambridge University Press, 2002: 292.
24. Cot, *Triumph of Treason*, 287.
25. Martin Thomas. *The French Empire Between the Wars: Imperialism, Politics, and Society.* New York: Manchester University Press, 2005: 212.
26. James S. Corum and Wray R. Johnson. *Airpower in Small Wars: Fighting Insurgents and Terrorists.* Lawrence: University Press of Kansas, 2003: 73.
27. Corum and Johnson, *Airpower in Small Wars*, 73–75.
28. Hebrard, "Sur le bombardement," 9.
29. Hebrard, "Sur le bombardement," 9.
30. Hebrard, "Sur le bombardement," 16.
31. Hebrard, "Sur le bombardement," 22.
32. Hebrard, "Sur le bombardement," 17.
33. Hebrard, "Sur le bombardement," 14.
34. Colonel Pierre Paquier. *L'aviation de bombardement française en 1939–1940.* Paris: Editions Berger-Lavrault, 1948: 199–202.
35. Pierre Barjot. *L'aviation militaire française.* Paris: J. de Gigord, 1939: 79.
36. Alistair Horne. *To Lose a Battle: France, 1940.* New York: Penguin, 1990: 278.
37. Horne, *To Lose a Battle*, 432.
38. "Composition detaille de l'Armée de l'Air Allemande." SHAA MO43/1: 64.
39. "Exercice sur la carte 1938–1939." SHAA MO43/1.
40. Robert A. Doughty. *Pyrrhic Victory: French Strategy and Operations in the Great War.* Cambridge, MA: Harvard, 2005: 516.
41. Karl-Heinz Frieser. *The Blitzkrieg Legend: The 1940 Campaign in the West.* Annapolis: Naval Institute Press, 2012: 20.
42. Lieutenant Colonel Pierre Tissier. *The Riom Trial.* New York: George G. Harap, 1942: 127.
43. Jérôme de Lespinois, ed. Document 20. *La doctrine des forces aériennes françaises 1912–1976.* Mayenne: Acheve d'imprimer par Jouve, 2010: 132.
44. de Lespinois, ed., Document 20, *La doctrine des forces*, 132.
45. de Lespinois, ed., Document 20, *La doctrine des forces*, 132–33.
46. de Lespinois, ed., Document 20, *La doctrine des forces*, 132–33.
47. de Lespinois, ed., Document 20, *La doctrine des forces*, 134–38.
48. de Lespinois, ed., Document 20, *La doctrine des forces*, 134.
49. de Lespinois, ed., Document 20, *La doctrine des forces*, 135.

50. de Lespinois, ed., Document 20, *La doctrine des forces*, 135.
51. de Lespinois, ed., Document 20, *La doctrine des forces*, 137.
52. Lieutenant Colonel H. H. Fuller. G-2 Report. 16 March 1936. "Distribution of Troops." 4711/136 France 6000/8. Maxwell Air Force Base, Montgomery, AL: Air Force Historical Foundation.
53. Jérôme de Lespinois, ed. Document 22. *La doctrine des forces aériennes françaises 1912–1976*. Mayenne: Acheve d'imprimer par Jouve, 2010: 139–41.
54. Jérôme de Lespinois, ed. Document 23. *La doctrine des forces aériennes françaises 1912–1976*. Mayenne: Acheve d'imprimer par Jouve, 2010: 143.
55. "Carte d'ensemble des moyens de défense de la D.C.A. du C.R.P. (Octobre 1918)." SHAA MO 23.
56. "Carte d'ensemble des moyens," SHAA MO 23, 143.
57. Jérôme de Lespinois, ed. Document 25. *La doctrine des forces aériennes françaises 1912–1976*. Mayenne: Acheve d'imprimer par Jouve, 2010: 149.
58. de Lespinois, ed., Document 25, 151.
59. de Lespinois, ed., Document 25, 152.
60. de Lespinois, ed., Document 25, 153.
61. de Lespinois, ed., Document 25, 159.
62. Corum, *Roots of Blitzkrieg*, 167.
63. Corum, *Roots of Blitzkrieg*, 167.
64. Eugenia C. Kiesling. *Arming Against Hitler: France and the Limits of Military Planning*. Lawrence: University Press of Kansas, 1996: 170.
65. Anonymous "*Intervention de l'aviation dans la bataille terrestre.*" SHAA MO 064/2–3.
66. Anon. "*Intervention de l'aviation,*" 9.
67. Anon. "*Intervention de l'aviation,*" 8.
68. Anon. "*Intervention de l'aviation,*" 1.
69. Anon. "*Intervention de l'aviation,*" 10.
70. Cot, *Triumph of Treason*, 297.
71. Robert Allan Doughty. *The Seeds of Disaster: The Development of French Army Doctrine, 1919–1939*. Hamden: Archon, 1985: 167.
72. Cot, *Triumph of Treason*, 15–16.
73. Doughty, *Breaking* Point, 239.
74. *Instruction sur l'emploi tactique des grandes unites aérienes, édition de 1937*. Paris: Imprimerie Nationale, 1937: 21–24.
75. *Instruction sur l'emploi tactique*, 37.
76. *Instruction sur l'emploi tactique*, 77–81.
77. Cot, *Triumph of Treason*, 302–303.
78. Patrick Facon. *Le bombardement stratégique*. Monaco: Éditions du Rocher, 1995: 15–16.
79. Charles Stephenson. *A Box of Sand: The Italo-Ottoman War 1911–1912, The First Land, Sea, and Air War*. Ticehurst: Tattered Flag Press, 2014. This is one of the very few works available in English on this subject.

80. L. E. O. Charlton. *War from the Air: Past, Present, Future*. London: Thomas Nelson and Sons, 1935: 166.
81. James S. Corum. *Airpower in Small Wars: Fighting Insurgents and Terrorists*. Lawrence: University Press of Kansas, 2003: 74.
82. Corum, *Airpower in Small Wars*, 77.
83. Corum, *Airpower in Small Wars*, 73–77.
84. Map: "Industrie aéronautique allemand et écoles aériennes." SHAA MO 43/1.
85. de Lespinois, ed., Document 25, 151.
86. Thomas Hippler. *Bombing the People: Giulio Douhet and the Foundations of Air-Power Strategy, 1884–1939*. Cambridge: Cambridge University Press, 2013, 254–55.
87. Corum, *The Luftwaffe*, 239–40.
88. Corum, *The Luftwaffe*, 239–40.
89. Tissier, *The Riom Trial*, 145.
90. Tissier, *The Riom Trial*, 148.
91. Cot, *Triumph of Treason*, 14–16.
92. Lieutenant Colonel Ralph C. Smith. "French Combat Estimate 1937–1940." Maxwell Air Force Base, Montgomery, AL. Air Force Historical Research Agency. Microfilm Reel 2873. 4109y.
93. Davis E. Johnson. *Fast Tanks and Heavy Bombers: Innovation in the U.S. Army 1917–1945*. Ithaca: Cornell University Press, 1998: 137–45.
94. "Carte d'ensemble des moyens," SHAA MO 23.
95. "Carte d'ensemble des moyens," SHAA MO 23.
96. Commandant Marcel Jauneaud. *L'aviation militaire et la guerre aérienne*. Paris: Ernest Flammarion, 1923: 129.
97. Hebrard, "Sur le bombardement," 9–16.
98. Cain, *Forgotten Air Force*, 56–57.
99. Cain, *Forgotten Air Force*, 113.
100. Cot, *Triumph of Treason*, 178.
101. Général Maurice Gamelin. *Servir*. Paris: Librairie Plon 1947: 167, 174–76.
102. Kiesling, *Arming Against Hitler*, 177.
103. Kiesling, *Arming Against Hitler*, 177.
104. Doughty, *Breaking Point*, 127.
105. "French Army Doctrine." Maxwell Air Force Base, Montgomery, AL. Air Force Historical Research Agency. Microfilm Reel A2873: 53.
106. "French Army Doctrine," 53.
107. "French Army Doctrine," 53.
108. Higham, *Two Roads to War*, 262.
109. Lieutenant Colonel H. H. Fuller. Report No. 24,113-W. 1. U.S. Air Force Historical Association, Maxwell Air Force Base, Montgomery, AL.
110. Cain, *Forgotten Air Force*, 70.
111. Cain, *Forgotten Air Force*, 66–67.
112. Cain, *Forgotten Air Force*, 72–73.

113. Lieutenant Colonel Ralph C. Smith. "French Combat Estimate 1937–1940." Maxwell Air Force Base, Montgomery, AL. Air Force Historical Research Agency. Microfilm A2873. 4109 ee.
114. Smith, "French Combat Estimate," 4109 ee.
115. Smith, "French Combat Estimate," 4109 ee.

CHAPTER 6. LUFTWAFFE DOCTRINE AND TRAINING, 1934 TO 1940

1. Robert M. Citino. *The Path to Blitzkrieg: Doctrine and Training in the German Army, 1920–1939*. Boulder, CO: Lynne Rienner, 1999: 44–45.
2. Hans von Seeckt. *Thoughts of a Soldier*. Trans. Gilbert Waterhouse. London: E. Benn, 1930: 56, 61–62.
3. James S. Corum. *The Luftwaffe: Creating the Operational Air War, 1918–1940*. Lawrence: University Press of Kansas, 1997: 275–80.
4. James S. Corum. "The Old Eagle as Phoenix: The Luftstreitkräfte Creates an Operational Air War Doctrine, 1919–1920." *Air Power History* 39, no. 1 (Spring 1992): 14.
5. Corum, "The Old Eagle," 13–15.
6. Corum, "The Old Eagle," 15–16.
7. Horst Boog. *Die Deutsche Luftwaffenführung 1935–1945: Führungsprobleme, Spitzengliederung, Generalstabsausbildung*. Stuttgart: Deutsche Verlags-Anstalt, 1982: 26–27.
8. James S. Corum. *Wolfram von Richthofen: Master of the German Air War*, 151.
9. Corum, *Richthofen*, 126–28.
10. Corum, *Richthofen*, 126–28.
11. Corum, *Richthofen*, 191.
12. Corum, *The Luftwaffe*, 201–3.
13. Williamson Murray. *Strategy for Defeat: The Luftwaffe 1933–1945*. Maxwell Air Force Base, Montgomery, AL: Air University Press, 1983: 7–10.
14. Murray, *Strategy for Defeat*, 16.
15. James S. Corum and Richard R. Muller. *The Luftwaffe's Way of War: German Air Force Doctrine 1911–1945*. Baltimore: Nautical and Aviation Publishing, 1998: 151–57.
16. Eugenia Kiesling. *Arming Against Hitler: France and the Limits of Military Planning*. Lawrence: University Press of Kansas, 1996: 176–77.
17. Robert A. Doughty. *The Breaking Point: Sedan and the Fall of France, 1940*. Hamden: Archon, 1990: 239.
18. Karl-Heinz Frieser. *The Blitzkrieg Legend: The 1940 Campaign in the West*. Annapolis: Naval Institute Press, 2005: 312.

CHAPTER 7. POLITICS AND AIRPOWER IN FRANCE

1. Pierre Tissier. *The Riom Trial*. London: George Harap, 1942: 5–6
2. Pierre Cot. *Triumph of Treason*. New York: Ziff Davis, 1944: 43.

3. Major General Edward Spears. *Assignment to Catastrophe: Prelude to Dunkirk. July 1939–May 1940*. Vol. 1. New York: A. A. Wyn, 1954: 287.
4. Spears, *Prelude to Dunkirk*, 287.
5. Lieutenant Colonel Ralph C. Smith. "French Combat Estimate 1937–1940." Maxwell Air Force Base, Montgomery, AL. Air Force Historical Research Agency. Microfilm Reel A2873. 4109 ee.
6. Smith, "French Combat Estimate," 4109 ee.
7. Smith, "French Combat Estimate," 4109 ee.
8. Smith, "French Combat Estimate," Annex 1, 16.
9. "Paris, June 1940." King's College, London. B. H. Liddell Hart Archive. Spears 11/1.
10. "The French Airforce [sic] in the Battle of France – 1940." n.d. YouTube video, 7:44. https://www.youtube.com/watch?v=TPOvYrvDv0Q.
11. Spears, *Prelude to Dunkirk*, 287.
12. Cot, *Triumph of Treason*, 274.
13. Cot, *Triumph of Treason*, 274–75.
14. James Sterrett. *Soviet Air Force Theory, 1918–1945*. New York: Routledge, 2007: 59.
15. James MacGregor Burns. *Roosevelt: Soldier of Freedom*. New York: Harcourt Brace Jovanovich, 1970: 601.
16. Robert A. Doughty. *The Breaking Point: Sedan and the Fall of France, 1940*. Hamden: Archon, 1990: 267.
17. Cot, *Triumph of Treason*, 65.
18. Cot, *Triumph of Treason*, 39.
19. General Maxime Weygand. *Recalled to Service*. New York: Doubleday, 1952.
20. Général Maurice Gamelin. *Servir*. Paris: Librairie Plon, 1946.
21. Charles de Gaulle. *The War Memoirs of Charles de Gaulle: The Call to Honour 1940–1942*. New York: Simon & Schuster, 1955: 99.
22. Charles de Gaulle. *The War Memoirs of Charles de Gaulle: Salvation 1944–1946*. Simon & Schuster, 1955: 223
23. Cot, *Triumph of Treason*, 24–25.
24. Cot, *Triumph of Treason*, 24–25
25. Pierre Cot. *L'Armée de l'Air 1936–1938*. Paris: Grasset, 1939: 11–13.
26. Colonel P[aul]. Vauthier. *La doctrine de guerre du Général Douhet*. Paris: Berger-Levrault: 1935.
27. Vauthier, *La doctrine de guerre*, vii–xiv.
28. Giulio Douhet. *Command of the Air*. Washington, DC: Air Force History and Museums Program, 1998: vii–x.
29. Douhet, *Command of the Air*, vii–x.
30. Pierre Cot. *L'Armée de l'Air*. Paris: Grasset, 1939: 48–61.
31. Cot, *Triumph of Treason*, 35–36.
32. Elizabeth Kier. *Imagining War: French and British Military Doctrine Between the Wars*. Princeton: Princeton University Press, 1997: 96.

33. Martin S. Alexander. *The Republic in Danger: General Maurice Gamelin and the Politics of French Defence 1933–1940*. Cambridge: Cambridge University Press, 1992: 291.
34. Alexander, *Republic in Danger*, 291.
35. Weygand, *Recalled to Service*, 11.
36. Alexander, *Republic in Danger*, 295.
37. General Sir Edmond Ironside. *Time Unguarded: The Ironside Diaries 1937–1940*. New York: David McKay, 1963: 213–14.
38. Weygand, *Recalled to Service*, 38–39.
39. Alexander, *Republic in Danger*, 291.
40. Cot, *Triumph of Treason*, 50–51.
41. Cot, *Triumph of Treason*, 50–51.
42. Cot, *Triumph of Treason*, 64–65.
43. Cot, *L'Armée de l'Air*, 111–24.
44. Kier, *Imagining War*, 25.
45. Cot, *Triumph of Treason*, 196–98.
46. Cot, *L'Armée de l'Air*, 73–78.
47. Herrick Chapman. *State Capitalism and Working-Class Radicalism in the French Aircraft Industry*. Berkeley: University of California Press, 1991: 103.
48. Cot, *L'Armée de l'Air*, 77–78.
49. Cot, *L'Armée de l'Air*, 77–78.
50. Cot, *Triumph of Treason*, 362–64.
51. Benjamin F. Martin. *France in 1938*. Baton Rouge: Louisiana State University Press, 2005: 73.
52. Herbert Romerstein and Eric Breindel. *The Venona Secrets: Exposing Soviet Espionage and America's Traitors*. Washington, DC: Regnery, 2000: 303–5.
53. Romerstein and Breindel, *Venona Secrets*, 303–5.
54. De Gaulle, *Call to Honour*, 99.
55. Susan B. Whitney. *Mobilizing Youth: Communists and Catholics in Interwar France*. Durham: Duke University Press, 2009: 44–50.
56. Cot, *Triumph of Treason*, 387.
57. Cot, *Triumph of Treason*, 46.
58. Colonel Pierre Paquier. *L'aviation bombardement française en 1939–1940*. Paris: Berger-Lavrault, 1946: 3–5.
59. Cot, *Triumph of Treason*, 44.
60. Cot, *Triumph of Treason*, 287.
61. Michel de Ladoucette. *Guy La Chambre: un Malouin illustre, homme de cœur et de devoir*. Dieppe: La Vigie: 3–9.
62. Cot, *Triumph of Treason*, 281–83.
63. Cot, *Triumph of Treason*, 281–83.
64. Ironside, *Time Unguarded*, 122.
65. Anthony Christopher Cain. "L'Armée de l'Air 1933–1940: Drifting Toward Defeat." In *Why Air Forces Fail*. Robin Higham and Stephen J. Harris, eds. Lexington: University of Kentucky Press, 2005, 41–70, 64–65.

66. Cain, "L'Armée de l'Air 1933–1940," 64–65.
67. Cot, *Triumph of Treason*, 280.
68. Spears, *Prelude to Dunkirk*, 272.
69. de Seversky, *Victory Through Air Power*, 190–91.
70. de Seversky, *Victory Through Air Power*, 190–91.
71. de Seversky, *Victory Through Air Power*, 190–91.
72. de Seversky, *Victory Through Air Power*, 190–91.
73. Cot, *Triumph of Treason*, 299–301.
74. Cot, *Triumph of Treason*, 1–3.
75. Spears, *Assignment to Catastrophe*, vol. 1, 17.
76. Robert J. Young. *In Command of France.* Cambridge: Harvard University Press, 1978: 198.
77. Spears, *Assignment to Catastrophe*, 17.
78. Cot, *Triumph of Treason*, 283.
79. Weygand, *Recalled to Service*, 50.
80. Cot, *Triumph of Treason*, 63.

CHAPTER 8. REASSESSING THE AIR BATTLE OVER FRANCE IN 1940

1. Marc Bloc. *Strange Defeat.* New York: Norton, 1968: 40.
2. Air Commodore Douglas Colyer. Report: "Paris, June 1940." 30 May 1940. Spears 11/1, 1–3.
3. Colyer, Liddell Hart Archive, Spears 11/1, 1.
4. Colyer, Liddell Hart Archive, Spears 11/1, 2.
5. Colyer, Liddell Hart Archive, Spears 11/1, 2.
6. Colyer, Liddell Hart Archive, Spears 11/1, 3.
7. Major General Sir Edward Spears. *Assignment to Catastrophe Volume 2: The Fall of France.* New York: A. A. Wyn, 1955.
8. Colyer, Liddell Hart Archive, Spears 11/1, 3.
9. Alistair Horne. *To Lose a Battle: France, 1940.* New York: Penguin, 1990: 640–41.
10. B. H. Liddell Hart. *History of the Second World War.* New York: Perigree, 1971: 68–84.
11. Meir Finkel. *On Flexibility: Recovery from Technological and Doctrinal Surprise on the Battlefield.* Stanford, CA: Stanford University Press, 2011: 205–22.
12. Stephen Budiansky. *Air Power: The Men, Machines, and Ideas That Revolutionized War from Kitty Hawk to Iraq.* New York: Penguin, 2005: 225.
13. Robin Higham. *Unflinching Zeal: The Air Battles Over France and Britain, May–October 1940.* Annapolis: Naval Institute Press, 2012: 193.
14. Williamson Murray. *Strategy for Defeat: The Luftwaffe 1933–1945.* Maxwell Air Force Base, Montgomery, AL: Air University Press, 1983.
15. Murray, *Strategy for Defeat*, 39.
16. Higham, *Unflinching Zeal*, 193.
17. Higham, *Unflinching Zeal*, 149.
18. Pierre Cot. *Triumph of Treason.* New York: Ziff Davis, 1944: 274–75.

19. Camille Rougeron. "Chasse française et chasse allemande." *L'Illustration*, no. 5053 (6 January 1940): 11–14.
20. Richard Heß. "Dem Ende entgegen." *Der Adler*. Heft 13 (25 June 1940): 290–94.
21. Higham, *Unflinching Zeal*, 166–86.
22. Williamson Murray. *Strategy for Defeat: The Luftwaffe 1933–1945*. Maxwell Air Force Base, Montgomery, AL: Air University Press, 1983: 299–303.
23. Murray, *Strategy for Defeat*, 40.
24. Murray, *Strategy for Defeat*, 40.
25. Robert Allan Doughty. *The Breaking Point: Sedan and the Fall of France, 1940*. Hamden: Archon, 1990: 119.
26. Cot, *Triumph of Treason*, 287–88.
27. Cot, *Triumph of Treason*, 287.
28. Cot, *Triumph of Treason*, 288.
29. Karl-Heinz Frieser. *The Blitzkrieg Legend: The 1940 Campaign in the West*. Annapolis: Naval Institute Press, 2005: 321.
30. *Manuel du gradé de D.C.A*. Paris: Charles Lavauzelle, 1940: 1–8.
31. *Manuel du gradé*, 1.
32. *Manuel du gradé*, 30.
33. Colonel P[aul]. Vauthier. *La doctrine de guerre du Général Douhet*. Paris: Berger-Levrault, 1935.
34. Général Niessel, Général Chabord, and Général de Guilhermy. *D.A.T. Défense aérienne du territoire*. Paris: Éditions Cosmopolites, 1934.
35. Niessel, Chabord, and de Guilhermy, *D.A.T.*, 57–74.
36. Commandant Marcel Jauneaud. *L'aviation militaire et la guerre aérienne*. Paris: Ernest Flammarion, 1923: 169–70.
37. Major General Sir Edward L. Spears. *Assignment to Catastrophe Volume I: Prelude to Dunkirk July 1939–May 1940*. New York: A. A. Wyn, 1954: 287.
38. Cot, *Triumph of Treason*, 288.
39. Patrick Facon. "Les mille victoires de l'Armée de l'Air en 1939–1940: Autopsie d'un mythe." *Revue historique des armées* 4 (November 1997): 83–84.
40. Facon, "Les mille victoires," 83–84.
41. Higham, *Unflinching Zeal*, 223.
42. Higham, *Unflinching Zeal*, 234.
43. Michael Balss. "Deutsche Luftwaffe Losses and Claims Part 2." Monograph, 2018: 5–207.
44. Balss, "Deutsche Luftwaffe Losses," 5–207.
45. Higham, *Unflinching Zeal*, xv.
46. Major Alexander de Seversky. *Victory Through Air Power*. New York: Simon & Schuster, 1942: 187.
47. Higham, *Unflinching Zeal*, 163–65.
48. Gaston Botquin. "The Morane Saulnier 406." *Profile Publications No. 147*: 8.
49. Cot, *Triumph of Treason*, 286.

50. Doughty, *The Breaking Point*, 239.
51. Doughty, *The Breaking Point*, 239.
52. General Heinz Guderian. *Panzer Leader*. Costa Mesa: Noontide Press, 1988: 97–98.
53. Lieutenant Colonel Pierre Tissier. *The Riom Trial*. New York: George G. Harap, 1942: 148.
54. Higham, *Unflinching Zeal*, 234.
55. Pierre Cot. *L'Armée de l'Air*. Paris: Grasset, 1939: 48–61.
56. Cot, *L'Armée de l'Air*, 48–61.
57. Herbert Romerstein and Eric Breindel. *The Venona Secrets: Exposing Soviet Espionage and America's Traitors*. Washington, DC: Regency, 2000: 303–5.
58. Cot, *Triumph of Treason*, 387.
59. Lieutenant Colonel Ralph C. Smith. "France Combat Estimate 1937–1940." Microfilm roll A2873. 248, Maxwell Air Force Base: Air Force Historical Research Agency. 248.501–56. Amendment April 1939. 4109 ee.
60. Maxwell AFB, "France Combat Estimate 1937–1940," 288–89.
61. Maxwell AFB, "France Combat Estimate 1937–1940," 63–65.
62. Higham, *Unflinching Zeal*, 235.
63. Spears, *Assignment to Catastrophe*, 306–7.
64. Higham, *Unflinching Zeal*, 234.
65. Murray, *Strategy for Defeat*, 40.
66. Murray, *Strategy for Defeat*, 8–11.

CONCLUSION

1. Robert A. Doughty. *The Breaking Point: Sedan and the Fall of France, 1940*. Hamden: Archon, 1990: 247.
2. Doughty, *Breaking Point*, 247.
3. Williamson Murray. *War, Strategy, and Military Effectiveness*. New York: Cambridge, 2011: 213.
4. James S. Corum. *The Luftwaffe: Creating the Operational Air War, 1918–1940*. Lawrence: University Press of Kansas, 1997: 275–77.

Bibliography

PRIMARY SOURCES—BOOKS

Bloc, Marc. *Strange Defeat*. New York: Norton, 1968.
Boog, Horst. *Die Deutsche Luftwaffenführung 1935–1945: Führungsprobleme, Spitzengliederung, Generalstabsausbildung*. Stuttgart: Deutsche Verlags-Anstalt, 1982.
Charlton, L. E. O. *War from the Air: Past, Present, and Future*. London: Thomas Nelson and Sons, 1935.
Cot, Pierre. *L'Armée de l'Air*. Paris: Grasset, 1939.
Cot, Pierre. *The Triumph of Treason*. New York: Ziff Davis, 1944.
Duval, Général Maurice. *Les leçons de la guerre d'Espagne*. Paris: Librairie Plon, 1938.
Gamelin, Maurice. *Servir: Les armées françaises de 1940*. Paris: Librarie Plon, 1947.
de Gaulle, Charles. *The War Memoirs of General Charles de Gaulle: The Call to Honour 1940–1942*. New York: Simon & Schuster, 1955.
———. *The War Memoirs of Charles de Gaulle: Salvation 1944–1946*. Simon & Schuster, 1955.
Guderian, Heinz. *Panzer Leader*. Costa Mesa: Noontide Press, 1988.
Ironside, Sir Edmund. *Time Unguarded: The Ironside Diaries 1937–1940*. New York: David McKay, 1963.
Jauneaud, Commandant Marcel. *L'aviation militaire et la guerre aérienne*. Paris: Ernest Flammarion, 1923.
Johnston, David. *German Eagles in Spanish Skies: The Messerschmitt Bf 109 in Service with the Legion Condor during the Spanish Civil War*. Atglen, PA: Schiffer, 2018.
de Ladoucette, Michel. *Guy La Chambre: Un Malouin illustre, homme de cœur et de devoir*. Dieppe: La Vigie, 1979.
de Lespinois, Jérôme, ed. *La doctrine des forces aériennes françaises 1912–1976*. Paris: L'Humanité, 2003.
Général Niessel, Général Chabord, and Général de Guilhermy. *D.A.T.: Défense aérienne du territoire*. Paris: Éditions Cosmopolites, 1934.
Paquier, Colonel Pierre. *L'aviation bombardement française en 1939–1940*. Paris: Berger-Lavrault, 1946.
———. *L'aviation militaire française*. Paris: J. de Gigord, 1939.

Rougeron, Camille. *Das Bombenflugwesen*. Berlin: Rowolht, 1938.
von Seeckt, Hans. *Thoughts of a Soldier*. Trans. Gilbert Waterhouse. London: Ernest Benn, 1930.
Severac, E. *Dans le ciel de France*. Paris: Cieux Collection, 1947.
de Seversky, Major Alexander. *Victory Through Air Power*. New York: Simon & Schuster, 1942.
Spears, Major-General Sir Edward L. *Assignment to Catastrophe: Prelude to Dunkirk July 1939 – May 1940*. Vol. 1. New York: A. A. Wyn, 1954.
———. *Assignment to Catastrophe: The Fall of France*. Vol. 2. New York: A. A. Wyn, 1955.
Strong, Major-General Sir Kenneth. *Intelligence at the Top: The Recollections of an Intelligence Officer*. London: Cassels, 1968.
Tissier, Lieutenant-Colonel Pierre. *The Riom Trial*. London: George Harap, 1942.
Vauthier, Colonel P[aul]. *La doctrine de guerre du Général Douhet*. Paris: Berger-Levrault, 1935.
Weygand, General Maxime. *Recalled to Service*. New York: Doubleday, 1952.

PRIMARY SOURCES—MANUALS

Instruction sur l'emploi tactique des grandes unités aériennes. Edition de 1937. Paris: Imprimerie Nationale, 1937.
Manuel du gradé de D.C.A. Paris: Charles Lavauzelle, 1940.
Ministère de l'Air. *Équipement et armement de l'avion Morane type 406, moteur Hispano-Suiza 12 y-31 1860 cv.*, 3 October 1938.
Ministère de l'Air. *Extrait du tableau de composition du l'avion Bloch 151*, 1939.
Notice technique de la mitrailleuse M.A.C. modèle 1934, type aile; type touselle, 1936.

PRIMARY SOURCES—ARTICLES AND PERIODICALS

Boog, Horst. "German Air Intelligence in World War II." *Aerospace Historian* 33, no. 2, June 1996: 121–29.
Eliot, Major George Fielding. "France's Weygand." *Life*, 20 May 1940: 94–106.
"The French Airforce [sic] in the Battle of France – 1940." n.d. YouTube video, 7:44. https://www.youtube.com/watch?v=TPOvYrvDvoQ (Note: This is an interview with Paul Cot).
Gagarin, G. "Aviation in Defensive Actions: Experiences of the Spanish Civil War." *Krasnaya Zvezda*, 16 May 1938. Translated by Charles Berman, U.S. Army War College, June 1938.
H. B. "La guerre aérienne en Espagne." *Revue de l'Armée de l'Air*, February 1937: 195–96.
Heß, Richard. "Dem Ende entgegen." *Der Adler*, Heft 13, 25 June 1940: 290–93.
Mikhailow, P. "Tactical Employment of Pursuit Aviation: Experience of the Spanish Civil War." *Krasnaya Zvezda*, 16 May 1938. Translated by Charles Berman, June 1938.

P. E. "La guerre d'Espagne." *Revue de l'Armée de l'Air.* May–June, 1938: 688–91.

———. "Une controverse italienne sur la chasse en Espagne." *Revue de l'Armée de l'Air.* May–June 1939: 313–19.

Rougeron, Camille. "Chasse française et chasse allemande." *L'illustration,* no. 5053, 6 January 1940: 11–14.

Sandys, M. Duncan. "Les bombardements aériens de Barcelone." *Revue de l'Armée de l'Air,* June 1938: 689–94.

PRIMARY SOURCES—ARCHIVAL

King's College London. B. H. Liddell Hart Archive

Colyer, Air Commodore Douglas. Report: "Paris, June 1940." 30 May 1940. Spears 11/1.

Maxwell Air Force Base. Air Force Base, Air Force Historical Research Agency

"Attaque et défense." SHAA, MO 064.

"Carte d'ensemble des moyens de défense de la D.C.A. du C.R.P., Octobre 1918." SHAA, MO 23.

"Carte d'ensemble des moyens de défense, Octobre 1918." SHAA, MO 064.

Centre des hautes études aériennes. "Dépôts d'essence et de munitions en Allemagne." Map. 1939. SHAA, MO 43/1.

"Composition detaille de l'Armée de l'Air Allemande." SHAA, MO 43/1.

"Difficulties with Gnome-Rhone Engines." 4711/136.

"Exercice sur la carte 1938–1939." SHAA, MO 43/1.

"French Army Doctrine." Microfilm roll A2873.

Fuller, Lieutenant Colonel H. H. G2 Report. 16 March 1936. "Distribution of Troops." 4711/136 France 6000/8.

Fuller, Lieutenant Colonel H. H. Report No. 24,326-W, 28 May 1938. "Government Contacts with Aeronautic Interests." Service Historique de l'Armée de l'Air. 4711/136.

G2 Report, 14 February 1936. "France: Bombardment in the Organization of the Air Army." Air Force Historical Research Association, 248.501–6.

"Géographie aérienne de l'Allemagne." SHAA, MO 61/2.

Hébrard, Jean. "Sur le bombardement aérien dans son interdiction diurne." SHAA, MO 38/8.

"Industrie aéronautique allemand et écoles aériennes." Map. SHAA, MO 43/1.

"Intervention de l'aviation dans la bataille terrestre." SHAA, MO 064.

"L'aviation de chasse en Espagne." SHAA, MO 064.

"La guerre en Espagne." SHAA, MO 064.

"Les troupes de transmissions de l'armée de l'air allemande." SHAA, MO 055.

Military Attaché Report France (Aviation), "General Disposition of French Air Army. In May 1940; Summary of Activity Prior to Armistice; Conclusions." Maxwell Air Force Base, Air Force Historical Research Association, 170.2278–28.

Nielsen, Generalleutnant a.D. Andreas L. *The Collection and Evaluation of Intelligence for the German Air Force High Command.* 8–115–20.
Odier, A. "Will the Pursuit Type Be Eliminated by New High Speeds?" *Revue de l'Armée de l'Air.* September 1936: 965–676. Translated by R. Garnier. 4624–47.
"Renseignements fournis par les aviateurs gouvernementaux sur la guerre d'Espagne." SHAA, MO 064.
Smith, Lieutenant Colonel Ralph C. "French Combat Estimate 1937–1940." Amendment 1939. 4109 ee. Microfilm roll A2873. 248: 501–56, "The Morane 406 Fighter." 4711/136.

Sciences Politiques, Paris

Cot, Pierre. Technical Mobilization: Hearings before a Subcommittee of the Committee of Military Affairs of the United States Senate. 77th Cong., 2nd sess. S.2721: A Bill to Establish an Office of Technical Mobilization, and for Other Purposes. Vol. 3, December 12, 14, 17, 18–19, 1942, Washington, DC: Government Printing Office, 1943: 605 (PC3, DC3).

SECONDARY SOURCES—BOOKS

Adamthwaite, Anthony. *Grandeur and Misery: France's Bid for Power in Europe 1914–1940.* New York: Arnold, 1995.
Alexander, Martin S. *The Republic in Danger: General Maurice Gamelin and the Politics of French Defence 1933–1940.* Cambridge: Cambridge University Press, 1992.
Angot, E. and R. de Lavergne. *Le Général Vuillemin.* Paris: La Palatine, 1965.
Breffort, Dominique and Andre Jouineau. *French Aircraft from 1939 to 1942: Fighters, Bombers, Reconnaissance and Observation Types.* Vol. 1, *From Amiot to Curtiss.* Paris: Histoire & Collections, 2004.
———. *French Aircraft from 1939 to 1942: Fighters, Bombers, Reconnaissance and Observation Types.* Vol. 2, *From Dewoitine to Potez.* Paris: Histoire & Collections, 2005.
Brindley, John F. *French Fighters of World War II.* Vol. 1. Windsor: Hylton Lacy, 1971.
Brown, Frederick. *The Embrace of Unreason.* New York: Knopf, 2014.
Buckley, John. *Air Power in the Age of Total War.* Bloomington: Indiana University Press, 1999.
Budiansky, Stephen. *Air Power: The Men, Machines, and Ideas That Revolutionized War from Kitty Hawk to Iraq.* New York: Penguin, 2005.
Burns, James MacGregor. *Roosevelt: Soldier of Freedom.* New York: Harcourt Brace Jovanovich, 1970.
Cain, Anthony Christopher. *The Forgotten Air Force: FAF Doctrine in the 1930s.* Washington, DC: Smithsonian Institution Press, 2002.
Chadeau, Emmanuel. *L'industrie aéronautique en France 1900–1950.* Paris: Fayard, 1987.
Chapman, Derrick. *State Capitalism and Working Class Radicalism in the French Aircraft Industry.* Berkeley: University of California Press, 1991.

Christienne, Général Charles, and Général Pierre Lissarrague. *Histoire de l'aviation militaire: L'Armée de l'Air 1928–1981*. Paris: Charles-Lavauzelle, 1981.

Citino, Robert M. *The Path to Blitzkrieg: Doctrine and Training in the German Army, 1920–1939*. Boulder, CO: Lynne Rienner, 1999.

Corum, James S. "From Biplanes to Blitzkrieg: The Development of German Air Doctrine Between the Wars." *War History* 3, no. 1 (1996): 98.

———. *The Luftwaffe: Creating the Operational Air War, 1918–1940*. Lawrence: University Press of Kansas, 1997.

———. *The Roots of Blitzkrieg*. Lawrence: University Press of Kansas, 1992.

Corum, James S. and Wray R. Johnson. *Air Power in Small Wars: Fighting Insurgents and Terrorists*. Lawrence: University Press of Kansas, 2003.

Corum, James S. and Richard R. Muller. *The Luftwaffe's Way of War: German Air Force Doctrine 1911–1945*. Baltimore: Nautical and Aviation Publishing, 1998.

Creek, Eddie J. *Junkers Ju 87: From Dive Bomber to Tank-Buster 1935–45*. Hersham: Ian Allen, 2012.

Davilla, Dr. James J. and Arthur M. Soltan. *French Aircraft of the First World War*. Stratford: Flying Machines Press, 1997.

Doughty, Robert A. *The Breaking Point: Sedan and the Fall of France, 1940*. Hamden: Archon, 1990.

———. *Phyrric Victory: French Strategy and Operation in the Great War*. Cambridge, MA: Belknap, 2005.

———. *The Seeds of Disaster: The Development of French Army Doctrine 1919–1939*. Hamden: Archon, 1985.

El Bied, Anis and André Jouineau. *The Messerschmitt Me 109*. Vol. 1, *From 1936 to 1942*. Paris: Histoire & Collections, 2001.

Facon, Patrick. *L'Armée de l'Air dans la tormente: La bataille de France 1939–1940*. Paris: Economica, 1992.

———. *Le bombardement stratégique*. Monaco: Éditions du Roche, 1995.

———. *Histoire de l'Armée de l'Air*. Paris: La Documentation Française, 2009.

Finkel, Meir. *On Flexibility: Recovery from Technological and Doctrinal Surprise on the Battlefield*. Stanford, CA: Stanford University Press, 2011.

Forczyk, Robert. *Case Red: The Collapse of France*. New York: Bloomsbury, 2017.

Friedenson, Patrick and Jean Lecuir. *La France et la Grande-Bretagne face aux problèmes aériens (1935–mai 1940)*. Vincennes: Service Historique de l'Armée de l'Air, 1976.

Frieser, Karl-Heinz. *The Blitzkrieg Legend: The 1940 Campaign in the West*. Annapolis: Naval Institute Press, 2005.

Gunston, Bill, ed. *Jane's Fighting Aircraft of World War II*. New York: Crescent Books, 1994.

Hallion, Richard P. *Strike from the Sky: The History of Battlefield Air Attack 1911–1945*. Washington, DC: Smithsonian, 1989.

Higham, Robin. *Two Roads to War: The French and British Air Arms from Versailles to Dunkirk*. Annapolis: Naval Institute Press, 2012.

---. *Unflinching Zeal: The Battles Over France and Britain, May–October, 1940*. Annapolis: Naval Institute Press, 2013.
Hippler, Thomas. *Bombing the People: Giulio Douhet and the Foundations of Air Power Strategy 1884–1939*. Cambridge: Cambridge University Press, 2013.
Homze, Edward L. *Arming the Luftwaffe: The Reich Air Ministry and the German Aircraft Industry 1919–39*. Lincoln: University of Nebraska Press, 1976.
Hooton, E. R. *The Luftwaffe: A Study in Air Power, 1933–1945*. Hersham, UK: Classic Books, 2010.
Horne, Alistair. *The Fall of Paris: The Siege and the Commune 1870–71*. London: Penguin, 1990.
---. *To Lose a Battle: France, 1940*. New York: Penguin, 2007.
House, Jonathan M. *Combined Arms Warfare in the Twentieth Century*. Lawrence: University Press of Kansas, 2001.
Jackson, Julian. *The Politics of Depression Era France: 1932–1936*. Cambridge: Cambridge University Press, 1985.
Jackson, Robert. *Spitfire: Life of the Legend*. New York: Metro Books, 2010.
Jensen, Sabine. *Pierre Cot: Un antifasciste radical*. Paris: Éditions Yves Michelet, 1990.
Johnson, Davis E. *Fast Tanks and Heavy Bombers: Innovation in the U.S. Army 1917–1945*. Ithaca: Cornell University Press, 1998.
Kier, Elizabeth. *Arming Against Hitler: France and the Limits of Military Planning*. Lawrence: University Press of Kansas, 1996.
---. *Imagining War: French and British Military Doctrine Between the Wars*. Princeton: Princeton University Press, 1997.
Kiesling, Eugenia. *Arming Against Hitler: France and the Limits of Military Planning*. Lawrence: University Press of Kansas, 1996.
Liddell Hart, B. H. *History of the Second World War*. New York: Perigree, 1980.
Martel, René. *French Strategic and Tactical Bombardment Forces of World War I*. Allan Suddaby and Steven Suddaby, translators. Lanham: Scarecrow, 2007.
Murray, Williamson. *Strategy for Defeat: The Luftwaffe 1933–1945*. Maxwell Air Force Base, Montgomery, AL: Air University Press, 1983.
Overy, Richard J. *The Air War: 1939–1945*. Dulles: Potomac Books, 2011.
---. *The Bombers and the Bombed: Allied Air War over Europe, 1940–1945*. New York: Viking, 2013.
Piekalkiewicz, Janusz. *Ziel Paris: Der Westfeldzug 1940*. Berlin: F. A. Herbig, 1986.
Posen, Barry R. *The Sources of Military Doctrine: France, Britain, and Germany between the World Wars*. Ithaca: Cornell University Press, 1984.
Pritchard, Anthony. *Messerschmitt*. New York: G. P. Putnam's Sons, 1975.
Romerstein, Herbert, and Eric Breindel. *The Venona Secrets: Exposing Soviet Espionage and America's Traitors*. Washington, DC: Regency, 2000.
Stephenson, Charles. *A Box of Sand: The Italo-Ottoman War 1911–1912: The First Air, Sea, and Air War*. Ticehurst: Tattered Flag Press, 2014.
Sterrett, James. *Soviet Air Force Theory, 1918–1945*. London: Routledge, 2007.

Thomas, Martin. *The French Empire Between the Wars: Imperialism, Politics, and Society*. New York: Manchester University Press, 2005.
Van Haute, Andre. *Pictorial History of the French Air Force: Volume I 1909–1940* London: Trinity Press, 1974.
Vivier, Thierry. *La politique aéronautique militaire de la France. Janvier 1933–Octobre 1940*. Paris: L'Harmattan, 2014.
Watt, Richard M. *Dare Call It Treason: The True Story of the French Army Mutinies of 1917*. New York: Dorset, 1969.
Whitney, Susan B. *Mobilizing Youth: Communists and Catholics in Interwar France*. Durham: Duke University Press, 2009.
Williams, Anthony G. and Emmanuel Gustin. *Flying Guns of World War II: Development of Aircraft Guns, Ammunition and Installations 1933–45*. Shrewsbury: Airlife, 2003.
Williams, George K. *Biplanes and Bombsights: British Bombing in World War I*. Maxwell Air Force Base, Montgomery, AL: Air University Press, 1999.
Young, Robert J. *In Command of France*. Cambridge: Harvard University Press, 1978.

SECONDARY SOURCES—ARTICLES AND CHAPTERS IN EDITED BOOKS

Alexander, Martin. "Force de frappe ou feu de paille? General Maurice Gamelin's Appraisal of Military Aviation before the Blitzkrieg of 1940." *Colloque International AIR 84*, 65–80.
Balss, Michael. "Deutsche Luftwaffe Losses and Claims Part 2." Monograph, 2018.
Botquin, Gaston. "The Morane Saulnier 406." *Profile Publications No. 147*, 1967.
Cain, Anthony Christopher. "L'Armée de l'Air: Drifting Toward Defeat." In *Why Air Forces Fail: The Anatomy of Defeat*. Robin Higham and Stephen J. Harris, eds. Lexington: University of Kentucky Press, 2006.
Facon, Patrick. "Les mille victoires de l'Armée de l'Air en 1939–1940: Autopsie d'un mythe." *Revue historique des armées* 4 (November 1997): 70–85.
Harvey, H. D. "The French Armée de l'Air in May–June 1940: A Failure of Conception." *Journal of Contemporary History* 25, no. 4 (1990): 447–65.
Higham, Robin. "Air Power in World War I, 1914–1918." In *The War in the Air, 1914–1994*. Edited by Alan Stephens. Maxwell Air Force Base, Montgomery, AL: Air University Press, 2001.
Martin, Thomas. "At the Heart of Things? French Imperial Defense Planning in the Late 1930s." *French Historical Studies* 21, no. 2 (1998): 325–61.
Overy, Richard. "Air Power, Armies, and the War in the West, 1940." *Harmon Memorial Lectures. No. 32*. Colorado Springs: United States Air Force Academy, 1989.
Terraine, John. *A Time for Courage*. New York: Macmillan, 1985.
Young, Robert J. "French Military Intelligence and Nazi Germany, 1938–1939." In *Knowing One's Enemies: Intelligence Assessment Before the Two World Wars*. Edited by Ernest R. May. Princeton: Princeton University Press, 1986.
———. "The Strategic Dream: French Air Doctrine in the Interwar Period 1919–1939." *Journal of Contemporary History* 9, no. 4 (1974): 35–67.

Index

Page numbers in *italics* indicate tables.

aero clubs, FAF, 169–70
air battle over France. *See* France, Battle of
air fleet (*Luftflotte*), 155–56
Air France, 168
"air superiority/dominance" model, 142–43
aircraft and equipment, 20–22, 28; in Battle of France, 9–10; bombers compared to fighters in Spanish Civil War, 85–86; of FAF compared to GAF, 3–4, 8–9, 29–30, 204–5; RAF bombers, 24; in World War I, 8. *See also* bombers, FAF; bombers, GAF; fighters, FAF; fighters, GAF; fighters, RAF
aircraft industry, British, 34–36
aircraft industry, French: BCR distractions for, 36; Colyer's report on, 181–82; downsizing, 34–36; foreign observations of, 36, 43–45; funding challenges of, 46–47; GAF bombers and strategic vulnerability of, 37–39; German modernization compared to, 50–51, 54; labor issues in, 39–40, 55; Maginot Line prioritization over, 35, 46; major works on, 33; nationalization of, 40–43, *41*, 45–46, 53; pilot training issues of, 134–36; production challenges of, 15–16, 27, 31–32, 54; production focus of, 134–35; safety issues of, 36–37; sociopolitical challenges of, 32–33, 47; standardization issues of, 152; technical challenges of, 32, 46; in World War I, 4, 33–34
aircraft industry, German: civilian aviation developments and, 49; designs based on purpose in, 52–53; French intelligence on production numbers of, 66–67, 191; French modernization compared to, 50–51, 54; labor and, 51; leadership and, 52–54; nationalization of, 53–54; shortages plaguing, 51–52, 55; in Soviet Union, 48–49, 95, 139; standardization advantages of, 152; Treaty of Versailles dodged by, 48–50; in World War I, 4, 34, 47–48
aircraft industry, Soviet, 34
aircraft industry, United States, 34–36
airpower doctrine, FAF: antiaircraft defenses and, 119–20; Army relations and, 108–9, 119–20, 123, 128–34, 136–37, 197–98; Battle of Verdun and, 115, 142; BCR concept and, 118–19; on blitzkrieg strategy, 115–16, 122; *Circulaire confidentielle pour les cadres de l'Armée de l'Air*, 117–18; Cot on, 165–67; defending, 125; defining, 120; Douhet and, 19–20, 102, 125–29; failures of, 107–8, 129–30, 136–37, 208–9;

GAF airpower doctrine compared to, 5, 108, 121–22, 156–57; Gamelin defending, 67–68; on ground attack role, 122–23; independent operations and, 116, 118, 120–21; *Instructions provisoire sur l'aviation légère de défense au combat*, 116–17; leadership conflicts over, 136; on light aviation, 116–17; literature on, 109–10, 190; Maginot Line and, 115, 125; morale bombing and, 111, 127; non-integration issues of, 130–34; offense to defense transition of, 124–25; order of operations in, 120–22; organization and, 156; pilot training issues of, 134–36; Poland's defeat impacting, 123; political divisions and, 108, 112; radio communication issues for, 133–34; on regular and special missions, 117; reprisal fears hampering, 114–15; Rif War in North Africa and, 112–13, 127; soundness of, 208; strategic bombing and, 110–14, 126–29, 208; studies on, 106–7; on technological advancements, 113; World War I policies of, 110–12

airpower doctrine, GAF: "air superiority/dominance" model and, 142–43; antiaircraft defense and, 147–48; Army cooperation and, 145–49; in Battle of France, 150–52; Battle of Verdun and, 115, 142–43; on early aerial combat, 141–42; effectiveness of, 209; evolution of, 110, 138–40; FAF airpower doctrine compared to, 5, 108, 121–22, 156–57; *Flivo* unit coordination in, 146–47; French intelligence assessment of, 65–66; goals of, 156–57; integration of ground and air in, 144; Kaiserschlacht offensive and, 143–44; morale bombing and, 143, 153, 190; order of operations in, 121–22; organization and, 155–56; Paris targeting in, 153–54; pilot training and, 154–55; radio communication and, 145–46, 150; strategic bombing and, 149–54; in World War I, 140–44

Alexander, Martin, 91–92

Amiot 351/4, 22

antiaircraft defenses, British, 143

antiaircraft defenses, French, 28; antiquated equipment of, 190; in Battle of France, 188–90; Cot on importance of, 89; FAF airpower doctrine and, 119–20; morale bombing and, 190; out-dated, 132; sabotage of, 189; shortcomings of, 206–7

antiaircraft defenses, German: effectiveness of, 206; French intelligence assessment of, 64–65; GAF airpower doctrine and, 147–48; Spanish Civil War lessons for, 100; technological advancements and, 100

Armée de l'Air. *See* French air force

L'Armée de l'Air (Cot), 89

Army, French: aerial attack weaknesses of, 132–33; in Battle of France, 188–91; Battle of France failures of, 207; communist fears of, 26; FAF leadership failures and, 160–61; FAF relations with, 108–9, 119–20, 123, 128–34, 136–37, 197–98; La Chambre and, 175; manpower issues of, 135; radio communication issues of, 123–24, 130, 133–34, 197, 206; in Riom Trials, 7; technophobic concerns of, 133, 150, 197, 206; training problems of, 132; U.S. Army influencing, 130; Vuillemin and, 177

Army, German: air attack training of, 148; *Flivo* units coordinating with,

146–47; GAF cooperation with, 145–49; Operation Barbarossa and, 186; radio communication of GAF with, 145–46, 150, 197–98; resources of, 52
Army, U.S.: French Army influencing, 130; World War II planning and revisions of, 93
Army Air Corps, U.S. (USAAC), 11; airpower doctrine of, 107, 110; Curtis Hawk H.75 and, 15; independent strategic role of, 128, 197; leadership of, 161–63

B. H. Liddell Hart Archive, 182
Barbarossa, Operation, 171, 186
battlefield air attack: in Battle of Guadalajara, 87–88; France on Spanish Civil War and, 86–90; of Germany in Spanish Civil War, 98–100; in World War I, 86–88, 98–99; in World War II, 86–87
BCR (Bombardment, Combat, Reconnaissance), FAF, 3–4, 36, 118–19
BEF (British Expeditionary Force), 2, 192
Belgium, xvi
Bell, Lawrence, 36
Bewegungskrieg, xiv
Bf 109: B, 17; in Battle of France, 196; E-1, 17–18; E-3, 18; firepower of, 60–61; French intelligence assessment of, 59–62; improvements of, 204–5; in Spanish Civil War, 59, 82–83, 96–97; testing and improvements of, 96–97
Bf 110, 18, 53
birth rates, during World War I, 135
blitzkrieg strategy, German: Cot on technique of, 57; FAF airpower doctrine on, 115–16, 122; Spanish Civil War and, 5, 63, 80, 94

Bloc, Marc, 186
Bloch 151/152, 13
Bloch M.B. 174/5, 21–22
Bombardment, Combat, Reconnaissance (BCR), FAF, 3–4, 36, 118–19
Bombenflugwesen, Das (Rougeron), 109
bombers, FAF: Amiot 351/4, 22; Bloch M.B. 174/5, 21–22; bomb types of, 22; Breguet 691/693, 20–21; combat efficacy of, 28–29; Douglas DB-7, 21; German intelligence on, 74–75; Glenn Martin 167F, 22; Lioré et Olivier LeO 451, 21; numbers of, 20, *20*; speed of, 26
bombers, GAF: combat efficacy of, 28; Dornier Do 17, 23; fighters guiding, 26–27, 62; French aircraft industry's strategic vulnerability to, 37–39; French intelligence assessment of, 62–63; He 111, 23, 97; He 177, 53; Ju 52, 49, 95–96; Ju 87 Stuka, 23–24, 63, 97; Ju 88, 53; numbers of, 20; speed of, 26; Udet's direction for, 53; vulnerabilities of, 103–4; in World War I, 19
bombers, Italian, 85–86
bombers, RAF, 24
Boog, Horst, 75–76
Botquin, Gaston, 11–12
Breguet 691/693, 20–21
Britain, Battle of, 77; GAF losses in, 154, 183, 185, 193; GAF strategic bombing in, 23, 103; RAF advantages in, 196
British Expeditionary Force (BEF), 2, 192
Budiansky, Stephen, 182

Cain, Anthony, 106
Case Red (Forczyk), 106–7
Chadeau, Emmanuel, 33
Chapman, Herrick, 33
Christienne, Charles, 11

Circulaire confidentielle pour les cadres de l'Armée de l'Air, 117–18
civilian morale, Spanish Civil War strategic bombing and, 84
Clarke, Arthur C., 140
Colyer, Douglas, 70, 159, 181–82
Command of the Air (Douhet), 118, 126–27
communism: Cot and, 43, 164, 173–74, 200; as dangerous, 166; factory workers and, 26, 39; FAF officer purge and, 174; French Army fears of, 26; Gamelin's fears of, 112, 167–68; labor and, 40; Soviet, 40, 166–67
Communist Party of France (Parti communiste français): factory cells of, 26, 39; French Right fears of, 200; persecution of, 168; Soviet Union and, 40, 112, 172; strength of, 39–40, 167
Condor Legion, German, in Spanish Civil War, 5, 23, 27, 94–95, 98–99, 101, 145, 207
Corum, James, 11
Cot, Pierre, xv, 162, 188; aero clubs and, 169–70; Air France and, 168; on airpower doctrine of FAF compared to GAF, 108; on antiaircraft defenses, 89; Battle of France, 199–200; on blitzkrieg strategy, 57; code name for, 172; communism and, 43, 164, 173–74, 200; de Gaulle and, 165, 172; divisiveness of, 164, 172, 179, 209; Douhet and, 165; on FAF airpower doctrine, 165–67; FAF leadership and, 164–75; FAF's rise and, 6; on fascism, 90, 92, 164, 172–73; on French aircraft industry's challenges, 15–16; French Left and, 164–65, 173; on GAF fighters compared to RAF fighters, 61–62; on German aircraft industry production numbers, 66–67, 191; on industrial relocation, 111–12; labor and, 174; nationalization of French aircraft industry led by, 40–43, *41*; officer purge of, 169–70, 174, 212; as Soviet spy, 171–72, 200; Soviet Union relationship pushed by, 26, 43, 73, 167–68, 170–71; on Spanish Civil War and France, 89–90; strategic bombing and, 173–74; Vuillemin questioned by, 160; in World War I, 165, 168
Curtis Hawk H.75, 15, 17, 196
Czechoslovakia, 171

Daimler-Benz DB 601 A Engine, 96
Daladier, Édouard, 165
DAT (Défense Aérienne du Territoire), 131
DCA (Défense Contre Aérienne), 28
de Gaulle, Charles, 165, 172
Défense Aérienne du Territoire (DAT), 131
Défense Contre Aérienne (DCA), 28
Denain, Victor, 25
Deuxième Bureau, 57–58, 70, 210
Dewoitine 510, 10
Dewoitine 520, 10, 196, 204
Dewoitine D.371, 81
doctrine and training. *See* airpower doctrine, FAF; airpower doctrine, GAF
Dornier Do 17, 23
Douglas DB-7, 21
Douhet, Giulio, 37; BCR and, 118; Cot and, 165; FAF airpower doctrine and, 19–20, 102, 125–29; Germans influenced by, 129
Dreyfus Affair, 27
Drôle de guerre. *See* Phony War
Dunkirk evacuation, 2
Duval, Maurice, 79, 80, 92
Dyle Plan, 184
Dynamo, Operation, 192

equipment. *See* aircraft and equipment

Facon, Patrick, 28
FAF. *See* French air force
Falkenhayn, Erich von, 142
Fall Gelb plan. *See* France, Battle of
fascism, 90, 92, 164, 172–73
fighters, FAF: in Battle of France, 196; Bloch 151/152, 13; capabilities and performance of, 16–17; Curtis Hawk H.75, 15, 17, 196; Dewoitine 510 and 520, 10, 196, 204; Dewoitine D.371, 81; German intelligence on, 74; machine gun performance of, 25–26; mitrailleuse M.A.C. modèle 1934 and, 14; Morane-Saulnier M.S.406, 11–12, 37, 44–45, 196, 205; numbers of, *10*, 10–11; Potez 630 and 631, 12–13; reliability and ammunition problems of, 14–15, 25–26; supply issues of, 27
fighters, GAF: in Battle of France, 196; Bf 109, 17–18, 59–62, 82–83, 96–97, 196, 204–5; Bf 110, 18, 53; bombers guided by, 26–27, 62; French intelligence assessment of, 59–62; machine gun performance of, 25–26; numbers of, 11; RAF fighters compared to, 61–62
fighters, RAF: in Battle of France, 196; GAF fighters compared to, 61–62; Hawker Hurricane, 18; machine gun performance of, 25–26; Spitfire, 18–19
Finkel, Meir, 182
Finland, 167
Fliegerverbingundsoffiziere (*Flivo*) units, 99, 146–47, 155, 207
Forczyk, Robert, 106–7
Forgotten Air Force, The (Cain), 106
France: division within, 7, 209–10; GAF airpower doctrine in, 150–52; German intelligence on war preparations of, 73–74; historical invasions in northwest, xiii–xiv; interwar lessons learned by, 78–79; Italy allyship issues for, 166; Maginot Line and national security of, xiv; socioeconomic-political divides in, 69–70; Soviet Union allyship issues for, 166–67, 171; as "weak democracy," 211. *See also* aircraft industry, French; antiaircraft defenses, French; intelligence, French; Maginot Line; Spanish Civil War, France and
France, Battle of: aerial bombing in, 63; aircraft and equipment in, 9–10; brevity of, 2–3; Cot and, 199–200; Coyler's report on, 181–82; Dyle Plan and, 184; FAF fighters in, 196; FAF mission in, xiv–xv; FAF pilot skills in, 201–2; FAF reactive stance in, 186, 201; French aircraft industry production problems and, 31–32; French antiaircraft defenses in, 188–90; French Army failures in, 207; French Army in, 188–91; GAF fighters in, 196; GAF losses during, 182–83, 185–88, *187*, *194*, 194–95; GAF victory in, 7; intelligence evaluation in, 56–57; organization command, control, communication in, 197–99; overview of, 184–85; politics, FAF leadership and, 199–201; RAF and, 191–93; RAF fighters in, 196; strategic bombing in, 149–51; technological advancements and, 195–96, 201–2
French air force (FAF), 2; aero clubs and, 169–70; Army relations with, 108–9, 119–20, 123, 128–34, 136–37, 197–98; Battle of France and pilot skills in, 201–2; Battle of France mission of, xiv–xv; Battle of France reactive stance

of, 186, 201; Battle of France technology inferiority of, 195–96, 201–2; BCR program of, 3–4, 36, 118–19; Colyer's report on, 181–82; Cot and rise of, 6; Deuxième Bureau of, 58, 70; fighters, *10*, 10–17, 25–27; GAF aircraft and equipment compared to, 3–4, 8–9, 29–30, 204–5; GAF losses caused by, *194*, 194–95; Gamelin blaming, 68, 119; independence of, 3, 197; intelligence usage failures of, 70–71, 210; internal problems of, 7; interwar lessons learned by, 78–79; manpower issues of, 135; nationalization impact on, 42–43; officer purge of, 169–70, 174, 212; organization of, 156; origin of, 169; pilot training challenges of, 134–36; radio communication used by, 206; recruitment strategies of, 135–36; reputation of airmen in, 212; Riom Trials and, 178; Spanish Civil War and, 27, 80; standardization issues of, 152; supply issues of, 27. *See also* aircraft industry, French; airpower doctrine, FAF; bombers, FAF; fighters, FAF; leadership, FAF

French Campaign. *See* France, Battle of

French Left, Cot and, 164–65, 173

French M1929, 14

French Revolution, 39

French Right, 89–90, 167, 174, 200

Front Populaire, 40, 89–90, 165, 212

Fuller, J. F. C., 8

GAF. *See* German air force

Gagarin, G., 91

Gamelin, Maurice, 164, 175; communist fears of, 112, 167–68; FAF blamed by, 68, 119; failures of, 160–61, 179; French airpower doctrine defended by, 67–68; radio communication missing for, 24, 124, 197, 211; Spanish Civil War lessons ignored by, 208

Georges, Alphonse, 69

German air force (GAF), 2; Army cooperation with, 145–49; Battle of Britain losses of, 154, 183, 185, 193; Battle of Britain strategic bombing by, 23, 103; Battle of France losses of, 182–83, 185–88, *187*, *194*, 194–95; Battle of France technology superiority of, 195–96, 201–2; Battle of France victory of, 7; FAF aircraft and equipment compared to, 3–4, 8–9, 29–30, 204–5; FAF causing losses to, *194*, 194–95; fighters of, 11, 17–18, 25–26; *Flivo* units of, 99, 146–47, 155, 207; genesis of, 3; leadership of, 161; Operation Barbarossa and, 186; organization of, 155–56; Paris target of strategic bombing by, 153–54; pilot training of, 154–55; radio communication of Army and, 145–46, 150, 197–98; RAF causing losses to, *194*, 194–95; rise of, 6; Spanish Civil War and, 27, 59, 95, 207–8; standardization advantages of, 152; Treaty of Versailles hindering, 9, 138. *See also* aircraft industry, German; airpower doctrine, GAF; bombers, GAF; fighters, GAF; Spanish Civil War, Germany and

Germany: Battle of France plan of, xiv–xv; *Bewegungskrieg* and, xiv; civilian aviation developments in, 49; Douhet's influence in, 129; financial woes of, 51–52; French intelligence on technological advancements of, 58–59; interwar military developments in, 169; Kaiserschlacht offensive of, 143–44;

natural resources of, 52, 55; Soviet nonaggression treaty with, 167; unity in, 7; Westwall and, xiv. *See also* aircraft industry, German; Army, German; blitzkrieg strategy; intelligence, German; Spanish Civil War, Germany and

Geschwader (squadron), 155

Glantz, David M., 2

Glenn Martin 167F, 22

Göring, Hermann, 95

Great Britain: aircraft industry of, 34–36; antiaircraft defenses of, 143; Battle of Britain, 77, 103; Dunkirk evacuation and, 2; interwar military developments in, 169; Italy allyship issues for, 166; Soviet Union allyship issues for, 166–67, 171. *See also* Royal Air Force

Gruppe (group), 155

Guadalajara, Battle of, 87–88

Guernica, bombing of, 101–2

Harris, Arthur "Bomber," 161

Hawker Hurricane, 18

He 111, 23, 97

He 177, 53

Hebrard, Colonel, 113, 131

Heer. *See* Army, German

Heinkel, 23, 49–50

Higham, Robin, 183, 193, 201, 202

Hitler, Adolf, 3, 6, 51, 53, 209

Hitlerjugend, 154

Horne, Alistair, 106, 182

L'industrie aéronautique en France 1900–1950 (Chadeau), 33

Instructions provisoire sur l'aviation légère de defense au combat, 116–17

intelligence, French, 4; accuracy of, 58–66, 210; Battle of France evaluation of, 56–57; Deuxième Bureau in, 57–58, 70, 210; FAF failure to properly use, 70–71, 210; GAF airpower doctrine assessment of, 65–66; GAF bombers assessment of, 62–63; GAF fighters assessment of, 59–62; on German aircraft industry production numbers, 66–67, 191; German antiaircraft defenses assessment of, 64–65; German intelligence compared to, 76–77; Germany's technological advancements assessment of, 58–59; internal enemies and distrust of, 71–73, 77; leadership underappreciating, 67–69; organization of, 57–58; Service de Renseignement in, 57–58; societal and cultural impact on, 69–70; on Spanish Civil War, 79

intelligence, German, 4; on FAF bombers, 74–75; on FAF fighters, 74; on FAF strengths and weaknesses, 74–76; French intelligence compared to, 76–77; on French war preparations, 73–74; shortcomings of, 76, 77, 210–11

Iraq, 93

Italy: in Battle of Guadalajara, 88; bombers of, 85–86; France allyship issues with, 166; strategic bombing and, 140–41

Jauneaud, Marcel, 63, 131

Johnson, Edwin C., 16, 61

Ju 52, 49, 95–96

Ju 87 *Sturzkampfflugzeug* (Stuka), 23–24, 63, 97–98

Ju 88, 53

Junkers, 49–50

Kaiserschlacht (Kaiser's battle) offensive, 143–44

Kesselring, Albert, 145

Kier, Elizabeth, 169
Krasnaya Zvezda, 90–91

La Chambre, Guy, 160; Army control and, 175; FAF leadership and, 175–77; modernization under, 180; protectionism and, 176–77
labor: communism and, 40; Cot and, 174; French aircraft industry issues with, 39–40, 55; German aircraft industry and, 51
leadership, FAF: aero clubs and, 169–70; air ministers of, 1933-1940, *163*; airpower doctrine conflicts of, 136; Army and failures of, 160–61; assessing, 159; Battle of France, politics and, 199–201; Cot and, 164–75; failures blamed on, 158–59, 179–80, 211–12; foreign views of, 159–60, 200; heads of, 1933-1940, *162*; intelligence underappreciated by, 67–69; La Chambre and, 175–77; officer purge of, 169–70, 174, 212; protectionism and, 176–77; sociopolitical issues of, 164; Soviet Union and, 167–68, 170–71; turnover and unstable, 161–63; Vuillemin and, 177–80
leçons de la guerre d'Espagne, Les (Duval), 79, 80, 92
light aviation, FAF airpower doctrine on, 116–17
Lioré et Olivier LeO 451, 21
Lissarrague, Pierre, 11
Loizeau, Lucien, 68
Luftflotte (air fleet), 155–56
Lufthansa, 49
Luftwaffe. *See* German air force

machine gun performance, of fighters compared, 25–26

Madrid, bombing of, 101–2
Maginot Line: Belgium's neutrality and, xvi; cost of prioritizing, 35, 46; FAF airpower doctrine and, 115, 125; France's national security and, xiv
Manuel du gradé de D.C.A, 189–90
Martin, Paul, 202
media: on Morane-Saulnier M.S.406, 12; on Spanish Civil War strategic bombing, 101–2; World War II analysis in, 1
Megargee, Geoffrey P., 1–2
Messerschmitt, 49–50
MG34 machine gun, in German antiaircraft defense, 148
Michael, Operation, 98
Mikhailow, P., 90
Milch, Erhard, 158, 161
Mitchell, Billy, 158, 161
mitrailleuse M.A.C. modèle 1934, 14
morale bombing, 111, 127, 143, 153, 190
Morane-Saulnier M.S.406: in Battle of France, 196; foreign reports on, 44–45; improvements to, 205; media touting, 12; production of, 11; safety issues of, 37; weaknesses of, 11–12, 196
Murray, Williamson, 182–83, 186–87

nationalization: of French aircraft industry, 40–43, *41*, 45–46, 53; of German aircraft industry, 53–54
Nationalsozialistisches Fliegerkorps (NSFK), 154
night bombing, Spanish Civil War and, 90
North Africa, Rif War in, 112–13, 127
NSFK (Nationalsozialistisches Fliegerkorps), 154

officer purge, FAF, 169–70, 174, 212

Paquier, Pierre, 113
Paris, as GAF strategic bombing target, 153–54
Parti communiste français. *See* Communist Party of France
Pétain, Philippe, 111
Phony War, 9, 184
pilot training: FAF, 134–36; GAF, 154–55
"Plan 1919," 8
Poland: Allied concern from invasion of, 191; defeat of, 67–68, 88–89, 93, 123; Soviet expansionism and, 171
politique aéronautique militaire de la France, La (Vivier), 33
Posen, Barry, 9, 106
Potez 630 and 631, 12–13
protectionism, FAF leadership and, 176–77

radio communication: FAF use of, 206; *Flivo* unit coordination through, 146–47; French Army issues with, 123–24, 130, 133–34, 197, 206; of GAF and Army, 145–46, 150, 197–98; Gamelin missing, 24, 124, 197, 211
RAF (Royal Air Force), xv
Recalled to Service (Weygand), 164
regular missions, FAF airpower doctrine on, 117
Revue de l'Armée de l'Air (journal), 80, 85
Reynaud, Paul, 116, 179
Richthofen, Wolfram von, 146
Rif War, in North Africa, 112–13, 127
Riom Trials, 7, 178
Rougeron, Camille, 109
Royal Air Force (RAF), xv; aircraft and equipment of, 9; airpower doctrine of, 107, 110; Battle of Britain advantages of, 196; Battle of France and, 191–93; bombers of, 24; fighters of, 18–19, 25–26; GAF losses caused by, *194*, 194–95; independent strategic role of, 128; leadership of, 161–62

Salamander, 10
Sandys, M. Duncan, 84
Seeckt, Hans von, 99
Service de Renseignement, 57–58
Seversky, Alexander de, 15
Sitzkrieg. *See* Phony War
Slessor, John, 92
Smith, Ralph C., 159–60, 200
Soviet Union: air generals of, 161; in Battle of Guadalajara, 88; collapse of, 1; communism in, 40, 166–67; Communist Party of France and, 40, 112, 172; Cot as spy for, 171–72, 200; Cot pushing relationship with, 26, 43, 73, 167–68, 170–71; FAF leadership and, 167–68, 170–71; France allyship issues with, 166–67, 171; German aircraft industry in, 48–49, 95, 139; German nonaggression treaty with, 167; interwar military developments in, 169; Poland and expansionism of, 171; in Spanish Civil War, 81; U.S. allyship with, 171. *See also* aircraft industry, Soviet
Spaatz, Carl, 161
Spain, Rif War and, 112–13, 127
Spanish Civil War, France and: amateurism in, 92–93; on battlefield air attack, 86–90; Bf 109 assessment in, 82–83; on bombers compared to fighters, 85–86; on civilian morale and strategic bombing, 84; Cot on, 89–90; FAF and, 27, 80; foreign reports backing up, 90–91; information flow in, 79–80; information quality and analysis in, 81–83, 93–94; intelligence on, 79; lessons of, 5, 91–92,

207–8; night bombing and, 90; politics and hesitations of, 89–90; on Soviet aircraft deployments, 81; on strategic bombing effects, 83–84; technical analysis of, 81

Spanish Civil War, Germany and: aerial combat lessons of, 104–5; aircraft design and improvement in, 95–96; aircraft testing and development in, 96–98; antiaircraft defense lessons of, 100; battlefield air attack and, 98–100; Bf 109 in, 59, 82–83, 96–97; blitzkrieg strategy and, 5, 63, 80, 94; Condor Legion in, 5, 23, 27, 94–95, 98–99, 101, 145, 207; *Flivo* units and, 207; GAF and, 27, 59, 95, 207–8; Guernica bombing and, 101–2; He 111 in, 97; Ju 52 in, 95–96; Ju 87 Stuka and, 63, 97–98; as laboratory, 94–95, 99; leadership developed in, 207–8; lessons of, 5, 94–95, 99–100, 104–5, 207; Madrid bombing and, 101–2; misunderstanding of, 4–5; strategic bombing and, 101–4

Spears, Edward L., 159, 182, 191

special missions, FAF airpower doctrine on, 117

Spitfire, 18–19

sports clubs, German, 49–50

squadron (*Geschwader*), 155

Stalingrad Trilogy, The (Glantz), 2

State Capitalism and Working Class Radicalism in the French Aircraft Industry (Chapman), 33

strategic airpower doctrine. *See* airpower doctrine, FAF; airpower doctrine, GAF

strategic bombing: in Battle of Britain by GAF, 23, 103; in Battle of France, 149–51; civilian morale in Spanish Civil War after, 84; Cot and, 173–74; FAF airpower doctrine and, 110–14, 126–29, 208; France on Spanish Civil War and effects of, 83–84; GAF airpower doctrine and, 149–54; of Guernica, 101–2; Italy and, 140–41; of Madrid, 101–2; media on Spanish Civil War and, 101–2; morale bombing and, 111, 127, 143, 153, 190; Paris targeted by GAF, 153–54; Rif War in North Africa and, 112–13, 127; in Spanish Civil War by Germany, 101–4; in World War I, 83–84, 102–3; in World War II, 83–84. *See also types of bombers*

Strategy for Defeat (Murray), 182–83

Stuka (Ju 87 *Sturzkampfflugzeug*), 23–24, 63, 97–98

technological advancements: Battle of France and, 195–96, 201–2; of bombers, 19–20; FAF airpower doctrine on, 113; French intelligence on Germany's, 58–59; German antiaircraft defenses and, 100; importance of, 205–6; between World War I and II, 8–9. *See also* aircraft and equipment; radio communication

Tiger I/II tanks, 24–25

To Lose a Battle (Horne), 106

Trenchard, Hugh, 158, 161

Triumph of Treason (Cot), 66–67, 89, 108, 173

Tukhachevsky, Mikhail, 161

Udet, Ernst, 53

United States (U.S.): aircraft industry of, 34–36; Army, 93, 130; French aircraft industry observations of, 43–45; interwar military developments in, 168–69; Soviet

allyship with, 171. *See also* Army Air Corps, U.S.
USAAC. *See* Army Air Corps, U.S.

Venona decrypts, 171–72
Verdun, Battle of, 115, 142–43
Versailles, Treaty of, 3; GAF hindered by, 9, 138; German aircraft industry dodging, 48–50
vie dell'aria, Le (journal), 85
Vivier, Thierry, 33
Vuillemin, Joseph, 134, 159; Army control and, 177; Cot questioning, 160; FAF leadership and, 177–80; inaction of, 178

War of Annihilation (Megargee), 1–2
Wells, H. G., 140
Westwall, xiv
Wever, Walther, 139, 145, 149
Weygand, Maxime, 79, 89, 164
Wimmer, Wilhelm, 23

wonder weapons (*Wunderwaffen*), 205
World War I: battlefield air attack in, 86–88, 98–99; birth rates during, 135; Cot in, 165, 168; FAF airpower doctrine policies from, 110–12; French aircraft industry in, 4, 33–34; GAF airpower doctrine in, 140–44; GAF bombers in, 19; German aircraft industry in, 4, 34, 47–48; Kaiserschlacht offensive in, 143–44; Operation Michael in, 98; strategic bombing in, 83–84, 102–3; technological advancements during, 8; technological advancements following, 8–9
World War II: battlefield air attack in, 86–87; historical narratives of, 1–2; media analysis of, 1; strategic bombing effects in, 83–84; technological advancements in, 8–9; U.S. Army planning and revisions in, 93. *See also* Britain, Battle of; France, Battle of
Wunderwaffen (wonder weapons), 205

About the Author

JAMES F. SLAUGHTER III is a course designer and an adjunct for Norwich University in Vermont. He has multiple degrees in history and education, including a PhD in history from the University of Wolverhampton. He has published numerous pieces on the history of World War II in Europe and regularly presents at conferences in the United States and abroad. He teaches and advises on many subjects at the university level in European and American history. His primary interests are France and Germany from 1870 to 1945, with an emphasis on the development of doctrine and security policy and the interaction of society and government. He is also interested in American topics from 1750 to 1877, with an emphasis on the causes, course, and outcome of the American Civil War. He resides in South Charleston, West Virginia, with his wife, son, and the family dog.

The Naval Institute Press is the book-publishing arm of the U.S. Naval Institute, a private, nonprofit, membership society for sea service professionals and others who share an interest in naval and maritime affairs. Established in 1873 at the U.S. Naval Academy in Annapolis, Maryland, where its offices remain today, the Naval Institute has members worldwide.

Members of the Naval Institute support the education programs of the society and receive the influential monthly magazine *Proceedings* or the colorful bimonthly magazine *Naval History* and discounts on fine nautical prints and on ship and aircraft photos. They also have access to the transcripts of the Institute's Oral History Program and get discounted admission to any of the Institute-sponsored seminars offered around the country.

The Naval Institute's book-publishing program, begun in 1898 with basic guides to naval practices, has broadened its scope to include books of more general interest. Now the Naval Institute Press publishes about seventy titles each year, ranging from how-to books on boating and navigation to battle histories, biographies, ship and aircraft guides, and novels. Institute members receive significant discounts on the Press' more than eight hundred books in print.

Full-time students are eligible for special half-price membership rates. Life memberships are also available.

For more information about Naval Institute Press books that are currently available, visit www.usni.org/press/books. To learn about joining the U.S. Naval Institute, please write to:

Member Services
U.S. Naval Institute
291 Wood Road
Annapolis, MD 21402-5034
Telephone: (800) 233-8764
Fax: (410) 571-1703
Web address: www.usni.org

www.ingramcontent.com/pod-product-compliance
Lightning Source LLC
Jackson TN
JSHW021654230325
81266JS00001B/1